"*A Teen's Guide to Christian Living* made God so real to me, and I found myself feeling loved, grounded and just made whole. I especially liked the stories from other teens because they helped me see how God works in our lives even when we're in the middle of all the ups and downs. And I thought it was so powerful and very cool to see how scriptures that were written thousands of years ago can fit so perfectly in our lives today."

Carson Hall, 16

"I have been so very inspired by reading *A Teen's Guide to Christian Living*. Young people are looking for answers, and this book offers thoughtful and practical ideas for living a Christian life in a secular world. This book will be a high priority for the many teens in my life."

Ronald D. Glosser
vice-chairman, Guideposts, Inc.

"As a twenty-three-year-old police officer, the greatest asset I have is my salvation. With Christ as my guide, there is no defeat—only life and forgiveness. As I perform my duties in a high-crime, high-risk area, I have realized that today's society is continuing to slip further into moral decay every day. In our present culture, there is a great peer influence leading teens to a life of crime and sin. The streets today are chaotic, violent and deadly. I could never sufficiently express how important it is for teens to establish and sharpen their relationship with God. God is the light, no matter how dark the path. It is important for teens to hear the stories of other teens and their triumphs through Christ. What important testimony—but it is so much more. This book is an excellent supplement to biblical study that offers an inspirational guide to spiritual growth."

Douglas R. Marx
police officer, Milwaukee, Wisconsin

"This book is to youth spiritual awareness what 9/11 became to patriotism. It is a call to walk upright in a world where turbulence and confusion often reign. In a world where our headlines are often filled with tragedy and violence, young people the world over want to believe that God still cares. *A Teen's Guide to Christian Living* is certain to help today's youth become more deeply and personally acquainted with the Christian faith—and thereby develop a personal relationship with God."

Linda and Millard Fuller
Habitat for Humanity International

"Sometimes my life can seem like it's full of so much drama—I don't always know how to deal with it all. I've always felt like I needed God to help me, but I guess I just didn't know how to go about it. *A Teen's Guide to Christian Living* made it easy to understand God and how to walk with Him. It is an awesome book that can change your life. I know it changed mine. I think every teen should read it because it can make life less complicated than we all seem to make it."

Rebecca Smithe, 16

"Today's youth often find themselves caught in a moral crossfire, the result being unsure what they're to believe and how to proceed in a world filled with duplicities. This wonderful book is part of the solution, giving young adults moral and internal guidance and confidence that God is the rock to rely on—always. Personally, as parents of young adults, we believe that parents, youth workers and anyone who cares about teens will do well to put this beautiful blueprint for Christian living into the hands of young adults."

Donna and Rev. Robert Schuller

"I always looked at those kids at my school who pray before they eat—right in the cafeteria. I'm a Christian, too, but I didn't exactly want to advertise it. After reading *A Teen's Guide to Christian Living*, I realized I need to think less of what the other kids think of me and more of what God means to me."

Brad Whiteside, 17

"In my youth ministry, I know firsthand how eager our youth are to find meaning, purpose and the passion of life. *A Teen's Guide to Christian Living* opens the door to a genuine fellowship with our Heavenly Father and will help teens see that it's what God offers. This book will take their faith to another level, helping them to see and know God as their Father, Healer, Guide, Provider, Teacher, Friend, Comforter, Helper, Protector, Shepherd and Deliverer."

Miles McPherson
senior pastor, The Rock Church
founder, Miles Ahead Youth Ministries

"From learning whether or not God cares who my friends are to how to pray, *A Teen's Guide to Christian Living* taught me the real importance of walking with God. I'd love for all my friends to read it."

Heather Burns, 14

"In a culture full of negative images and messages that either omit or profane faith, *A Teen's Guide to Christian Living* provides a positive, easy-to-understand response to a smorgasbord of God and faith issues that young people are dealing with. This book will make sense to teenagers."

Dr. Steve Vandegriff
Professor of Youth Ministries, Liberty University
author, *Timeless Youth Ministry*

"A few years ago, I went to a special service at church and raised my hand to ask Jesus into my heart, but I didn't really change the way I lived. I don't think I even knew what it meant to give my life to Christ. This book showed me what it means. It also helped me learn how to live a life where God is number one."

Chad Whitcomb, 16

"In a world that centers around social activities, popularity and grades, *A Teen's Guide to Christian Living* earns an A⁺. It is the ultimate study guide for every major exam in life."

Cheryl Barber
host of *Goodnews!* (a Christian TV talk show)

"You hear about having a 'personal relationship' with God. I think almost everyone would want to have that kind of relationship. I know I always have. *A Teen's Guide to Christian Living* pointed out the way for me to know God as a loving Father and as a forever friend."

Brianna Lynn Butler, 16

"*A Teen's Guide to Christian Living* is one of the most balanced books for teens I have had the privilege of reading. Having studied the Bible extensively and having been involved with the Christian community all my life, I can tell you this will be an invaluable book for teens."

Cathy Slovensky
Christian editor

"I love this book because it showed me how God is really working in the lives of other teens—even in the tough times. I've never seen another book on being a Christian that gave me real-life inspiration straight from other teens and the Bible-based facts, too. This book made it so easy to 'get it' that God is there for me, always and forever."

Samantha Comer, 13

"With easy-to-understand language and clear teaching, *A Teen's Guide to Christian Living* delivers a much-needed resource for teens. Whether a young person is struggling to understand who God is, what happens when we die or why God would allow events such as 9/11, this book provides answers. This book should be on the nightstand of every teenager."

Brittany Waggoner
author, *Prayers for When You're Mad, Sad or Just Totally Confused*

"This truly excellent book has the potential to optimize the spirit of Christ in our lives and contribute to a vastly better world. It is truly a masterpiece!"

Joe Batten
author, *The Leadership Principles of Jesus*

"If any Christian parent is searching for a book to help their teen grow spiritually, this is it. This loving and beautifully written book will provide the biblical promises and guidelines for a joyful life, now and forever."

Cheryl Nason
host, *Metroplex Today*

"There is an ache in the heart of so many to integrate Christian values with everyday life. Bravo for *A Teen's Guide to Christian Living,* a simply magnificent book providing practical answers to young people on how to use their own lives as a reflection of God's love."

Nancy Rivard
founder and president, Airline Ambassadors

"Teens will benefit wholeheartedly from this wonderfully written and Spirit-filled book, and inspire them as they go about living the Christian Walk on a daily basis."

Rachel Rauch
publicist, Servant Publications

"Wonderful! Outstanding! I can't say enough about this book. I absolutely encourage every parent to get a copy and read it to your kids. Make room for this book in your home and in your hearts. Allow it to become a part of your everyday lives."

Terry Bradshaw
Hall of Fame quarterback, four-time Super Bowl winner
Emmy-winning co-host, *Fox NFL Sunday*

"I believe God will use this book powerfully in the lives of everyone who reads it."

Pastor Ron Kallem

"Wow! A totally awesome book that helps today's young people answer questions about how to talk to God and how to walk with God. Most compelling are the touching stories from teens who have had their faith tested and, as a result, instead of chasing the futile winds of happiness have found the key to face the winds of change with clarity, courage and integrity. Young people the world over are in great need of this important work. Help make it happen: Give a copy to every youth leader you know."

Jeanne and Karl Anthony
youth entertainers, founders of Strike-A-Chord

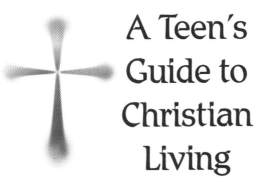

A Teen's Guide to Christian Living

Practical Answers to Tough Questions About God and Faith

Bettie B. Youngs, Ph.D., Ed.D.
Jennifer Leigh Youngs

**Authors of the bestselling
Taste Berries™ for Teens series**

Debbie Thurman

Faith Communications
A Division of Health Communications, Inc.®

Health Communications, Inc.
Deerfield Beach, Florida

www.faithcombooks.com
www.tasteberriesforteens.com

We would like to acknowledge the following publishers and individuals for permission to reprint the following material. (Note: The stories that were penned anonymously, that are public domain or were previously unpublished stories written by Bettie B. Youngs, Jennifer Leigh Youngs or Debbie Thurman are not included in this listing. Also not included in this listing but credited within the text are those stories contributed or based upon stories by teens.)

All Scripture quotations, unless otherwise indicated, are taken from the Holy Bible, New International Version® (NIV®). Copyright 1973, 1978, 1984 by International Bible Society. Used by permission of Zondervan Publishing House. All rights reserved.

Scriptures also taken from the New American Standard Bible, ©1960, 1962, 1963, 1968, 1971, 1972, 1973, 1975, 1977, by The Lockman Foundation. Used by permission. Other Scriptures from the King James Version.

(Continued on page 355)

Library of Congress Cataloging-in-Publication Data

Youngs, Bettie B.
    A teen's guide to Christian living : practical answers to tough questions about God and faith / Bettie B. Youngs, Jennifer Leigh Youngs with Debbie Thurman.
      p.   cm.
    Includes bibliographical references.
    ISBN 0-7573-0101-0
    1. Christian teenagers—Religious life.   2. Christianity—Miscellanea.
I. Youngs, Jennifer Leigh, date. II. Thurman, Debbie. III. Title.

BV4531.3.Y68 2003
248.8'3—dc21

                                  2003042335

©2003 Bettie B. Youngs and Jennifer Leigh Youngs
ISBN 0-7573-0101-0 (trade paper)

Faith Communications (FC), its Logos and Marks are trademarks of Health Communications, Inc.

Publisher: Faith Communications
               An Imprint of Health Communications, Inc.
               3201 S.W. 15th Street
               Deerfield Beach, Florida 33442-8190

Cover illustration and design by Andrea Perrine Brower
Inside book formatting by Dawn Von Strolley Grove

To: _Bethany_____

With Blessings!

From: _Your Secret Angel_____

Also by Bettie B. Youngs, Ph.D., Ed.D.

12 Months of Faith: A Devotional Journal for Teens (Faith Communications)
365 Days of Taste-Berry Inspiration for Teens (Health Communications, Inc.)
A Teen's Guide to Living Drug-Free (Health Communications, Inc.)
A Taste-Berry Teen's Guide to Setting & Achieving Goals (Health Communications, Inc.)
Taste Berries for Teens #3: Inspirational Stories and Encouragement on Life, Love, Friends and the Face in the Mirror (Health Communications, Inc.)
A Taste-Berry Teen's Guide to Managing the Stress and Pressures of Life (Health Communications, Inc.)
More Taste Berries for Teens: A Second Collection of Inspirational Short Stories and Encouragement on Life, Love, Friendship and Tough Issues (Health Communications, Inc.)
Taste Berries for Teens Journal: My Thoughts on Life, Love and Making a Difference (Health Communications, Inc.)
Taste Berries for Teens: Inspirational Short Stories and Encouragement on Life, Love, Friendship and Tough Issues (Health Communications, Inc.)
Taste-Berry Tales: Stories to Lift the Spirit, Fill the Heart and Feed the Soul (Health Communications, Inc.)
A String of Pearls: Inspirational Stories Celebrating the Resiliency of the Human Spirit (Adams Media)
Gifts of the Heart: Stories That Celebrate Life's Defining Moments (Health Communications, Inc.)
Values from the Heartland: Stories of an American Farmgirl (Health Communications, Inc.)
Stress & Your Child: Helping Kids Cope with the Strains & Pressures of Life (Random House)
Helping Your Child Succeed in School (Active Parenting)
Safeguarding Your Teenager from the Dragons of Life: A Guide to the Adolescent Years (Health Communications, Inc.)
How to Develop Self-Esteem in Your Child: 6 Vital Ingredients (Macmillan/Ballantine)
Keeping Our Children Safe: A Guide to Emotional, Physical, Intellectual and Spiritual Wellness (John Knox/Westminster Press)
Is Your Net-Working? A Complete Guide to Building Contacts and Career Visibility (John Wiley)

Also by Jennifer Leigh Youngs

365 Days of Taste-Berry Inspiration for Teens (Health Communications, Inc.)
A Teen's Guide to Living Drug-Free (Health Communications, Inc.)
A Taste-Berry Teen's Guide to Setting & Achieving Goals (Health Communications, Inc.)
Taste Berries for Teens #3: Inspirational Stories and Encouragement on Life, Love, Friends and the Face in the Mirror (Health Communications, Inc.)
A Taste-Berry Teen's Guide to Managing the Stress and Pressures of Life (Health Communications, Inc.)
More Taste Berries for Teens: A Second Collection of Inspirational Short Stories and Encouragement on Life, Love, Friendship and Tough Issues (Health Communications, Inc.)
Feeling Great, Looking Hot & Loving Yourself: Health, Fitness and Beauty for Teens (Health Communications, Inc.)
Taste Berries for Teens Journal: My Thoughts on Life, Love and Making a Difference (Health Communications, Inc.)
Taste Berries for Teens: Inspirational Short Stories and Encouragement on Life, Love, Friendship and Tough Issues (Health Communications, Inc.)

Also by Debbie Thurman

12 Months of Faith: A Devotional Journal for Teens (Faith Communications)
From Depression to Wholeness: The Anatomy of Healing (Cedar House Publishers)
Journaling from Depression to Wholeness: A 12-Week Program for Healing (Cedar House Publishers)
Hold My Heart: A Teen's Journal for Healing and Personal Growth (Cedar House Publishers)

Contents

PART 4: MATURING IN MY FAITH— LETTING GOD "GROW ME UP"

Acknowledgments

This book has been a divine journey, and we'd like to thank those who have played a part in bringing it to the hearts and hands of our readers. First, to the many teens who were a part of this new undertaking: Thank you for so generously opening your hearts and sharing your experiences so that other teens might have the courage and desire to talk and walk with God. This is our eleventh book for teen readers, so we know how important and powerful your views are to your peers. In this book, your words witness in a most profound way.

As always, we extend our heartfelt gratitude to our publisher, Peter Vegso, whose publishing mission is "to change the world one book at a time." To be in his presence is to both enjoy his eminent playfulness, as well as to feel the indelible majesty of a mission borne out of its own personal destiny. Thank you, Peter, for making work fun—and so very purposeful! Thank you as well to the talented staff at HCI, most especially those with whom we work most closely: Lisa Drucker, Susan Tobias, Christine Belleris, Lori Golden, Kim Weiss, Randee Feldman, Terry Burke, Kelly Johnson Maragni, Tom Sand, Larissa Henoch, Elisabeth Rinaldi and Brian Peluso—as well as to the many others who play an intricate role in transporting this labor of love into the hands and hearts of our readers. As always, a special thanks to Andrea Perrine Brower for her beautiful cover designs on our books. As with many of our books for teens, we work with many students, educators and school administrators and we are deeply grateful to those of you who were a part of this one—thank you.

And to the many important blessings in our personal lives.

Bettie: Thank you to my family for helping me understand that while we are born into the arms of those we call "relatives," we are all—everyone in the world—brothers and sisters. Feeling as interdependent as I do paves the way for feeling the collective joy and energy of the human family, and yet to feel that it is deeply wrong that anyone on Earth be in jeopardy, be it from oppression, deprivation, starvation, violence or war. We do need God. Thank you, Debbie, for all your love and soul and work on this important book for teen readers. Years ago upon meeting, we knew intuitively we'd been called together for a reason, and this book is one of them! I'd also like to pay tribute to my beloved daughter: Jennifer, as always, I honor the tenderness of who you are, and deeply respect the privilege of being your mother and friend. Your soul-search has been an intense one, and you've responded by aligning your life with God's will. That you walk with God deepens my faith, and praise is His just knowing that the single most important experience a mother wants for her child—knowing God's love—has been gifted to you, completely humbles and melts my heart. Imagine, eternal life, together.

Jennifer: First, thank you, Mom (Bettie Youngs), for yet another expression of love and soulship. Working together is always a joy, and since this has been a book we've wanted to do for some time, doing it together is one more totally awesome memory between us. It is with so much love that I touch it one last time as it makes its way into the hands of readers. A very special thanks to my dad and to my grandfather, as well as to friends Jimmy, Genta, Fred, Tyla, Laura, Clayt, Paula and Shari for their support and love. The time we've spent together has been a big part of my own growth, and I thank you from the bottom of my heart.

Debbie: First and foremost, thank you to my husband Russ, and to daughters Jenni and Natalie, for your encouragement, love and patience, as always. Our standard family joke is that writer's block is not a problem; it's figuring out how to turn the stuff off! Thanks to all those who blessed this book with their prayers and encouragement. You know who you are. Hugs to Bettie and Jennifer for allowing me to be a part of this wonderful undertaking and for their heart for teens. You're the best! Finally, I thank my Lord and Savior, Jesus Christ, who gives me the seeds to sow and the grace to grow. I am truly blessed.

And from all of us, to our many *brothers* and *sisters everywhere in the world*, thank you for sharing the journey and for touching our hearts.

As always, we give all glory to God from whom all blessings flow.

Introduction

Dear Readers,

It is with great joy and humility that we bring you *A Teen's Guide to Christian Living: Practical Answers to Tough Questions About God and Faith*. The desire to live life the way our Creator intended is at the very heart of human existence. What could be more important than knowing God and experiencing the peace, joy and comfort of a personal relationship with Him? What could be more reassuring than knowing that in each and every choice we make and in each and every step we take, clarity and godly wisdom are ours for the asking?

Open your heart to the asking; certainly God is ever ready to guard and guide the heart of His teens in seeking "truth." Listen to the encouragement behind His gentle yet firm instruction: "Do not let anyone look down on you because you are young, but set an example in word, in conduct, in life, in love" (1 Tim. 4:12). As you know all too well, standing this tall won't always be easy. We work with and hear from teens worldwide, and so learn of the struggles you face as you strive to live according to your values and beliefs—and yet be counted among your peers as "one of us."

We are also well aware that as you prepare to step into adulthood—thinking more independently and making choices accordingly—you will desire to know God *on your own terms*. Perhaps Brandon Lange explained it best: "In my home, faith was a family affair. We went to church together; we prayed at mealtimes. I accepted God on 'family terms.' Now, at seventeen, I'm thinking for myself, and I'm asking: 'What do I believe, and why? What is *my* relationship with God, and how do *God and I* live my life?' As I ask these questions, I realize I'm in new territory. I want to know what God expects of me personally, even if that means I'll be *different* from who I am now."

Many teens find themselves filled with similar questions. Think about it: Is there supposed to be a difference between the way a Christian lives and the way a nonbeliever lives? We're all human when you look beneath the surface. We have the same needs, the same basic desires, the same fears and amazingly similar dreams. It's our choices—what we choose to display as our character—that sets us apart from one another.

So how do we know what is expected of us as Christians? Well, we can go to "God's Big Instruction Book"—the Bible—and check out its rules and examples. There really is no other blueprint for Christian living. Perhaps you are somewhat familiar with the Bible, and perhaps you have never read it. Maybe no one has ever told you that you should. Despite the occasional controversy over what role biblical concepts have played in world history, governments or other institutions, the fact remains that there are universally accepted truths and values that keep the world from falling into chaos. They sprang from common belief in an authority higher than any human being on Earth. For thousands of years, mankind has looked to God as the creator of the universe and all its laws. The obvious next question is, *Will we choose to live according to what He expects of us?* Each of us must answer for ourselves.

This book is our best human attempt to present the answers to questions teens ask most frequently about God, faith and applying Christian principles to everyday life. It is based on our collective knowledge and experience in traveling the Christian road. The answers don't originate with us, however, but come from the collective wisdom of the ages and from the Word of God, which we accept as the ultimate God-breathed truth. We believe that you will discover more happiness and peace in those who are living their lives according to this truth than you will in those who live according to their own rules.

God gives us unique insights into His Word when we ask to

receive His truth. Naturally, the real truth will not be obvious to a casual reader of the Bible, no matter how wise and intellectual. It makes for interesting reading on any level, but it does not speak to our souls unless we truly know God.

If this is your first real exposure to God's truth and the principles of Christian living, we believe this book can be a real eye-opener for you and can even change your life. If you have been looking to go deeper into the Christian experience, this book can guide that exploration, as well. As you'll note, this book is divided into six units. In parts 1 through 5, you'll get a chance to explore particular topics and learn how Scripture explains and supports each one. Each chapter then closes with a "Personal Reflection" section that consists of thought-provoking questions to help you examine your own life and put Christian principles into practice. We wholeheartedly invite you to discuss these with your friends and within your youth group. We especially encourage you to share them at the dinner table with your family members.

In part 6, "Teen Talk," you'll find true stories contributed by real teens who each share an experience that made them see how real God is in their lives. In each story, you'll see how teens like you learned to rely on God during a moment of truth in their lives. May each of their stories inspire you, give you hope to face life's challenges and encourage you in similar struggles that you (or a friend or family member) may be going through.

A Teen's Guide to Christian Living will help you better understand the Christian faith and know *who God is*. Obviously, you will spend the rest of your life getting to know God personally, but this book is a start. It will help you gain insight into questions such as:

- Who is God, and why should I believe in Him?
- What does God expect of me, and how will I discover this?
- How well does God know me, and does He love me, no

matter what is in my past or in spite of the things I've said and done?

- Does God have a plan for me? Specifically, does He care who my friends are or what kind of work I do? Does He have someone in mind for me to love?
- Is there a "best" way to pray, and how does prayer make a difference?
- Does God watch over my family—even if other family members don't believe in God?
- Does loving God mean I can't go to parties, kiss or flirt?
- Does loving God mean I can only associate with those of my own religious beliefs?
- How can I serve and follow God and still be a "regular" teen with "regular" friends and a "regular" life?

So here, from our heart to yours, is a book to help you know more about God and how to serve Him "in word, in conduct, in life, in love" (1 Tim. 4:12). It is our prayer that *A Teen's Guide to Christian Living* will become a resource you treasure for years to come, second perhaps only to your Bible.

Bettie, Jennifer and Debbie

A Special Word from the Authors

For the sake of simplicity and clarity, personal pronoun references to God in this book will be capitalized (i.e., He) while references to the person of Jesus Christ will be lowercased (he). This in no way makes a doctrinal statement, but serves to make clear the distinction between the two entities.

Part 1

Who Is God (and Why Does It Matter)?

*I am Alpha and Omega, the beginning
and the end, the first and the last.*
—Revelation 22:13

*If the peace of God is our only goal, then we will
succeed, no matter what the outcome of a situation.
We detach from what things look like,
and embrace the love that is always present.
That is the rock on which we stand.*
—Marianne Williamson

*To believe in God for me is to feel
that there is a God, a living one,
who with irresistible force urges us
towards more loving.*
—Vincent van Gogh

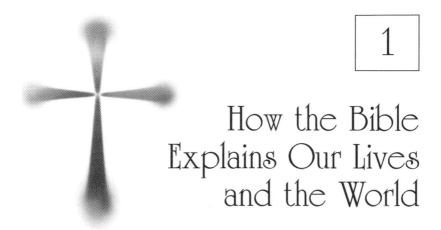

How the Bible Explains Our Lives and the World

The Bible opens with the words, "In the beginning, God . . . " Have you ever really wondered what "in the beginning" is all about? Time is a fascinating concept, so much so that some of our favorite science-fiction stories deal with altering time or traveling through time. As little children, we might have heard our parents or Sunday school teachers say that God has always existed. Always? Those of us who like to dig deeper and want to know the hows and whys of life are sure to ask the obvious question: "How?"

There was a beginning. No matter how we believe it all got started, it *did* get started, and because it did, you are here. It is only natural to ask, "How, and by what or whom?" It isn't so important to know when the beginning was (yes, we know about carbon dating) as it is to know that it was an event of great magnitude. A famous scientist decided the term "Big Bang" was appropriate. There have been all sorts of theories through the ages, some of them amusing myths, about how the universe came into being. Some want to say the Big Bang was a spontaneous event that just happened once upon a time when all the elements were exactly right. Just as seventeen-year-old Lance Waldrop (whose story you'll read in part 6) believed, there's only one little problem with that thought. Where did the elements

3

come from? As we walk back through time to consider when the beginning was, we have to come to a point when we realize something can't come from nothing. It takes a Big God to make a Big Bang.

This brings us back to the question of how God existed before the beginning. It's kind of like having two mirrors reflect off of each other. Can they reflect nothing? Hardly. They can reflect an image back and forth to infinity, one would have to suppose. We've no doubt all sat mesmerized at one time or another as we've tried to see how far into infinity we can actually glimpse with two mirrors. Fascinating, isn't it?

Is God infinity, then? The old hymns your grandparents liked to sing, reflecting the words of Scripture, spoke of God as the Alpha and the Omega. That's A to Z, in case you don't know any of the Greek alphabet. In other words, man sees God as the everything. How does God see God? When He revealed Himself to Moses in the Old Testament, God called Himself "I AM" (Exod. 3:14). If God existed before the beginning (remember, "in the beginning, God . . . "), then He would have to be infinite, or existing beyond what we know as time. I AM. Period. That may boggle the human mind, but He's God. We're not.

The next word after God in Genesis 1:1 is "created." The God who always was, is and will be, acted. He created the heavens and the Earth, and everything else. That creative force brought human beings into existence. Those people, as God commanded, were "fruitful" and multiplied into nations that covered the world. God's people. It began with the first two people, Adam and Eve, who were "made in God's image" (Gen. 1:27). Although God considered His creation of man to be "very good" (Gen. 1:31), sin (rebellion) was already lurking in the world. It didn't take long for it to capture the heart of mankind as Satan appeared to Adam and Eve, tempting them with divine knowledge and power. We know this as "the fall" or "original sin." Because of this event, every person from that point on was considered to be born with a sinful heredity. What's more, we are all considered lost or separated from God through this sin unless we allow Him to redeem us.

God's Promises: From Abraham to a Jewish Carpenter

Why God chose a certain people through whom to work in early history we cannot know. After a number of generations (all those "begats" in the Old Testament) and God's disappointment with the sinfulness of His people, He chose to form an important covenant (or agreement) with Abraham, originally known as Abram.

Israel and generations beyond grew out of God's promise to Abraham that his descendants would be as plentiful as the stars, even though he and his wife Sarai (later renamed Sarah) were old and childless. The story of Abraham's faith is a fascinating one that begins in Genesis 12. It explains how the Jewish nation descended from Isaac, the miracle son of the elderly Abraham and Sarah, while the Arab nation descended from Ishmael, the earlier illegitimate son of Abraham and his wife's Egyptian maid, Hagar. Now you know why the Jewish and Arab worlds have been at odds since the beginning.

Of course, there is much history leading up to this covenant between God and Abraham, including the Great Flood (which God used to rebuild His creation) and the scattering of nations from the tower of Babel. Hollywood has taken much of its epic film material from the early chapters of the Bible. Those old classical stories, along with every element of the Bible that is inspired (literally, breathed into) by God, have influenced a lot of the world's great literature. Do they still have lessons to teach us today? You bet. Faith always matters; sin is still highly contagious; God always has a plan, and He still keeps His promises, to name just a few.

The Old Testament foreshadows the New Testament by

speaking, sometimes quite poetically, about the coming of Jesus Christ. Much of early biblical history consists of God beginning to work out His secondary plan in mankind because the first plan, which was paradise on Earth, was rejected by Adam and Eve, allowing the father of lies—Satan—to operate freely in the world. Human nature became corrupt. It's not hard to imagine why, since even the angels had their problems. Lucifer (Satan) was the brightest among them before he and others rebelled against God.

Why Did God Give Man "Free Will"?

Had God not given man (and angels) the free will to choose what he wanted, His creation would have been meaningless. Love that is dictated is not love. Man chose poorly, egged on by the lost angels who wanted company in their misery, and for generations, sin grew and corrupted the hearts of mankind. God would have to form a new covenant with His beloved children, one that would give clearer meaning to the old laws and make some of them no longer necessary. Isaiah 53, for instance, is a well-known description of Jesus, the Son of God and Son of Man—"a man of sorrows and familiar with suffering"—and a glimpse into his earthly life, and sacrificial death, to come. You may be familiar with the famous verse, "We all, like sheep, have gone astray, each of us has turned to his own way; and the Lord has laid on him the iniquity (sin) of us all" (Isa. 53:6). Jesus was God's plan to set the world right by answering for the sins of man.

Why Is the Bible "The" Book (Sacred to the Christian Faith)?

It is important to know that the Bible must be seen as a large mosaic, with all the pieces fitting together to make a picture. It will certainly make far more sense when taken as a whole, not in isolated bits and pieces. We must all read it for ourselves over a period of time to gain a sense of the scope of its plan and purpose. Some read it as literature, and it is certainly both beautiful and fascinating as such. However, a person who has accepted Christ as personal Savior then receives a deeper understanding of the Bible's meaning. The more one truly studies God's Word, the clearer it becomes. It is not unusual to discover more and more truth, even after reading it for a great many years.

If you placed all the holy books or scriptures of major religions or worldviews side by side, you would find many similar passages or teachings. So why is the Bible different, and what makes it so sacred to the Christian faith? The first five books of the Bible chronicle (tell a story of) many generations of God's chosen people, including the conflicts among those who were scattered abroad. Some of these people were heroic people of faith; some were singled out for the mistakes they made. God is seen in the Old Testament over and over as a loving God who wants to protect His people, but also as a God who naturally becomes angry with the fickle nature, ingratitude and forgetfulness of His people as they try to figure out what they perceive to be a better way than the one God has outlined for them. They even choose to reject God and to worship other false gods or idols.

God sent various prophets out into the world to remind His people of the promises He had made and of His deliverance from their former slavery and hardship. The prophets spoke for God and gave warnings of the discipline that awaited His people unless they turned back to Him. Prophets sometimes performed miracles in God's name and provided signs of His power to convince the people that He was still who He said He was. Still, many continued to stray and fall out of God's grace. God had no choice but to make a new covenant with His people because He had promised that He would not destroy the world again as He had done in the form of the great flood of Noah's time. Instead of abolishing all of the old laws, He chose to send His own son to Earth to embody a new covenant that would make the old one more meaningful, but also provide a solution to the problem of sin in man. The New Testament opens with the hope that arrives in the world through the birth of Jesus. It had been hundreds of years since God had spoken through any prophet, and a dark cloud of sin had fallen over the Earth. Faithful men and women of God still awaited some sign that God had not forgotten them.

Why and How the Bible Is Unique from Any Other Holy Book

The Bible, in its entirety, is unique from any other holy book because it combines these two covenants and outlines the plan of salvation through Jesus Christ, who is clearly shown to be not just a man, but the divine son of God. Furthermore, through Jesus a very important entity came into the world—the Holy Spirit—who God sent after Jesus had fulfilled the new covenant to each believing person as a guide and a comforter and a means of knowing God through a deeply personal relationship. The Holy Spirit is meant to connect us directly to God and to give us the means through which to communicate with Him and to know the truth of the Scriptures. "The Spirit helps us in our weakness," the apostle Paul writes in the book of Romans. "We do not know what we ought to pray for, but the Spirit himself intercedes for us with groans that words cannot express. And He who searches our hearts knows the mind of the Spirit because the Spirit intercedes for the saints (believers) in accordance with God's will" (Rom. 8: 26–27). We will discuss the Holy Spirit in more detail in chapter 3.

The Bible, the most widely read of all books, is recognized among true followers of Christ as the divinely inspired Word of God. That is one of the fundamental beliefs of the Christian church. It is not to be proved or disproved, but merely accepted as truth on the basis of faith. The Bible was written over a period of more than 1,500 years by a series of authors who wrote according to the instruction of God Himself. It predates by far all known writings of significance and is unique in that it has survived throughout all those centuries, despite the great hatred of those who have opposed its teaching. Many people have wanted to deny the authenticity of the Bible, but the longer we live the more proof we find that it is both historically and scientifically accurate.

What Does It Mean to Be a Christian?

Through his brief ministry on Earth, Jesus began what would become a worldwide impact on the lives of people. Oh, he wouldn't be universally accepted. We still have free will. The plan has never changed, however. As we have seen, God originally chose the nation of Israel to carry His truth to the world. Christ himself was born a Jewish descendant of one of the original twelve tribes of Israel through the line of King David. In turn, he chose twelve disciples whom he taught and equipped to do the work of building the early church after his death. This was the birthing stage of Christianity. The twelve became eleven because one deserted and betrayed him. These disciples, who walked alongside Jesus during his three-year ministry on Earth, went on to plant churches around the Middle East, Asia and parts of Europe. Others who came after them, the most famous being Paul (originally Saul of Tarsus), writer of the well-known epistles or letters to the various churches we see in the New Testament, expanded the church even more.

The result of all that work of the early church is a movement that has never stopped growing and changing lives. We see its impact all around us today, in every corner of the world. Jesus told Peter, one of his beloved disciples, that he would build his church upon "this rock" (Matt. 16:18), which was Peter's literal name, and that not even the gates of hell would conquer it. Peter helped fulfill that prophecy.

It is hard for much of the world to understand the depth of

faith that drove the early church fathers to face loneliness, hunger, sickness, extreme danger and even death while serving the God they loved. They did all this so that they could carry out the Great Commission of Jesus Christ to take his saving message of good news to the ends of the Earth. It was a God-breathed mission that continues to this day. While the mission has been attacked from all sides, it has never in these more than 2,000 years been derailed.

Nine Beliefs That Set Christians Apart from Other Faiths

Christians adhere to nine fundamental beliefs that set them apart from other faiths. Because it is important for you to know what they are, we are including them here. The questions that are raised by this list will be answered in the remainder of this book. This particular version was prepared by the editors of *Christianity Today* magazine:

1) Christians believe that the Bible is the uniquely inspired and fully trustworthy word of God. It is the final authority for Christians in matters of belief and practice, and though it was written long ago, it continues to speak to believers today.

2) Christians believe in one God in three persons. He is distinct from His creation, yet intimately involved with it as its sustainer and redeemer.

3) Christians believe that the world was created once by the divine will, was corrupted by sin, yet under God's providence moves toward final perfection.

4) Christians believe that, through God's grace and favor, lost sinners are rescued from the guilt, power and eternal consequences of their evil thoughts, words and deeds.

5) Christians believe that it is appointed for human beings to die once and after that face judgment. In Adam's sin, the human race was spiritually alienated from God, and that those who are called by God and respond to His grace will have eternal life. Those who persist in rebellion will be lost eternally.

6) Christians believe that spirit beings inhabit the universe, some good and some evil, but worship is due to God alone.

7) Christians believe that God has given us a clear revelation of Himself in Jesus and the sacred Scriptures. He has empowered by His Spirit prophets, apostles, evangelists and pastors who are teachers charged to guide us into faith and holiness in accordance with His Word.

8) Christians believe that life is to be highly esteemed but that it must be subordinated in the service of Biblical love and justice.

9) Christians believe that Jesus is God incarnate and, therefore, the only sure path to salvation. Many religions may offer ethical and spiritual insights, but only Jesus is the Way, the Truth and the Life.

Today, we are all still free to receive the good news or to reject it. And what is this good news? Simply that Jesus died for our sins and that all those who believe he is the son of God and who accept him as their personal Savior—"the way, the truth and the life" (John 14:16)—will spend eternal life with him. Believing in this—and living according to the Word of God—is what it means to be a Christian.

Persecution of Christians still goes on in some parts of the world. But wherever free people gather to worship God as they choose, the truth of old rings out. The line of David extends to the present and into the future. Amazing!

Personal Reflection

1. Have I struggled to understand God's role in creation? If so, why?
2. Is it hard for me to accept the Old Testament stories as history? Why or why not?
3. Do I believe that we all have a corrupt or "sin nature" and that I need God's help to avoid temptation and poor choices? Have I ever been taught, instead, that I am basically good?
4. Do I believe that I have a personal relationship with God through Jesus and the Holy Spirit?
5. Do I or my family own a Bible? How is it used in my home?

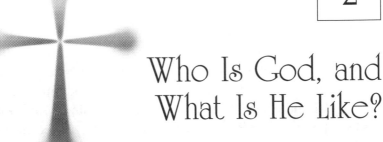

Who Is God, and What Is He Like?

When you consider that we are all "made in God's image," what comes to mind? "As a little kid, I struggled to grasp what God looked like or how I could see Him," seventeen-year-old Teresa Allen remembers. "I finally decided He was a kind old man, sort of like my grandfather, who had passed away. I had a deep need to know God as tender and fatherly."

Teresa believed God loved her, but that He also kept track of her sins in His "Book of Life," as she had been told by her mother. Teresa also learned at her mother's knee and from Sunday school teachers that she could go to God with anything in her heart and talk to Him about it—that He was her personal heavenly father, and a God of love and compassion. "Not having much of a relationship with my alcoholic father, this mattered a great deal to me," she says.

It is true that we first learn how to relate to God from our parents and the significant adults in our lives. You may not fully understand at this point in your life why you may distrust God, have total blind faith in Him or fall somewhere in between. Think for a moment about your home life or where your first impressions of God were formed. Have you had a loving, fatherly presence in your life or, like Teresa, have you been brought up in a home that is marred by the absence of a parent or one who has been distant, ill or abusive? Naturally, your ability to know God as a loving, trustworthy father will be affected by your experiences in your own family.

Scott Gilbert, sixteen, never really knew his father. He walked out on him and his mother when he was only two years old, leaving a boy who could have grown up angry and bitter. "I was hurt, and I knew something essential was missing," said Scott, "but what is amazing is the way that other godly men came into my life to be role models and to restore my faith in God." That kind of love changed Scott's perception of himself and of God. He no longer sees himself as that abandoned little boy.

Six Attributes of God

Who is this God we serve? What do we mean when we speak of godly character? It's interesting to see how God's character is revealed over and over in the Psalms, sometimes called "the little Bible." While we can note more specific attributes for God, six major ones come to light through the Bible. God exists as powerful Creator of all, as holy, as a God of justice, love and patience, and yes, anger when appropriate.

Creator/Sustainer: How Does God "Run" His Universe?

Since the beginning of time, people have had a sense that they are not alone in this world, but are connected in some essential way to a power that gives them life and purpose. We could call this our God-sense, or the desire that He has placed in each of us to connect with His creative force and to know Him on a deep and personal level. Biblical history demonstrates that we humans can be pretty good at failing to recognize that God-voice within us. The Psalms are perhaps the clearest historical illustration of the desire to know God in the Bible because they uncover the emotions we feel in our universal struggle and the whole range of needs that really only God can meet.

One of the most heavily quoted verses from the Bible comes from the beginning of Psalm 121: "I lift up my eyes to the hills—where does my help come from?" The question is already answered, even before the next statement, "My help comes from the Lord, the Maker of heaven and Earth." While there is only one God, the different sides of His character are shown in the various biblical names that were used for Him. Entire books have been written just on this subject.

God's control over nature and all the elements is both an awesome thing to contemplate and a nagging mystery to us. When we hear of a natural disaster such as a deadly flood or an earthquake, we feel so helpless. We want to cry out to God right away to halt the destruction. And so we should, at the same time realizing that He is also the author of all the beauty in the world and is our divine protector. But He is God, and it all happens on His timetable. We can't question His purposes, no matter how strange they may seem.

Since the devastating events of September 11, 2001, people of all ages have taken a hard look at their lives and the priorities that govern them. This time of fear and uncertainty has brought some people back to a faith that they may have taken for granted. Others have wondered if there is any reason to believe at all. Those are valid concerns, and this book is one attempt to address them in language that teens (and their parents) can understand. Is God still "on the throne"? Does He still care for us? Is He really everywhere at once or omnipresent? We shall see.

Worthy of Worship: How "Holy" Is God?

It is surprising to most of us to see God referred to in the Bible as jealous. Isn't that a rather petty emotion? How can God actually let the green-eyed monster of jealousy live in Him? After a little scholarly investigation, we learn that the Hebrew word used for jealousy when God refers to Himself does not mean

what we think it does. It means He desires—in fact, demands—
our best love. He is to be our first love, and in turn He promises
to love us with "an everlasting love." Do you know the first of
the Ten Commandments that Moses brought down off the
mountain? "I am the Lord your God. . . . You shall have no other
gods before Me" (Exod. 20:2–3). The second commandment
builds on the first: "You shall not make for yourself an idol in the
form of anything in heaven above or on the Earth beneath or in
the waters below. You shall not bow down to them or worship
them; for I, the Lord your God am a jealous God" (Exod. 20:5).
While the image of a golden calf is not exactly what we may be
longing to bow down before, modern-day "gods" can come in all
sorts of packages: other people, money and personal possessions, success, status or popularity. You get the picture. Notice
the deeply personal nature of the commandments. God did not
speak to His people as a group, but as individuals, reinforcing
the nature of His relationship with each one.

God goes to great lengths to remind us in His Word that if we
honor His holiness and place Him first in our lives, other blessings can then follow. "Do not worry, saying 'What shall we eat?'
or 'What shall we drink?' or 'What shall we wear?' . . . Your
Heavenly Father knows that you need [these things]. But seek
first His kingdom and His righteousness and all these things
shall be given to you as well" (Matt. 6:31, 33). When we get it
backwards, we find ourselves in trouble.

While we don't see godly men or women with their faces literally glowing as Moses' face did in God's presence, we can still
know that God is no less holy today than He was then. Have you
been in the presence of someone who you just knew had a special relationship with God? Isn't it amazing how we can sometimes "feel" God's presence through others? What's even more
amazing is when other people can feel His presence through us.
Bible teachers may tell you that we are in the presence of God,
experiencing His holiness and His mind, when we feel deep

conviction (a sense of guilt and a desire to change) about something we've done wrong. When we are out of step with Him, running headlong toward our own selfish desires, it is much more difficult for God to get our attention.

Compassionate Judge:
Is God Always Just and Merciful?

The knowledge that God will be just or fair in His dealings with us is a double-edged sword. We certainly want Him to deal out justice, which we may see as deserving punishment, to those who have offended us or who throw their weight around and take advantage of the little guys of the world. But what about when that justice is applied to us? Then the shoe is on the other foot, and we don't much like it.

Perhaps you've heard the term "just war" being used to describe the current fight against terrorism in the world. While there are some who believe no war is just, there are others who look to history and point out that God Himself used warfare to pass judgment on His people. War terminology is used in many different ways in the Bible. It describes the basic conflict between good and evil, God and Satan. We are told in the New Testament to "put on the armor of God" (Eph. 6) to defend ourselves against the forces of evil in the world, and that our greatest struggle is not against physical, earthly powers, but against spiritual ones. Sometimes real people or nations represent that evil, however.

That infernal struggle can be reduced right down to the inner battles we all fight sometimes. *Do I really need to listen to my parents? Can't I have a little fun without anyone knowing or being hurt?* you may sometimes wonder. Cartoonists over the years have depicted our inner warfare by placing a little angel on one shoulder and a devil on the other who alternately whisper or shout in our ears to try to move us to their side. It's not quite that simple, but that animated illustration does open our eyes a bit. It's a battle none of us can escape. As sixteen-year-old Kay Jennings says, "It's easy to ignore what God is trying to tell you until after you've made the mistake." In the end, we can be thankful that God's evenhanded justice reaches to us all.

"Woe to You": Does God Ever Get Angry?

Does God ever get angry? Afraid so. No one wants to be on the receiving end of God's anger, but there can be no justice without some occasional anger. Anger is an emotion that is confusing to many of us. Have you ever wondered if you are even supposed to feel angry? If God does not want us ever to be angry, then why does His own anger come through so clearly in biblical history? Whenever you see the words "Woe to you" or something similar in the Bible, you can be sure an unpleasant word or a judgment from God is about to follow. Listen to one of these warnings from the prophet Isaiah: " . . . for they have rejected the law of the Lord Almighty and spurned the word of the Holy One of Israel. Therefore the Lord's anger burns against His people; His hand is raised and He strikes them down" (Isa. 5:24–25). Yikes! God means business.

If we are made in God's image, then we are to experience all of His character, right? That's a pretty safe assumption. In fact, just to make sure we can get that point, God gave instruction through Jesus Christ's ministry, also echoed by his disciples, that we may be angry when it is appropriate, but we may not sin in our anger. In other words, we are not to lose control or give our enemy an opportunity to use our anger against us or "give the devil a foothold" (Eph. 4:26–27). One can hardly imagine an angrier Christ than the one who drove the greedy moneychangers out of the temple because they were defiling God's holy place of worship. As we are justified in feeling anger toward others at times, God is justified in occasionally putting us in our place. That anger is balanced by yet another pair of God's characteristics, the ones for which we are most grateful.

Loving Father: Does God Love Me *No Matter What?*

Just as anger sometimes must enter into the justice equation, so must compassion. God may be angry on occasion, but—thankfully for us—it takes Him a long time to get there. No earthly parent has that kind of patience. It's as if there is a big cup into which He pours his anger. It holds a lot, but when it is so full it begins to overflow, then judgment is sure to follow. We can't know exactly when that is going to be, but we can be assured it will not be a moment before we truly deserve it. This is a truth we don't like to talk about much. To simplify this concept, just ask yourself what loving parent would *never* discipline his own child. This pain is a necessary one at times. It's never pleasant, but it's how we learn. This knowledge gives us the healthy respect for God we need, but it can be abused by misguided parents or teachers who overuse fear tactics "for our own good." Perhaps you've experienced this kind of "discipline" in your own life. Parents aren't perfect. They will make mistakes, just as you will, but God doesn't allow any of us excuses for making the same ones over and over. We will naturally respect those in authority who are consistent and whose love comes through in their discipline. God represents the standard for that kind of fairness.

As individual children of God, we are given ample opportunity to change our ways before He takes action, and His discipline will be suited to the crime—no more, no less than we need. Despite what preachers or so-called prophets may say, no one truly knows if an act of God is a judgment or a wake-up call. Only God knows. If there is fear in this, it is a healthy fear. And if God should figuratively "spank" us, He also will allow us to come immediately to Him and nestle in His comforting presence. No loving father or mother takes any joy in correcting their children or watching them go through a painful lesson. Okay, so you're a little old to climb into Mommy's or Daddy's lap. Perish the thought! But you need to know that a parent or loving counselor will be there for you. We can come to God with the same familiarity that we bring to our parents. Just as Jesus cried out to God in anguish before he was to be crucified (see Mark 14:36), we can cry out that same familiar "Abba!" (Daddy!) and know we will be comforted.

Our Love—Sweet Perfume to God

It is love that caused us to be here in the first place. God wanted a people who could love and serve Him, but who He could also love, protect and bless. His original plan did not call for all the pain and heartache we see around us. So that our love for Him would be meaningful, He designed us with the free will to choose to act as we desired. The rules were pretty simple in the beginning, but temptation overcame us and the rules had to change for our own good. Human nature can cause us to do some ugly things. At the same time, our divine nature gives us heroic strength. Why? Here it comes again: We are made in God's image and according to the blueprint of His own character. Just as we are loved, we are to love God, or as Jennifer's grandmother so eloquently detailed (see Jennifer's story in part 6) to be "sweet perfume to God." Still, we are not gods ourselves, so we struggle with the human, corruptible side of our nature. It is God's loving compassion toward us, with all our weaknesses, that allows us to celebrate our own humanness. The principles laid down in the creation story assure us that God was highly pleased with His most wonderful achievement—us! He declared this work "very good," as we see in Genesis 1:31.

It is fascinating to see more and more scientific research today that points to a personal force behind the universe. The complex genetic structure we discover in everything around us could only have been purposefully designed, we are told over and over. There is great comfort in this. How could we live in this world and have any hope at all if everything were based on random, meaningless events? There are rules, and they hold everything together. It is upon this foundation that we base government and other institutions. If we did not have the innate ability to govern ourselves as God governs us, everything would fall apart.

The Ten Commandments: The Law of All Laws

Man has generally looked to the original laws God handed down through Moses to His people—the Ten Commandments—as the basis for all civilized institutions. They serve as our guide to knowing what God expects of us, and therefore what we should expect of each other. The boundaries established by godly law allow all people to enjoy the "inalienable rights" referred to in the foundational documents of our nation.

While most of us think we know the Ten Commandments, few people can actually recite them all, and rarely in order. Here is the entire list from Exodus 20:1–17 (the bracketed numbers represent the order of the commandments, not the actual verses): "And God spoke all these words: 'I am the Lord, your God, who brought you out of Egypt, out of the land of slavery.

[1] 'You shall have no other gods before me.

[2] 'You shall not make for yourself any idol in the form of anything in heaven above or on the Earth beneath or in the waters below. You shall not bow down to them or worship them; for I, the Lord your God, am a jealous God, punishing the children for the sin of the fathers to the third and fourth generation of those who hate me, but showing love to a thousand generations of those who love me and keep my commandments.

[3] 'You shall not misuse the name of the Lord your God, for
     the Lord will not hold anyone guiltless who misuses His
     name.
[4] 'Remember the Sabbath day by keeping it holy. Six days
     you shall labor and do all your work, but the seventh day
     is a Sabbath to the Lord your God. . . . For in six days the
     Lord made the heavens and the Earth, the sea and all that
     is in them, but He rested on the seventh day. Therefore the
     Lord blessed the Sabbath day and made it holy.
[5] 'Honor your father and your mother, so that you may live
     long in the land the Lord your God is giving you.
[6] 'You shall not murder.
[7] 'You shall not commit adultery.
[8] 'You shall not steal.
[9] 'You shall not give false testimony against your neighbor.
[10] 'You shall not covet your neighbor's house. You shall not
     covet your neighbor's wife, or his manservant or maid-
     servant, his ox or donkey, or anything that belongs to
     your neighbor.'"

We will be referring to most of the commandments in later
chapters where they are applicable. Most are self-explanatory,
but some may need a little clarification. What does it mean to
"misuse" the name of God, for instance? It refers to swearing an
oath by His name or cursing in His name. The word "covet" is
not in general use anymore, but it means to want something that
is not yours or to envy someone their possessions or blessings.
Do you see how coveting can lead to stealing, committing adultery (having sex outside your own marriage), lying (bearing
"false witness") or even to murder? God may have placed this
commandment last on the list, but it is hardly the least
important.

So, there really does appear to be a purpose for everything.
We want a world where love and harmony are the rule, not the

exception. Yet our human weakness takes over sometimes, and God's even hand of justice must be called in to set things right again. It's like living in a great big family. Someone has to be in charge—someone we can look up to, honor, trust, love and be loved by. Without that someone, there would be chaos.

It's not unusual to wonder who God is or where He is from time to time. It's not unusual for us to think that we need to put on our Sunday faces to come into God's presence. In truth, He lets us come just as we are, with all our doubts and faults. You see, He knows all about us already. He made us just the way He wanted us, and He made us to know Him. He is holy, He is God, but He is not so far away that we can't "touch" Him.

Personal Reflection

1. Who is God to me? Is He my loving Heavenly Father, or do I feel He has no interest in me or He is "out to get me"? In what ways do I feel I can "touch" Him?
2. Do I struggle with any of God's characteristics? If so, which ones?
3. Do I feel that God has disciplined me in some way? If so, what did I learn from it?
4. Do I remember some times when I asked God to comfort me? What happened?
5. Do I believe God is just as present today as He was in days of old?

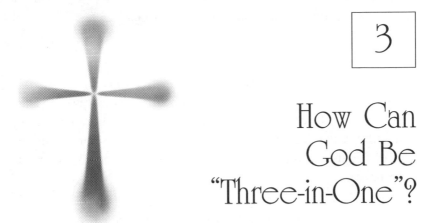

How Can God Be "Three-in-One"?

Have you found yourself confused, even if you have been raised in the church, by the concept (also called doctrine) of the "Holy Trinity"? You may have heard it referred to as "the Godhead." This is the blending of three separate entities or beings into one God, and is the origin of the term "triune," or three-in-one. In the Catholic church, one pays visible respect to the Trinity by making the sign of the cross, or touching the forehead, the abdomen and each shoulder to represent God the Father, God the Son and God the Holy Spirit. The custom or sacrament of water baptism includes a reference by the baptizer to each person of the Trinity as the believer is immersed or sprinkled. Protestants affirm the Trinity in their creeds, such as the Apostle's Creed, and statements of faith. Many people don't understand the meaning behind these rituals or references, however.

While we can at least accept and perhaps visualize in some way God as our Heavenly Father, and we know Jesus as an historical figure, we have a harder time understanding who, what and why the Holy Spirit is. It is not unusual for younger children to be confused and even a little frightened by the third element in the Trinity because the word "spirit" is interchangeable with the word "ghost." We begin to understand somewhere during our youth that we can't see, feel or touch God in the usual sense—that He is a spiritual being—but the idea of a ghost flying around trying to communicate with us, whether holy or not, is just a little unsettling. We seem much more comfortable with the idea of angels among us and have less trouble accepting them as spiritual beings.

Who Is the Holy Spirit?

The very earliest recorded history of the church, which Jesus commanded his disciples (then and now) to establish, began with his "Great Commission" at the end of Matthew's gospel: "All authority in heaven and on Earth has been given to me. . . . Go and make disciples of all nations, baptizing them in the name of the Father and of the Son and of the Holy Spirit, and teaching them to obey everything I have commanded you" (Matt. 28:18–20).

Other gospels record additional details about what Jesus told his disciples before his earthly life was over. Luke's gospel, John's gospel and the Book of Acts, also written by Luke, contain Jesus' promise that he would send a "power from on high" to the eleven remaining disciples after they had waited for a while. "I will ask the Father, and He will give you another Counselor to be with you forever—the Spirit of truth" (John 14:16). In fact, Jesus told them they would be "baptized with the Holy Spirit" (Acts 1:5). Biblical history tells us this divine gift was given to them while they waited in a secluded room in Jerusalem, as Jesus had told them to do, following his death and resurrection. This initial arrival of the Holy Spirit to followers of Christ (described in Acts 2:1–21) is known as "The Pentecost" because it happened on the Feast of Pentecost, a Jewish custom. Following this event, Jesus' disciples were filled with supernatural insights, and they preached powerful sermons that converted a great many people to Christianity. This is even more amazing when you consider how confused and afraid they were following Jesus' death.

"Spirit-Filled"—Recognizing
God's Presence Within Us

This God-presence we know as the Holy Spirit was intended for all followers of Christ who simply ask to receive it. It is Christ who sent it back from the Father to all of mankind, according to his own words and the acts recorded in the New Testament. The Holy Spirit, simply put, is God *alive in us,* just as He was alive in Jesus. It is God's way of providing us with the power to know Him and His will for us. When you hear of someone referred to as "Spirit-filled," it means that person is believed to be in close relationship with God or is living according to His will instead of his own self-focused desires. It is certainly the goal of every devoted Christian.

A new or young believer generally finds this concept more than a little weird. How, you might wonder, will I know if something is from God or from Mars? What about negative interference from the enemy, which can blind us to the real truth? How can we even know if we have the presence of the Holy Spirit? One way is to check the "fruit on the tree." Do I or others tend to exhibit the so-called "fruit of the Spirit"? A list of these qualities appears in Galatians 5:22–23: "love, joy, peace, patience, kindness, goodness, faithfulness, gentleness and self-control." These traits are the gold standard we desire to live by more and more as we mature into the Christian life. It is the Holy Spirit that helps us acquire the discipline for more of the character of God. Not only will we become aware of this change in us, but it will show to others, as well.

A Greek word commonly used in the New Testament for the Holy Spirit is *Paracletos,* or a helper who comes alongside. This term beautifully represents the comforting, healing, teaching and even the rebuking or correcting nature of the Holy Spirit. A familiar representation in your parents' day of the conscience, that inner voice that keeps us on the straight and narrow, was little Jiminy Cricket in the Disney film *Pinocchio*. Disney movies are still a big part of our culture, so you probably saw that old movie yourself when you were little. Some children (kids were more naive in those days) were so taken with Pinocchio's Jiminy-conscience that they wouldn't harm a cricket in case it was someone's conscience.

We have the ageless spirit of God Himself mysteriously knowing what we need even before we ask. If you wrestle with all this, you might want to ask yourself how you can so easily get caught up in some sci-fi movie magic that seems real enough to have you wondering about telepathic alien life-forms one day, yet get freaked out the next by the thought of the real God of the universe seeking to talk to you.

Why Is Jesus Called "Son of God, Son of Man"?

To be a true Christian is not only to accept the Holy Spirit as a divine part of God and begin to understand how this gift operates in us, but also to accept the divine nature of Jesus, the middle part of the Trinity. The linchpin of the Christian faith—what holds it all together—is to know Jesus Christ as both the Son of God and the Son of Man, sent by God through the most humble of births to live among us. Sinless. Miracle worker. Crucified to death—a tragedy on the surface, yet a wonderful fulfillment of God's plan to set humanity right. Bodily risen from the dead and enthroned in heaven once again with God. Whew! That's a lot for anybody to take in. Some won't take it in. Jesus is a unique figure in history. It is tempting to take what is so lofty and divine and want to bring it down to Earth, to our level. Yet, isn't that just what God did through the life of Jesus? Think about it.

Jesus called himself "the way, the truth and the life" (John 14:6). He meant he is a door to God. In a sense, it is God's divine chain of command. Jesus is working through the Spirit to get us before the Father. We are never really aware that we are going through the other two elements to be in God's presence. It all happens instantaneously.

But wait. Couldn't God have done it without Jesus? Well, He tried it once. The problem wasn't in Him, but in us, His stubborn, strong-willed children. In God's view, we needed a bridge. To the Christian (literally, "little Christ"), that bridge is Jesus Christ. As we know, there are other worldviews, other perceived roads to God's heaven. Still, everyone has to face the same question sooner or later: Does God just want me to live a good, moral life? How do I fit Jesus into the equation? When we accept Christ into our hearts, we also receive the Holy Spirit, the "still, small voice" that combines Father and Son. This is Jesus' gift back to us.

How Can I Believe What I Can't See?

The very essence of Christianity is believing in the unseen. This is faith. We know that God can't be God if we can fully understand Him, and that is okay . . . or is it? In today's world, we encounter people all the time who want to understand God on every level and feel entitled to it. It seems illogical to believe, to have that kind of faith. An ever-present God? How can that be? Maybe you've met some of these folks, or you wrestle with it yourself. Certainly many teens do. Sometimes it just takes traveling down the road far enough to really begin to see through the eyes of faith, as you'll gather from reading many of the stories by teens in part 6 of this book. It may take being on the receiving end of something miraculous or experiencing something that could only be from God. He has the patience to let us find our way.

"I thought I'd learned to cope pretty well," said fifteen-year-old Marie Trembath, who lost both parents in separate tragedies before she was eight. "Then my aunt sent me to live with a cousin hundreds of miles away so that I could attend a Christian high school and earn a guaranteed scholarship to a Christian university. I couldn't afford college any other way." Christian friends at her new school helped Marie, she remembers. "Before long, I began to feel loved again, and I had hope. It's still tough because my home life isn't ideal, but I'm learning to have patience, and I pray more."

The Christian walk is a journey. Marie might feel down at times, but she is learning to know that God (all of Him) is present in her life. As we continue on our path, we come to know a deepening of our faith. We can eventually see God in everything and take great comfort in knowing He is there, even when we don't understand all that is happening.

Why did God need to be three persons? Through Jesus Christ, He chose to come down to our human level at a particular time in history and minister to everyday needs. More importantly, He needed a way to bring His wandering people back into relationship with Him. This He accomplished through the sacrifice of His son Jesus Christ, a price that only needed to be paid once for all time. In turn, God sent the same divine Spirit that empowered Christ on Earth to all people—an awesome plan that was perfectly accomplished by a loving God.

What Does God (in All Three Parts) Expect from Me?

The one thing that distinguishes Christianity from other worldviews or religions is the emphasis on a personal relationship with God, which is enhanced in the "person" of the Holy Spirit. This is truly a beautiful and awesome gift, when you think about it. God is not the Big Judge in the Sky, just waiting for an opportunity to catch you off guard and hurl a lightning bolt at you. He isn't out to take all your fun away. He instead desires to have a relationship with you on a deeply personal level. God wants to teach you what His specific plan is for your life. He already knows you intimately. How well do you know Him? Can you take your problems and life's concerns to Him and wait for Him to give you answers through His Holy Spirit? It's not hard. God made us to know Him, and none of us can escape that desire deep in our hearts.

You may be unique, but you cannot live outside of God's purpose and have true happiness. You can only find a mere reflection of meaning in your life until you come to know God. Some take the long, hard route—the fifty-year or more plan—while others choose to take the most direct route—the five-minute plan. One prayer to open your heart and ask God to live in it is all it takes to begin that relationship.

Personal Reflection

1. Do I have difficulty accepting God in all three persons—Father, Son and Holy Spirit? Why or why not?
2. Have I asked for or possibly received God's Holy Spirit into my own life? Is there proof?
3. Has there been a time when I've felt the Spirit possibly leading me in a particular direction? What happened?
4. Does my life reflect God's presence to others? If so, in what ways?
5. If I am not yet a Christian, have I felt myself coming to the point where I believe I'm ready to know God? If I'm there now, I can say "A Prayer for Salvation" on page 342 and seal that decision, or I can ask a pastor, a family member or a Christian friend to pray with me.

How Well Does God *Really* Know Me?

Think for a moment about the complex genetic structure of DNA. Most of us don't have enough knowledge to think for more than a brief moment about it. Perhaps you haven't studied genetics in biology class yet, but you will. What could be more detailed and ordered than the smallest components that make us who we are as individuals? We are amazingly put together and surely no accidents of nature. God is the perfect author of all things.

Psalm 139 is a most beautiful reminder of the depth of God's love for us and the lengths to which He goes to know us and to care for us. "O Lord, You have searched me and You know me," begins this beautiful psalm. "Before a word is on my tongue, you know it completely, O Lord" (verse 4). "For You created my inmost being; You knit me together in my mother's womb. I praise You because I am fearfully and wonderfully made" (verses 13–14a). "How precious to me are Your thoughts, O God! How vast is the sum of them!" (verse 17). "Search me, O God, and know my heart; test me and know my anxious thoughts" (verse 23).

We would "totally die" (well, at least be "stressed-to-the-max") if anyone on Earth knew our innermost thoughts! Luckily, no human has the capacity to fully understand who we are and why we think or feel as we do. But God knows everything about us and still loves us! He is with us every waking and sleeping moment of our lives. To the person who is trying to run away from God or who can't even face himself, that's a scary thought. For the rest of us, it brings an awesome peace. That person who is trying to escape will eventually have to stop running when he or she meets God at every turn. That's when fear and uncertainty can turn into comfort and true insight. God's not out to get us and make us miserable. He just wants us to know there is no real peace of mind without Him.

"Made in God's Image": Do I See God in the Mirror?

Can we even comprehend exactly what it means to be made in God's image? Does it mean that God knows us as well as He knows Himself? Does it also mean that we can know Him as well as we know ourselves? It has been said that God must have made men in His physical image and women in His emotional image. Together as mankind, we form a more complete image of God. You may think you know quite a lot about yourself, but actually, none of us can begin to mine the depths of our "inmost being." That's God's territory. As we grow in our knowledge of the Lord, it stands to reason that we will know more of ourselves, but we will never know everything until God chooses to reveal it to us. That is not promised in this life, but is reserved only for eternity with God. "Now we see but a poor reflection as in a mirror; then we shall see face to face. Now I know in part, then I shall know fully, even as I am fully known," wrote the apostle Paul (1 Cor. 13:12).

So many people strive through their own inventions to know the mind of God here on Earth just as they try to find real and lasting happiness in this limited human life. They may believe we can become one with the universe or become gods ourselves as we tap into the universal mind of God and transcend our common lives through some mystical form of meditation. They're on to something, but not quite what they think they've grasped. You will see that we have briefly examined other major religions and philosophies in chapter 11. It can be helpful for you to know where your friends and classmates who may practice other faiths are coming from. Some of these religions accept the "universal mind of God" concept, or a variation of it. This is not the same as the Christian believer's maturing into the wisdom of the "mind of Christ." Please don't confuse the two ideas. The gift of the Holy Spirit, which helps us to become more Christlike, is a simple act that does not require us to go through all sorts of gyrations to seek out a "higher consciousness." "Ask and you will receive," promised Jesus in Matthew 7:7. It's that simple.

God leaves us free to search out the truth for ourselves, but the Judeo-Christian concept of eternal life has captured more hearts than any other single system of religious thought. According to the Barna Research Group, 85 percent of Americans identify themselves as Christians. More than one-third of the world's population is considered Christian, nearly twice the number of its closet rival, which is Islam (see statistics at the end of this chapter). You may be curious about the claims of other faiths at some point in time, but allowing God to "search your heart" will bring the truth to light for you.

What's It Like to Get a "Hug" from God?

The personal, intimate relationship that we can have with God sets us apart from the animal kingdom (and even other faiths) and gives us a hope that we can't find anywhere else. You may have been introduced to God or Jesus as your friend as a little child in Sunday school, or maybe you discovered you had an innate sense of God's presence even if you didn't learn about Him as a child.

There is a popular country song that tells the story of a little girl living in a terrible home situation with both parents either drinking or doing drugs nonstop. She is left to watch television and fend for herself while her parents go out carousing with friends or fall asleep on the couch, drunk or stoned. When they curse and scream and hit each other, she hides, trembling, behind the couch. One night, the violence gets out of hand. Her father ends up shooting her mother, then turns the gun on himself in desperation as the child hides behind the couch. She ends up being adopted by a Christian family who takes her to church for the first time. As she looks up on the wall of her Sunday school class, she sees a picture of Jesus on the cross. She tells her teacher that she knows he got down off that cross because he was there with her, holding her in his arms the night her parents died.

It's hard to listen to that song with a dry eye, so moving is the story. Unfortunately, that scenario occurs far too many times. If you have lived or are living in an unhappy, unsafe home environment, you may take comfort in knowing that you are never alone in your heartache. Have you ever experienced being held by God when you were confused, hurt or had a broken heart?

We can still be encouraged today by the words of God through the prophet Isaiah as he spoke to God's disheartened chosen people, the Jewish nation. "I, even I, am He who comforts you. . . . I have put My words in your mouth and covered you with the shadow of My hand—I Who set the heavens in place, Who laid the foundations of the Earth, and Who say to Zion, you are My people" (Isa. 51:12a, 16).

Does God Care About the Little Things in My Life? (Will He Help Me Get a Date for the Prom?)

We can easily forget that God really is the author of all, so we don't always bother to include Him in the small and seemingly insignificant areas of our lives. Is anything really unimportant to us, though? If it matters to us, why wouldn't it matter to our Heavenly Father? You are as important to God as any of the other six billion plus inhabitants of this planet. He is your personal God the same as He is our personal God.

Don't be embarrassed to take your problems, no matter how small, before God in prayer. We are told in pop culture that it's all small stuff—don't sweat it. That's sort of half right. It's not all small, but God can handle it without ever breaking a sweat. So why should we even try to do His job? Save the towels. Yes, He wants you to learn how to stand on your own feet and make some decisions, but He will never make you feel dumb or petty for bringing Him into the picture. It's far more dangerous to be too self-sufficient and credit your success only to your efforts.

As for that date for the prom . . . well, God does care about your relationships, but it's tough to know what He has in mind in each of them.

We can become so attached to someone or become so giddy over the possibility of being with a special person that this "hottie" can occupy too much space in our minds from God's point of view. Remember, He's a tad jealous over us. He wants to be your first love (remember that second commandment), although He certainly understands your feelings. The great commandment that God instructed Moses to pass on to the Israelites in Deuteronomy 6:5 was, "Love the Lord your God with all your heart and with all your soul and with all your strength." Jesus also emphasized this commandment in Mark 12:30 when asked which commandment was the most important. He simply added the word "mind" to the same list, i.e., "with all your heart . . . soul . . . mind . . . and strength."

You may succeed in getting that special date without God's help, or you may bomb out. Then again, as Sarah Erdman discovered when competing for a place on her school's Wind Symphony (see her story in part 6), He may know something you don't. Time has a way of revealing some things to us that we just can't see when we're living in the middle of a situation. It's best to trust God with the desires of your heart and learn to live with the result. How can we not trust Him? Isn't it kind of silly to think we know more than He does?

What are you to your Heavenly Father? You are *His* child. You are loved and protected by the greatest one of all.

Personal Reflection

1. What do the biblical phrases "fearfully and wonderfully made" and "inmost being" mean to me?
2. Do I believe I have a personal relationship with God right now? If so, what is it? If not, am I ready to ask so that I will receive that gift?
3. Do I remember having any experiences before understanding who God was that caused me to believe God or Jesus was helping me in a special way?
4. Why do I think the phrase "it's all small stuff" is so popular?
5. Have I ever felt that God was speaking to me about some little area of my life that needed to change? If so, what did I do?

85% of Americans Identify Themselves as Christians

- 5% of U.S. adults classify themselves as Evangelicals
- 35% of U.S. adults classify themselves as born-again, but not Evangelical
- 37% are self-described Christians, but are neither Evangelical nor born-again
- 8% of adults nationwide maintain self-identity as atheists or agnostics
- 9% of the U.S. population identify with a faith other than Christianity
- 95% believe in God (1997)
- 72% believe in God when described as the all-powerful, all-knowing, perfect Creator of the universe who rules the world today (2001)
- 10% believe that God represents a state of higher consciousness (2001)
- 7% believe that God is the total realization of personal human potential (2001)
- 15% say God is no longer involved in their lives (1997)
- Almost nine out of ten people (87 percent) say the universe was originally created by God (2000)

Source: Barna Research Group

5

Talking with God: What Is Prayer? Does God Have a Preference for How We Do It?

If you asked ten different people for a definition of prayer, you would likely get ten different answers. The responses might range from something like "Huh?" to an elaborate jumble of words that would make even a theology professor scratch his head. Prayer is a reflection of each individual heart as we seek God, so to an extent, we do define it for ourselves. Yet God has given us some clear guidelines to help us know His intentions for prayer. Our mission here is to give you a better understanding of what prayer really is and to help you see how it can make a difference in your life and in the world around you. The most important thing to remember is that prayer is our personal link to God. It's how we involve our Heavenly Father directly in our lives.

Seeking to focus their prayers, people have invented cute acrostic formulas as prayer aids over the years. The most common is ACTS: Adoration—Confession—Thanksgiving—Supplication (humbly asking), but there are others. There is nothing wrong with that kind of memory aid. You could come up with one of your own. We tend to remember things better that way. As we grow older and our relationship with God deepens, we may find we no longer need those simple reminders. Prayer can become as natural as breathing, and when it does, something tremendous is happening to us and in us.

We spoke of the Christian's desire to have the "mind of Christ" at the beginning of this unit. As we come closer to that state of mind, our communications with our Heavenly Father begin to resemble conversations that are as easy and flowing as the ones Jesus must have had with Him while on Earth. This is our goal in prayer.

What Is the Purpose of Prayer, and What Difference Does It Make in Our Lives?

Is prayer any different for the twenty-first-century Christian than it was in the days immediately following Christ's death and resurrection? Not really. It is every bit as necessary and meaningful today as at any time in history and certainly serves the same purposes. We're even better equipped to understand the instantaneous and far-reaching impact of prayer today. We have the Internet, satellite television and microwave communications.

As God is ageless and changeless, so is the nature of our communication with Him. Around the world, we speak many different languages, dress differently, eat differently and have a variety of customs. However, prayer language to the Almighty is universal—kind of like music, when you think about it. Music is a language that touches the soul. We're told in the Scriptures that heavenly music is more beautiful than we can imagine here on Earth. Is it possible that the faithful prayers of His children fall also like music on the ears of God?

Why do we pray, and what difference does it make in our

lives? First, we pray because God expects us to. He created us for a personal relationship with Him. We also pray to:

- draw on God's grace for daily living and to receive His blessing;
- ask for God's protection and His divine wisdom;
- ask God to be present in the lives of those we love and to draw them to Himself;
- thank God for who He is and what He has done, and even for what He will do;
- ask for healing and comfort in times of trouble;
- ask God to increase our belief if we are struggling with our own faith;
- ask for God's justice, but also for His mercy;
- ask for God's will to be done in our lives and all around us;
- know Him, or as author Marianne Williamson said, "The highest level of prayer is not a prayer for anything. It is a deep and profound silence in which we allow ourselves to be still and know Him. In that silence, our hearts and minds are illuminated."

If we believe that our loving and all-powerful Heavenly Father really wants what is best for His children, then it will only be natural for us to pray for His will to be done, even if we don't understand it at the time. Prayer is our way of acknowledging that the Creator is intimately involved in the lives and activities of all people and that He can alter our circumstances if He so chooses. Our part is to do the praying; His part is to hear and respond. That gives us the further responsibility to listen for that response. As the old saying goes, God gave us two ears and one mouth for a reason. Prayer will be much more meaningful to us when we remember that.

What if we don't feel like praying or we hurt too much to pray? This is when we most need to talk to our Heavenly Father.

Isn't it a crisis that usually brings the thought of praying to mind? When things are going all right, we tend to ignore God. When we become angry or really sad, we can feel like defying God and refuse to pray. The sooner we get over that feeling, the better off we will be.

How Do I Know God Answers Prayer? Are There Signs?

How can we know what God is saying to us? First, we must allow ourselves to have enough quiet time to get tuned in to Him. He speaks to us in various ways. No, it's not necessarily in a real audible voice, although that soft little voice that sometimes whispers in your ear or activates your conscience could well be God's Holy Spirit. Scripture tells us to "be still before the Lord and wait patiently for Him" (Ps. 37:7). The psalmist also says to "delight yourself in the Lord and He will give you the desires of your heart" (Ps. 37:4). Does that mean we can get anything we want from God? It depends on our motives. Look at verse twenty-three of Psalm 37: "If the Lord delights in a man's way, He makes His steps firm." Over and over in that Psalm, we are told that God will support us with whatever we need if we stay true to Him. The word "delight" is used to describe our feelings for God as well as His for us. To delight in someone is to take great pleasure or joy in his or her company. If we delight in God, our motives (the desires of our hearts) will automatically be pure. We will want to draw near to Him, and He will honor that.

Sometimes we realize that we have gained more insight into a situation after taking it to the Lord in prayer, such as was true for Lorenza Martinez (whom you'll meet in part 6) when she asked God to help her pass a particularly difficult test only to discover He was telling her to not just rely on faith, but to apply herself to preparing for the test. And sometimes the results of prayer may happen almost immediately (as was the case for Samantha Long—another teen you'll meet in part 6 of this book—who asked God for a "comeback" to quell the smart-aleck remarks from her boss). Answers are more likely to come to us later as a sense of peace and direction, however God sends us His answers even in the form of other people or events. You've heard it said that He can close a door, blocking our path in one direction, but that He might then open a window to a new direction. His answers can come today in the form of opportunities that weren't there yesterday.

Have You Ever Felt God Was Trying to Get Your Attention?

It may be God rather than you who begins a conversation. Have you ever felt that God was trying to get your attention? There would be no mistaking His voice if it came to us in the night as He called the young Samuel from a sound sleep in the Old Testament. (The story is in Samuel 3.) You may have had the experience of waking in the night without realizing why and feeling the urge to pray for someone or some situation in your life or feel some deep sense of comfort in the midst of turmoil. The still of the night is often the best time for God to get our attention. With the busyness in our schedules, we tend to crowd Him out during our waking hours. Still, if we listen, we will "hear."

Lindsey Wells, sixteen, realized that she had been having a strong impression for more than a week that she was supposed to take a summer job at a local restaurant, even though she had applied for good jobs at one of those companies. Besides, she really wanted to get one of those positions because one of her friends was already working at that company. When she was offered the waitress job, she wanted to say no, but found herself instead saying yes. "I went down to talk with the owner and found out she was a Christian," says Lindsey. "It turned out to be a great place to work, and I met some really interesting people. One day, a girl about my age came in and sat at a table in the corner by herself. She had been crying and looked really depressed. I went over to take her order and saw that she was writing something. It wasn't busy at the time, so I kept an eye on her and finally asked the owner if I could talk with her. I thought the girl might want me to go away, but she let me sit down. I introduced myself and asked her if she'd like to talk. She began to cry, and when she finally was able to say something, she told me she was writing a letter to her parents. She'd planned to catch a bus at the nearby station after she left the restaurant. She was running away from home. I got her talking about her problems. Pretty soon, the owner came over, and we sat and prayed with her. She said no one had ever cared enough to do that before. We got her to call her parents, and her mom came right over to get her. When I saw them hug each other, I knew that God had sent me there for a reason. That girl needed a friend, and I decided to be that friend. Today, we go to the same church and youth group. She is getting the help she needs."

Understanding God's "Answers"

The longer we walk with God, the better we can understand His answers to our prayers or His directives to us. We learn to hear His voice in our circumstances, our inner thoughts or through interactions with others, for instance. We learn over time that going against His will for us, once we've actually figured out what that is in a given set of circumstances, is not a good idea. Sometimes doing God's will for us takes changing our will, and that's the challenge. We can go in any direction that we want, but why would we go down a path that God has not chosen for us if we know that His path leads to the greater blessing? How we wish we could see far enough down the road, but there's always a bend that blocks our vision. Have you ever played with one of those small toy periscopes? It's a kick to be able to see around obstacles and spy where we couldn't see before. Prayer becomes our periscope, in a sense, and allows us to see what we just can't see on our own. Be patient. Persist. Do this, and your faith will grow as well.

God needs for us to be moving before He can steer us. Have you ever felt you needed to just sit and wait for an unmistakable word from God before you undertook something? He could have you sitting for a long time. He wants us to do and to listen. He never lets us stray too far off the path if we keep on praying and listening. "Trust in the Lord with all your heart, and do not lean on your own understanding. In all your ways acknowledge Him, and He will make your paths straight" (Prov. 3:5).

Is There One *Best* Way to Pray?

Do you sometimes feel a deep need to pray, but just can't form the words to convey the desires of your heart? Perhaps you've heard some great, flowery prayers being offered in public by others, and you know you could never pray like that. You don't have to. No one is grading you when you pray. Some of us think if we don't dot every "i" and cross every "t" just right, God won't hear us. He gives us guidelines, but prayer based on a rigid formula would eventually become meaningless, and God knows this.

Though you may pray in the company of others at times, praying from the heart is mostly a private conversation between you and God. He hears the desires of your heart and instantly knows the emotions that live there before you even form the words. When you're too upset or afraid to pray, just turning your feelings over to God is enough. These are the times when the Holy Spirit carries our thoughts and prayers directly to God's ear. Paul explains it in the book of Romans: "We do not know what we ought to pray for, but the Spirit himself intercedes for us with groans that words cannot express" (Rom. 8:26). Remembering that prayer is also an attitude of the heart, in addition to being an action, will help us. How else could we "pray continually," as Paul reminds Christians to do in the New Testament? God "searches the heart" through the Holy Spirit, and the Spirit reveals our desires and prayers directly to God. This is what the word "intercede" means. What could be more personal and loving than a Father who is that concerned for us?

What if God Answers "Yes," "No" or "Not Now"?

Patience is perhaps the hardest part of the prayer process. Have you heard of the man who prayed, "Oh, God, give me patience, and give it to me *now!*"? We chuckle, but how many times are we like that man? Waiting is not easy. It does serve a purpose, however, and that is to strengthen us and build patience into us. *You mean it's one of those character things?* Afraid so. While it seems God is nowhere to be found at times, we really have no reason to doubt His promise: "I will never leave you nor forsake you" (Josh. 1:5).

We are far more likely to forget about Him than the other way around. How many people have walked away from God, bitter and feeling rejected, when all they had to do was wait a little longer for Him to show up? We don't know what we don't know. Fog may cover the top of the mountain temporarily, but the mountain is still there. Would you run a race if you had no idea where the finish line was, even if you could get a nifty reward? Perhaps not. What if someone promised to run it alongside you, pacing and encouraging you until you both found the finish line together? Would you run it then?

God wants us to live life as if we were running that kind of race. After the author of the book of Hebrews reminds us of the great old heroes of faith (Heb. 11), he goes on to tell us, "Therefore, since we are surrounded by such a great cloud of witnesses, let us throw off everything that hinders and the sin that so easily entangles, and let us run with perseverance the race marked out for us" (Heb. 12:1). Life is for the long haul. We don't have to have all the answers today. We couldn't handle them anyway. Life comes to us moment by moment, and so must our prayers go to God.

One essential point we often forget is that our prayers may be blocked if we are ignoring something that we need to put right with God. How can we expect Him to hear and honor our prayer if He knows that we are holding a grudge against someone that we need to let go? "Forgive us our debts as we forgive our debtors" (Matt. 6:12). It works both ways. We have to be reconciled or get right with others in order to experience the blessings of God. (We can do this through prayer.) Jesus included this principle in his Sermon on the Mount (Matt. 5: 23–24). That puts an exclamation point on it.

In essence, prayer is our immediate link to the one who created us. He means it to be as necessary to our life as the air we breathe.

What Does "The Lord's Prayer" Really Mean?

Jesus gave his disciples a model for prayer that came to be known as "The Lord's Prayer," the one that we so often recite, although it is more properly called the Disciples' Prayer. Jesus' prayers to his Father were of a different nature (see John 17 for a true Lord's prayer). It was this simple prayer, recited with a calm telephone operator, that helped spur Todd Beamer's resolve and courage to lead a charge on September 11, 2001, to overpower militant hijackers on United Flight 93, actions that most assuredly saved the loss of even further life and property as that plane was bound for another terrorist strike in the nation's capital. Beamer, a man of deep faith, and others went to their deaths as heroes that day.

There are several important principles from that simple model prayer Jesus offered (Matt. 6:9–13). You will see that the acrostic ACTS with its four cornerstones (Adoration—Confession—Thanksgiving—Supplication) comes from this instructional prayer. Here is the poetic King James Version (KJV), the one most familiar to us:

> *Our Father which art in heaven,*
> *Hallowed be Thy name.*
> *Thy kingdom come.*
> *Thy will be done*
> *on Earth, as it is in heaven. (verses 9–10)*

This first part of the prayer is the Adoration or praise we are to give to God because His will is sovereign or all-powerful, both in heaven and on Earth.

> *Give us this day our daily bread. (verse 11)*

This verse stands alone and is an important one. It is part of the S in ACTS, or Supplication, but also the T for Thanksgiving. It tells us to pray for what we need for each day only and implies that we are to be grateful for it. A weakness of our human nature is to focus too far ahead. This is what worry is all about. We can only live one moment at a time, one day at a time, and this is what Jesus wanted to emphasize. God gives us grace for each day and expects us to spend it all because He intends to give us more the following day and every day thereafter.

> *And forgive us our debts,*
> *as we forgive our debtors. (verse 12)*

This is an obvious reference to the C of ACTS or Confession. We are to acknowledge our sins, referred to here as debts or shortcomings, before God. He does not want us to miss the double-edged concept of forgiveness, however: We must also forgive those who have sinned against us.

> *And lead us not into temptation,*
> *but deliver us from evil: (verse 13a)*

Here is the other part of S as these two important requests also represent our asking for God's mercy and intervention in the daily temptation we face in our lives.

> *For Thine is the kingdom*
> *and the power and the glory forever. Amen. (verse 13b)*

Once again, praise and adoration are offered to God. Note this double emphasis at the beginning and end of the prayer. We can never praise God too much.

These are guidelines, not commands, to follow a set formula for prayer. Likewise, *we are not commanded to pray at certain times or in any particular location.* Many find it helpful to form the habit of daily prayer at a given time, say in the morning along with Bible or devotional reading. Some feel best when both starting and closing their day in prayer. As we become aware of needs, we can come to God even briefly at any time of the day. Can you pray silently sitting in your classroom at school? Of course. How many silent prayers do you think are offered before a test or exam? Driving down the road or in the midst of work or any activity, we can take a few moments to turn to God in prayer, even if it's a so-called bullet prayer or foxhole prayer. That's the "Oh, help" prayer we quickly shoot up to heaven when we're in dire need. Even unbelievers tend to do that just in case God might be there.

The examples set by Jesus while he walked on the Earth remind us to pray often and pray sincerely. You can take comfort in knowing that a regular, committed prayer life is hard for even the most disciplined Christian. It takes a lifetime to perfect, as we are constantly being distracted by the world around us.

Personal Reflection

1. What does prayer mean to me?
2. How have I seen prayer make a difference in my life or in another's life?
3. Have I found it hard to pray regularly? What might help me to overcome my distractions? What would be a good time for me to pray?
4. Does God have me on hold with a prayer request at the moment? If so, why do I suppose that is?
5. Read Jesus' prayer in John 17. What does this teach me about the power of prayer?

Part 2

Answers to Questions I've Always Wanted to Ask

We are closest to God in the darkness.
—Madeleine L'Engle

As we are healed, the world is healed. Doing anything for a purpose other than love means reliving our original separation from God, then perpetuating and maintaining that split.
—Marianne Williamson

Man is certainly crazy. He could not make a mite, and he makes gods by the dozen!
—Michel de Montaigne

6

Eye in the Sky:
Is God Watching
the Decisions I Make?

What's the biggest decision you've made in your life so far? It is possible you've been thrust into making some painful choices, such as having to decide which parent to live with after their divorce. Some of you have faced the option of becoming sexually active and have even dealt with an unplanned pregnancy. If you've chosen to remain a teen parent, you are on your way to gaining a maturity that few can claim at your age. You may have been confronted with the opportunity to use tobacco, alcohol or drugs—and may even be struggling with addiction. Some of you have contemplated dropping out of school or running away from home and living with a boyfriend or girlfriend. Wondering which college you will attend or even whether you will pursue a college education is also a major decision.

Have you chosen wisely, or have you slipped up and wish you could live that part of your life over? Life happens, they say. Make lemonade from lemons. True, but we also make life happen.

Maybe you've avoided having to make any really big decisions up to this point in your life, but you know it's only a matter of time before you will be staring all these choices right in the face. Are you going to face these tough decisions alone, or will you bring the wisest of all counselors into the picture? Just as teens

Kristen Cartwright and Jennifer Stripe (whose stories you'll read in part 6) discovered, God cares about every aspect of your life—whether it be decisions about premarital sex or overcoming personal grief and shame and illness. While it is natural for us to want to consult someone older and more experienced in life (hopefully, a parent or pastor), we can't go wrong when we filter all our decisions through God and His Word.

Let's look at some "biggie" decisions of life and how God can help us to choose wisely.

Does God Care Who My Friends Are?

If God knows you intimately, is it reasonable to assume He has an interest in those with whom you associate? It would appear so. Scripture certainly confirms that and is full of advice concerning the importance of choosing friends wisely and the consequences for associating with the wrong people. "Do not set foot on the path of the wicked or walk in the way of evil men" (Prov. 4:14). "Blessed is the man who does not walk in the counsel of the wicked or stand in the way of sinners" (Ps. 1:1). Look at the promise that follows in Psalm 1:3: "He is like a tree planted by streams of water . . . Whatever he does prospers." The apostle Paul writes in 1 Corinthians 15:33: "Do not be misled: 'Bad company corrupts good character.'"

Common sense and experience eventually show us if we've made a mistake in choosing a particular friend. If we're lucky, the consequences won't be too serious. How can we be sure about a person's character? Are we to wall ourselves up in a fortress and never venture out into the world to befriend those who don't know God just because we're afraid of being influenced by them? Not exactly. Look at the example of Jesus who angered the Jewish leaders of his day by sitting down to eat with those who were considered unclean or unworthy, or by healing those who were deemed untouchable. He drew them into his circle of influence.

However, there is one important thing to remember: We're not Jesus. We don't quite have his insight or his resistance to the influence of others. Therefore, it's best for us to be cautious until we reach a higher level of maturity and judgment.

For now, it may be easier to positively influence others while in the company of several Christian friends who can be there to support us. A stronger "brother" or "sister" helping a weaker one is part of what Christian growth is all about. As you grow in knowledge and become wiser, you gain the ability to stand more firmly on your beliefs and to exert a stronger influence on the world than it exerts on you. You can't expect to live and operate in the "real" world unless you experience some of it firsthand. But that doesn't mean you're given a blank check to experiment with things you know to be wrong just so you can better relate to what others are thinking and feeling.

Surrounding Myself with Friends Who Share My Faith

You should be given leeway, however, to reach out and extend a hand of friendship to someone who is in need of some positive influence in his or her life. Just remember to have some other friends come alongside you to weigh the odds in your favor (but not to gang up on the person). You may be rejected, but more often than not, you can turn that around. Sometimes the home life of a lonely and seemingly lost individual is too much to overcome. If you feel you're getting in over your head, stop and regroup. Bring a parent or a youth pastor in on your endeavors or just talk it over. We can't solve every problem, but we can pray for God's intervention. Sometimes, we're meant to be the seed planter while someone else comes along later to do the watering. It's okay if you're on the receiving end of this friendship rather than the giving end. Because we're all subject to temptation and down times, none of us can be the giver all of the time.

Surrounding yourself with friends who share your faith and

your outlook on life will be a habit you will want to cultivate for a lifetime. God's grace is never more evident than when He sends us a special friend or friends to walk with us and share both our joy and our pain. Be that friend, but also seek those friends for yourself. If you've made some mistakes, it's not the end of the world. God can restore you and help you to learn from those mistakes. "He who began a good work in you will carry it on to completion until the day of Christ Jesus" (Phil. 1:6). Satan will seek to pull you down with feelings of guilt and unworthiness over any poor choices you have made. You need to feel the pain of a mistake only as long as it takes for you to repent and ask for God's forgiveness. Once that's done, you can let it go and refuse to listen to those taunting lies that rattle around in your head.

Does God Care What Career I Choose?

Very few decisions are of more importance to us than what we choose to do for our career or life's work. It's true you are "bent" in a certain way, meaning you have particular gifts and abilities that will cause you to prefer one kind of work over others. Some of us have difficulty in making that choice, nonetheless. You pretty much have to fall into one of three categories: You have known what you want to do for as long as you can remember; you have several fields of interest and might be happy in any of them; you haven't a clue what the right path is for you.

There is sometimes a fourth category, and that is you are being or will be groomed for a particular career or lifestyle by a parent, whether you like it or not. That can be the toughest place to be, even more than not knowing what you want. Will you be compliant and go peacefully in that direction, or will you go kicking and screaming all the way—or not go at all?

Does God Have Something in Mind for Me
and, if So, How Do I Discover What It Is?

So where does God fit in here? He made you; He knows you better than you know yourself. Surely, He must have the answer. It's reasonable to believe He does know what's best (even more than your parents), but if you look around at the lives of other people, you will find that He doesn't always roll out the red carpet to the ultimate choice right away. He may well let you do what you desire to do, and in most cases, you will choose well if you put the right amount of prayerful thought into it. "Commit to the Lord whatever you do, and your plans will succeed" (Prov. 16:3).

Many of us incorrectly assume that we only get to choose our life's work once, but that's not the way it has to be. Making a decision that you only get to make once is like being in a pressure cooker! Ever answer one of those dinnertime phone calls from a solicitor who has a deal that sounds too good to be true (that means it is), but you only get it if you act NOW? Not so. God tends to build our lives layer upon layer, decision upon decision. We learn from what's gone before. He is not so rigid as to force us to make such an important decision early in life before we've had enough experience to really know what best suits us. You may certainly change your mind down the road and feel that God is leading you in another direction.

Some of you will have the exciting experience of seeing God take you to places to which you never dreamed you would go. Others of you will watch your apparent hopes crumble as the open doors to your preferred dreams suddenly close for no apparent reason. In those cases, your faith will be tested, but if you keep placing your trust in God, the way will become clear again. How can you know if you are being tested by God or tempted by the enemy? Isn't it true that Satan will try to keep you from finding God's purpose? That's one of the ways He operates, all right. But God owns your life and your path. He knows what He's doing: "'For I know the plans I have for you,' declares the Lord, 'plans to prosper you . . . plans to give you hope and a future'" (Jer. 29:11). Satan may offer up a career choice that looks attractive, but if it puts you in a position where you have to lie, cheat, steal or in any way dishonor God, then you will know it's the wrong choice. If you refuse to go in that direction, God will put you in fertile soil where you will bloom in good time, and you will be like that tree planted by the water "which yields its fruit in season and its leaf does not wither" (Ps. 1:3). The important thing is to not let money and the lure of material things become your God. God knows you need money. "Seek first His kingdom and His righteousness and all these things will be given to you as well" (Matt. 6:33). "For we brought nothing into this world, and it is certain we can carry nothing out" (1 Tim. 6:3).

Is There Only One "Soul Mate" for Me?

While the choice of your life's work is surely important, it is eclipsed by the choice of your future life's partner. *Have I met him yet?* You may wonder from time to time. *Maybe he sits near me in class,* you may daydream. More likely, he or she is years down the road.

As you read in the section "Does God Care Who My Friends Are?" it stands to reason that yes, God cares who your "special someone" is as well. It is entirely possible that you've already fallen in and out of love several times in your life and that your heart has even been broken in one of these relationships. Each person you loved may have seemed to you to be your soul mate until you were proven wrong. If you long day and night for that one perfect person—your only true love—you're not alone. Everyone longs to be with someone, to have an especially close "exclusive" bond with someone of their own choosing. Love is serious business. It is the most wonderful and the most painful experience on Earth. Tough as it can be, most of us wouldn't trade it for anything. It's hard to imagine anyone sadder than a person who is afraid to risk loving and being loved. Certainly the Song of Solomon speaks to the power of love's feelings: "Your lips are like a strand of scarlet . . . You have ravished my heart with one look of your eyes, with one link of your necklace . . . I sleep, but my heart is awake! . . . Tell my beloved that I am lovesick! . . . How beautiful are your feet in sandals" (4:3, 5:2, 5:8, 7:1).

And you thought you could write a torrid love note! Just as you know that love is a powerful feeling, so is the pain of love gone wrong. If you're in a relationship right now, you may find yourself wondering what is proper and what is not. *Am I really in love?* you might ask yourself. *Is this the one for me? How far can we go if we're really in love?* Those are important questions, and God's Word provides answers. Proverbs, the book of wisdom, has some warnings: "Above all else, guard your heart for it is the wellspring of life" (Prov. 4:23). "For the lips of an adulteress drip honey, and her speech is smoother than oil; but in the end, she is bitter as gall, sharp as a double-edged sword" (Prov. 5:3–4). Girls, you can substitute "him" for "her" in that verse. The father who is writing those words does not want his son or daughter to have to say one day, "How I hated discipline! How my heart spurned correction! I would not obey my teachers or listen to my instructors. I have come to the brink of utter ruin" (Prov. 5:12–14).

Have you ever thought that those old proverbs or commandments are just not suited for this day and age? After all, this is the twenty-first century. Times have changed. Well, yes and no. We live in a fast-paced world and don't ride camels or horses much anymore. We're hip and smart, right? Then why are we dying from AIDS in record numbers? Why do teens suffer from so much depression and such high suicide rates? Maybe we're not as invincible as we think.

If I'm Really in Love, "How Far" Can I Go?

Hopefully, you have established some boundaries for intimacy in your relationships with the opposite sex. If not, it's time to do that. It's so easy to believe you can keep your physical touching and romantic actions to a minimum, or you can just stop if things start to get out of hand. Those who are older and have been down that road know the real truth. It's hard to stop a runaway train, and sexual intimacy is like that. You may have succeeded in stopping once or twice, but it will become harder to continue holding back those feelings that are a natural part of your emotional and physical makeup. Those feelings are God-given and are not wrong, per se. They are just meant to be expressed freely in married relationships. You don't have to "prove" anything to a boyfriend or girlfriend, and you surely don't have to prove anything to other friends who may want to know how far you will go. Anyone who respects himself or herself will also respect you. One touch or kiss that seems innocent enough is capable of leading to much more. Are we saying you should keep each other at arm's length or wear a strand of garlic around your neck? Of course not. Date, if you wish, but in accordance with your parents' or guardians' guidelines. Just be aware of your feelings. You can use the old "safety in numbers" adage to your advantage and choose to go out in groups. Remember, "God is faithful; He will not let you be tempted beyond what you can bear. But when you are tempted, He will also provide a way out so that you can stand up under it" (1 Cor. 10:13).

Is it wrong to even think about having sex with someone you really like a lot? According to God's Word, it is. "You have heard that it was said, 'Do not commit adultery.' But I tell you that anyone who looks on a woman (or man) lustfully has already committed adultery with her (or him) in his heart" (Matt. 5:28). Jesus preached these words in his famous Sermon on the Mount. Does this mean that you are condemned the moment your thoughts stray to sex? Of course not. You are human. We tend to sin more in our thought life than anywhere else. Others may not know it, but God does. "Can a man scoop fire into his lap without his clothes being burned?" we are asked in Proverbs 6:27, referring to the power of sexual lust. Large portions of Scripture are devoted to warnings about avoiding the traps of sex. That means we can go to Him and offer our thoughts and temptations up to Him while asking for His help to replace them with more appropriate ones. Don't deceive yourself. If you think about something long enough, you will find yourself doing it at some point in time. You may have heard it said, "You always fall in the direction in which you're leaning." You can control your thought life, however, with God's help.

How Can I Prepare for Marriage?

You don't live in a bubble, but you may or may not know that about half of all marriages, including Christian marriages, end in divorce. You are likely, then, to have lived in one of those homes. Those grim statistics may cause you to wonder what may happen to you, no matter how wisely you choose. *Am I doomed to fail?* you may be wondering. Even many marriages that don't end up in divorce are not happy marriages, and some couples who do split up could have saved their marriages by working on them instead of giving in to their own selfish desires. Still, the good news is there are many wonderful marriages out there.

A dangerous trend has been developing among young married couples in today's fast-paced world. Many are in love with the idea of marriage, or more to the point, with the dream of a lovely storybook of wedding memories. Some couples are actually thinking of a first marriage as a practice session for the real one later on. Amazing! Sounds like playing Barbie and Ken, doesn't it? Marriage is no game. You can be sure God takes it very seriously. *Oh, no problem,* you may be thinking. *I'll just live with my fiancé until we figure out if we're right for each other. At least we won't be a divorce statistic.* Nice try, but God's not impressed. Last time we checked, He had not removed "Do not commit adultery" from the Ten Commandments. In case you're thinking that God was only referring here to sex with someone else's wife or husband, think again. The proper word for any sex between couples who are not married to each other is "fornication," and the Bible is full of warnings against it.

Make no mistake; you're up against some tough odds for a successful marriage in today's world. Some young people just assume there are no real virgins left anymore and that virginity is just a nice, antiquated idea whose time has come and gone— that it's just too hard to save themselves for marriage. You may be surprised to know there is a growing number of teens in the world who are challenging that idea and are making commit-ments—covenants between themselves, their future spouses and God—to keep themselves sexually pure until marriage. These teens are looking around at their friends' shattered lives and at the epidemic of sexually transmitted diseases and AIDS and are deciding it can and will be different for them.

Marriage Has Always Been a Primary Concern for God

The idea of marriage is so esteemed by the Creator that He used the image of a bridegroom and his bride to describe the relationship between Christ and his church. The blueprint for the ideal marriage is laid out in God's Word. There is an entire poetic book in the Bible (Song of Solomon) devoted to the beauty of mar-ried love. "Each one of you must also love his wife as he loves him-self, and the wife must respect her husband" (Eph. 5:33). You have the ability, no matter what your age, to look at a relationship and figure out if that couple is genuinely loving and respecting one another. The marriage with which you are most familiar is the one going on under your own roof, if your parents are living together.

You already are beginning to form an image in your mind of your ideal mate. Depending on how you view your parents' marriage, past or present, you will either look for someone with some of the qualities of your own father or mother, or you will go in a totally different direction. You're fortunate if you've had the privilege of living in a home with two loving parents. That doesn't mean that you can't happily marry if you haven't had that example. No matter your experience, there is hope for you. You may even choose to model your future marriage after that of a couple you know in your church or elsewhere in your family.

Does God Have a Specific Someone in Mind for Me?

Many Christians have the notion that God has specifically chosen a future husband or wife for them. That may be true in rare cases, but it doesn't hold true for everyone. You have the ability to meet and fall in love with any number of people in your lifetime. Rare is the person who meets the right one the first time out. You will almost surely fall in and out of love several times before you find the person who is right for you. When you make that commitment, it is intended to be for life. The Genesis story so beautifully tells of the first woman literally coming from man—"'bone of my bones and flesh of my flesh.' . . . For this reason a man will leave his father and mother and be united to his wife, and they will become one flesh" (Gen. 2:23–24). Marriage is a sacred covenant, not the joke that you see depicted on many television sitcoms or in movies today. As long as you and your partner are "equally yoked" (2 Cor. 6:14), meaning you share the same faith in God and enough similar interests, your future marriage can be as blessed as any under the sun.

Many wonderful books have been written on the subject of marriage, and if you're interested, you might check some of them out. (See Suggested Readings and Resources for some suggestions.) Just know that you don't have to be in a rush to get into a serious relationship. If you do find yourself unusually attracted to the kind of person who meets your list of criteria for a life mate, take it slow and stay prayerfully before God in order to know His will for you. We strongly urge you to go through a premarital counseling course with your pastor or other qualified counselor before you actually marry. God will bless your patience and your planning.

Personal Reflection

1. Have I made any choices or decisions that I regret? How would I choose differently today?
2. Am I having a greater influence on others around me than they are having on me? Is this a good thing or a bad thing?
3. Of the four categories related to my future life's work, which one best applies to me?
4. Do I choose the people I may want to date wisely? Have I needed to use God's escape route from sexual temptation?
5. What are the three most important qualities I will look for in a marriage partner when the time is right, remembering the importance of being "equally yoked"?

7

The Great Epic: What *Is* "Truth"?

One of the most endearing superheroes ever to be created in comic book "literature" was Superman. Your parents' generation grew up with the "Man of Steel," and some teenagers today still flock to reruns of a more recent television series depicting him in an updated Metropolis. Despite seeing the concept of truth become more and more watered down in this present age, the producers of *Lois and Clark: The New Adventures of Superman* chose to make upholding "truth, justice and the American way" the centerpiece of the hit television series. Though he is not presented as a man of any particular faith, Superman's character is so solid, he simply cannot lie. Oh, that we could all really have that kind of moral strength!

Imagine for a moment a world that is under assault at all times by the forces of darkness and evil. Masses of people are continually deceived by evil masquerading as something good and desirable. Too late, they learn the truth. Their will is not strong enough to resist this monstrous evil. They need a hero, one who will lead them out of their darkness and oppression and defeat the dreaded enemy once and for all. One day, word begins to spread of such a superhuman man among them. He represents all that is good. Can his light and truth conquer this dreaded enemy? Is his strength greater?

Yeah! Where can I see the movie? Is the book out? Before you rush out to look for this latest rival to *Star Wars* or Tolkien's *Lord of the Rings*, you might want to consider looking closer to home.

This is the epic, the continuing saga that outsells all others year after year. It was first printed with real, movable type in Germany by a fellow named Gutenberg in the fifteenth century, although it was written by hand for many hundreds of years prior. Oh, there's another thing you ought to know. You're a character in this story. We all are. You know the book and parts of the story— Alpha to Omega, Genesis to Revelation, Adam to Christ.

Jesus Christ has been depicted as everything from a divine superhero to a simple Jewish carpenter who was a teacher of moral truths. It was easy for the Jewish people among whom Jesus lived and who first heard his gospel message to accept him as their rabbi or teacher. It was much more difficult for them to believe he could actually be the Messiah, the one promised in Scriptures of old as a king who would restore Israel to her former glory and conquer her evil enemies. God presented the most incredible and powerful event in history in the humblest and simplest of packages. He considered His truth and the future of all mankind, and placed their fate in the hands of a Savior whose grand entrance into this world was by birth on animal bedding in a stable to a young mother, who simply and without reservation trusted the God who had chosen her for this purpose. No scriptwriter in Hollywood could invent a story to rival this one, although they are all inspired by it—even if they don't know it. It overshadows all our imaginations.

In Search of Truth

This same Jesus Christ began his formal ministry on Earth at the age of thirty. It would last only three years. That was all the time needed to accomplish God's purpose of redeeming mankind and to begin His church. In the last days of his life on Earth, Jesus made the most powerful of statements concerning who he was and what he represented. As he approached Jerusalem where he would for the last time speak to his fellow Jews—the same people who would soon put him to death—

about his relationship with God, the father, Jesus said, "If you hold to my teaching, you are really my disciples. Then you will know the truth, and the truth will set you free" (John 8:31). To those who did not believe, he said, "Why is my language not clear to you? Because you are unable to hear what I say. . . . He who belongs to God hears what God says. The reason you do not hear is that you do not belong to God" (John 8:43, 47). Sounds tough, but Jesus also grieved for his people and their unbelief. In fact, he wept as he looked out over his beloved Jerusalem and longed for his people to know and love him.

We live in a world today where it is not considered "politically correct" to believe that Jesus is both the Son of God and the Son of Man. Tolerance is the answer for many. Christianity is not "inclusive" enough, they complain. What about all the other "good" people? There are many roads to knowing God, we hear. Messages that are contrary to the teachings of Christ bombard the young and the old alike. Consider this statement of Jesus to his eleven beloved disciples while the twelfth, Judas Iscariot, was in the very act of betraying him to his death: "I am the way and the truth and the life. No one comes to the Father except through me" (John 14:6). Pretty straightforward, isn't it?

We all have to decide whether Jesus was (and is) who he said he was or whether he was the biggest liar and pretender who ever walked the Earth. If he is not the Son of God, then Christians, as Paul reminds us in his New Testament writings, are to be pitied more than anyone because of their deception. Do you think that kind of deception could have endured for 2,000 years? Think about it. If we are deceived by our own God, then what is truth? Could it, then, even exist? Why even live if there is no truth to hold everything together? Upon what would we build our relationships if not for truth? So-called wise men or women can ponder these questions all day long. They might go so far as to attempt to reinvent truth or rewrite history. Truth simply is. It cannot change. There is great freedom in knowing that.

God Has Often Chosen Young People to Accomplish Great Things

Consider the numbers of teenagers chosen by God to be a part of His plan. A teenager (David) was chosen to become champion and king of Israel and part of the royal lineage of Jesus himself. A teenager (Daniel) was chosen to face the lion's den for his beliefs (and survived). Why was a teenager (Mary) chosen to give birth to the Savior of the world? We are all given the option of believing or not believing. God has often chosen young people to accomplish great things. Why? Because He had a purpose for them. Was their youth a factor? Maybe, maybe not. You don't know whether God will choose you, a teen, to accomplish some special purpose through you or not, so have your heart ready and be willing— because He does choose young people, just as seventeen-year-old Paul Cattaneo describes in part 6. It could be because of their purity and simple faith. It could be because of a gift He has given them that they don't even know about yet. We can't second-guess God, but we can make some assumptions based on common sense.

No one has ever successfully argued against the logic or the truth of Christ's teachings in the gospels, although many have tried. One was C. S. Lewis, whom you may know from his classic tales, *The Chronicles of Narnia*. He decided he was an atheist at an earlier time in his life and attempted to disprove Christianity. What happened was not at all what he expected. His scholarly training led him to believe and accept that Christ is who he said he was. Lewis became one of the most outspoken Christians of the twentieth century, and the world remains indebted to him for his wonderful teaching.

Why Do We Need to Be "Set Free" by the Truth?

The writers of the gospels tell us that Jesus went obediently to his death, knowing all along what was to happen, and that he sealed the fate of the enemy and his dark forces, defeating forever the "father of lies" (John 8:44). Heroic for the Son of Man. Divine destiny for the Son of God. Freedom for all mankind. Why do we need to be set free? Because we are captive to our sinful desires and powerless to rise above them on our own. And, of course, we live in a world filled with temptations. While some may wish to believe that it's somehow too old-fashioned and uncomfortable to talk about the dark side of our human nature, not talking about it doesn't change things.

It is interesting to note that many people today have simply removed the word "sin" from their vocabulary. How? By moving more and more in the direction of *moral relativity*. Do you know what that means? It means that to them, there is no absolute right or wrong, no one standard to live by—if it feels good or it doesn't appear to harm anyone else, then do it. Do you believe that we can live under such a philosophy without there being some consequences for our actions? We have laws to protect us from the bullies of the world who feel they can have what they want, when they want it and at anyone's expense.

Under Certain Circumstances, Is Stealing or Cheating Sometimes Justified?

A few years ago, a group of nine students from one high school was involved in a famous cheating scandal in a national competition between schools from every state. One of them appeared in her early twenties on a television talk show to say that *she didn't think what they did was wrong.* She still believes, she said, that cheating is justified in certain circumstances. Amazing! Cheating is serious business, and every reputable college and university has its own students enforce an honor code that says any student caught cheating can be expelled. If you've been flirting with the idea of cheating to get a better grade or have already done it, ask yourself why you think it's okay. Is it fair to the other students who study hard and take tests honestly? What about financially strapped students who are competing for limited scholarships to colleges or graduate schools? Shouldn't one's character also weigh in as a factor in the decision-making process? A person who cheats does hurt someone else by gaining an unfair advantage. It is wrong, period.

Cheating isn't only for students, you know. You must have heard at least a little about the recent "cheating" (theft) that has been exposed in the business world, causing top executives who took advantage of their employees and investors and pocketed fortunes to lose their jobs and face possible prison sentences. How does all that start? Perhaps back in school with a little "harmless" cheating here and there. Do you want to work for a company such as that one day? Hardly. If not for godly standards of moral behavior, what is to keep such crimes in check? Perhaps the most insightful verses in the Bible, when it comes to addressing moral corruptness, are these from Proverbs: "There are six things the Lord hates, seven that are detestable to Him: haughty (proud) eyes, a lying tongue, hands that shed innocent blood, a heart that devises wicked schemes, feet that are quick to rush into evil, a false witness who pours out lies and a man who stirs up dissension among brothers" (Prov. 6:16–19). We are expected to keep on measuring ourselves with this ruler. It is our truth stick, in one sense.

Sin is alive and well in many forms, no matter how many people want to ignore it. To think that any of us can escape its consequences is to make a big mistake. Your parents or grandparents were much more likely to hear the warning "Your sins will find you out" (Num. 32:23) when they were younger than you may be today. A moral standard—and fear of breaking it— is meant to keep us on the straight and narrow. It is ideally passed from generation to generation, but sometimes it gets lost. Incidentally, it was a teacher—the very person entrusted with their training—who helped the students cited above to cheat on their competition. Pretty shameful. Cheating comes in all sizes.

What Is the "Living Word"?

No discussion of Christianity is meaningful without reference to the truthfulness of "the Word" as represented in the Bible. We have chosen John's gospel here because it offers such a clear explanation of the mysterious relationship between God and truth, as expressed in the person of Jesus Christ. In fact, "the Word" is a phrase that actually refers to Christ. The very opening verses of John say, "In the beginning was the Word, and the Word was with God and the Word was God. *He* was with God in the beginning" (John 1:1–2, our italics). All of the Bible is really an unfolding of history that points to the Word becoming "flesh" and providing the way for all who receive him to know God and His truth for all eternity. It is this truth that Jesus said would set us free from the misery that accompanies the lies of Satan, the prince of this world.

As always, God provides the truth, but does not force us to accept it. It is simple and logical, even available to a child. When do we get to the age where we start becoming sophisticated? For some of you reading this, it has already happened. Regarding Jesus, the living Word, his disciple John wrote: "In him was life, and that life was the light of men. The light shines in the darkness, but the darkness has not understood it" (John 1:4). To this day, the truth that comes in the form of Jesus is not understood by many. Sin and selfishness continue to blind unbelievers to that truth, even though it is there for anyone who seeks it. Jesus says in John's gospel, "Everyone who does evil hates the light, and will not come into the light for fear that his deeds will be exposed. But whoever lives by the truth comes into the light, so that it may be seen plainly that what he has done has been done through God" (John 3:20–21). Light and truth are often interchangeable words in the New Testament. Kind of makes sense, doesn't it? Light, truth and life vs. darkness, lies and death.

If the truth is difficult for you to understand right now, take heart. If a stuffed-shirt, skeptical professor at both Oxford and Cambridge Universities like C. S. Lewis can accept Christ as genuine Savior, so can anyone. It's not a matter of how much gray matter you have. Lewis had a lot more to sort out than you do. The important thing is not to hinder the truth from getting through. Your faith is as genuine as anyone's. Simple, childlike faith is what Jesus said we should have: "Whoever humbles himself like [a] child is the greatest in the kingdom of heaven" (Matt. 18:3).

Personal Reflection

1. What does the phrase "absolute truth" mean to me?
2. Do I see Christianity as restricting and limiting to my freedom? What does Jesus' statement, "You will know the truth, and the truth will set you free" (John 8:32) mean to me, personally?
3. Do I know someone whose life was changed radically after accepting Christ? Perhaps that someone is me. What was he/she/I like before God's truth made that change?
4. What worldly influence (fake truth) do I have the most trouble dealing with? What should I do about this?
5. Does seeing Jesus as the "living Word" make the Bible more meaningful to me? How?

What Is (and Isn't) Sin?

Sin. It's a simple little word, but one that has surely rocked our world over the ages. We're not as likely today to hear those old-fashioned fire-and-brimstone sermons that our grandparents used to hear. The question still remains: What is sin, and what do we do about it? The simplest, bare-bones definition of sin is *anything that separates us from God and keeps us from knowing Him.* It is not living up to our end of His covenant: God created us to be holy, ultimately, like Himself. Sin blocks our route to holiness or the perfection that we are seeking as children of God.

Sin: Anything That Keeps Us from Knowing God

None of us is indestructible. Each of us will die one day when our bodies are ready to shut down. It may be from old age, or it may be from the trauma of an accident, a crime or a terminal illness. None of us knows how or when we will check out of this life, but we know we will. It's inevitable. In part 6 of this book, you'll meet one of our favorite teens, Mandy Martinez, a teen who has written a story for four of the books in our *Taste Berries for Teens* series as well as *A Teen's Guide to Living Drug-Free.* As we were working with Mandy on another story for this book, her young mother suddenly lost her life in a fatal car crash. Our hearts go out to Mandy and her family, as well as to Jenny King and Jenna Peterson who also lost beloved family members (see part 6). We know that many teens face the reality of death, whether it is family members, classmates or friends. Death is supposed to be too far off to contemplate for a teen; this is not always the case.

Having said that, you need to know that if you personally are preoccupied with death, you may be dealing with an emotional problem that needs attention. Suicidal thoughts are not to be taken lightly, whether your own or a friend's, as sixteen-year-old Emily Whitney knows from having been diagnosed with depression (you'll find her ordeal profiled in part 6). To be depressed or to have thoughts of wanting to die is not necessarily a sin. In many cases it's the sin of someone else, often an abusive person, that drives a person to such desperate thoughts. Please tell someone safe and responsible if you or a friend have been victimized or are being threatened by someone. Get help. (See Suggested Readings and Resources at the end of the book.)

The End of Life Is Just a Beginning

While we're not to run around like Chicken Little, fearing the end of the world, there is a death that should concern us—the death of the soul. That one is not a given. Jesus instructed his disciples, "Do not be afraid of those who kill the body, but cannot kill the soul. Rather, be afraid of the One who can destroy both soul and body in hell" (Matt. 10:28). Let's stop right here. That's a heavy thought, and it may even frighten you. It would be easy for us just to gloss over it, but we can't. It's not our truth; it's God's. The end of life on this Earth is just a beginning to something far more significant. The creator of a well-known animated television sitcom said a few years ago, "When I die, the world will be over." Not to burst this luminary's bubble, but planet Earth will be alive and well when he leaves it. So it will be with all of us, unless

Christ returns first, in which case we will finally get to answer the question of whether there really will be a "Rapture" (understood as the instant translation of true believers into eternal afterlife).

There's a story about two preachers who were fishing by a riverbank when a man drove up and stopped short upon seeing a handwritten sign they had obviously erected: "The End Is Near. Turn Around." "Hey, I don't appreciate that kind of blatant sermonizing," the man shouted to the fishing clerics, and he drove on in a huff. A few moments later came the sound of screeching tires followed by a loud splash. "I told you we should have written 'Bridge Out Ahead,'" said one preacher to the other.

Some people do run headlong into life's traps, resenting being told to slow down or turn around. Perhaps we, too, shake our heads at the apparent foolishness of those who would preach doom and gloom to us when it's much more fun to listen to a positive, uplifting message about how wonderful we are. We like it even more if we can feel good each day by simply blowing ourselves a kiss in the mirror. God wants us to know how special and loved we are, but He also wants to keep us from falling into the clutches of sin, which can destroy us.

Why Sin *Feels* Bad

Did you ever wonder why your conscience hurts when you do something that is wrong? Consider this: We're *supposed* to feel bad when we come under conviction of some sin in our lives. Nobody likes it. *But it's fun to cross the line and not get caught*, you may be thinking. Right you are. Sin is often attractive and inviting, and we are easily drawn into its clutches. In reality, it's the fact that we can get away with something that makes it more appealing even than the act itself. You know what the flip side of that attraction is? Addiction—the constant craving for a bigger thrill and the sad realization that wanting it is not the same as having it. It's like waking up one day and finding out that someone moved all the furniture out of your room overnight. The sun is shining, but you don't feel it as you stand in that empty and hollow space. Meanwhile, the thief is off somewhere laughing at how easily you were robbed while you slept.

While sin is powerful and attractive and addictive, it has its own Achilles' heel, a weakness that can be exploited just as it exploits us. Yes, you can outsmart the enemy and his bag of tricks. How? Simply by acknowledging your own human weakness (sinful nature) and asking your big brother, Jesus, to come and stand alongside you with his sword of truth. The enemy can't stand up to the real truth! He runs like a scared puppy when confronted with the risen Lord. Throw a Bible verse at him like, "I can do everything through him who strengthens me" (Phil. 4:13). Use the name of Jesus. Keeping the truth of the living Word before you will shield you from sin's snare.

That's all? No Jedi knight light-saber duels, no dark force vs. light force cosmic battles? Not necessary. "The battle is the Lord's" (1 Sam. 17:47). Period. We are not equipped to go toe-to-toe with the great deceiver. We don't have to. Moreover, our human nature won't permit it. Part of his cunning and deception is in luring us into a fight we can't win on his turf. That's why God tells us to run from temptation. If you can't swim, would you dive into the deepest end of the pool?

Even when we're not looking for it (and sometimes we are), sin can hit us on the blind side, appearing as the proverbial wolf in sheep's clothing. It wears many disguises in order to gain the upper hand. If the devil himself popped up in your face looking like Darth Maul, of course you'd recognize him. The problem is, he doesn't do that. So turn the tables on him; change the turf. It's that simple. Childlike, maybe. Effective? Oh, yeah.

What Is "Original Sin"?

A godly judicial system, such as we have in the United States, operates under the principle that a person standing accused of a crime is considered innocent until proven guilty, either by the defendant's own admission or by a trial in a court of law. We are thankful for that protection of individual rights because no one down here is God. Meanwhile, God comes along and tells us that we are all guilty of sin because our ancestors messed it up, but that the punishment we deserve has been given to Jesus in our place. The fancy term for this good news in Christian doctrine is "substitutionary atonement." In plain English, Jesus died so we could live. "For God so loved the world [that's all of us] that He gave His one and only Son, that whoever believes in Him shall not perish but have eternal life" (John 3:16).

Imagined Shortcomings in the Areas of Service or Witnessing Are Heavy Chains to Drag Around

Conviction is the authentic pain or guilt we feel when we contemplate our true sins. Without it, we would have no motivation to seek forgiveness and to change. However, Christians of all ages are vulnerable to a trap that pagans (people of no faith) don't have to worry about. When we try to live with Christ at the center of our lives, we are acutely aware of the possibility of our sins. Because it matters to us, we can find ourselves feeling guilty for things that really don't matter or reasons that don't even exist. Have you ever beat yourself up for some imagined shortcoming? Our perceived failures in the areas of service or witnessing to others can be some of the heaviest chains we drag around. We convince ourselves that God is not all that pleased with us because we aren't doing enough for Him or we can never do enough to get right with Him. We forget John 3:16 ("For God so loved the world that . . .").

There is an interesting motivation for subtle guilt in our churches. Some churches are strong in the witnessing department, and this goes for the youth programs, too. While it's true that we all come under the Great Commission that commands us to go and tell everyone we can the good news of Christ's atonement, not all of us are gifted in this way. We confuse the gifts and talents of others with what God expects of us. We're not all called to be soul-winning evangelists. Did you know that none of us can save even one soul? That's God's job. Period. He uses us, with our own unique gifts, to reach out to others, but He doesn't place the burden for their salvation on us.

We likewise carry burdens of false guilt for some secret sin that we feel must be unforgivable. We could clear our churches in a hurry if everyone knew everyone else's hidden life. We're all sinners. Though all "have sinned and fall short of the glory of God" (Rom. 3:23), the good news is we're not condemned before God because "we are justified freely by His grace through the redemption that came by Christ Jesus" (Rom. 3:24). Our sin debt has been paid by Jesus. This is the good news that God wants to shout from every rooftop: "I'm not angry with you. I love you. You are forgiven. You are my precious child."

While some might have us believe we must earn our way into God's good graces, nothing could be further from the truth.

Will I Always "Reap What I Sow"?

The Bible is full of parables and illustrations that use farming imagery to teach us object lessons about life. One is the principle of sowing and reaping. In other words, you can't plant corn and get tomatoes. A seed must bear its own fruit. We are also told that seeds can fall on different kinds of soil with different results. If we plant in rich, fertile soil, we get the best crops. If we plant in shallow, rocky soil, we won't see much of a harvest. Seeds sown among weeds will come up, but will soon be choked out by the weeds.

We are all seeds put here by our Creator. One extremely important seed principle is that a seed must die in order to bear fruit. After going through this process, the seed becomes something else entirely. Through a mysterious transformation, it grows into a tiny seedling and then into a fully mature plant. It's amazing to contemplate how tough this tiny seed-plant must be to push its way through the ground in order to produce whatever fruit it is intended to bear. Many plants reseed themselves, bearing many more of their kind the following season.

What does this principle mean to us, and how does it relate to sin? Simply that we must want our sinful nature to "die" so that we can become what God intends us to be. Whatever fruit He means for us to bear, He will produce in us if we first submit to being placed into the fertile soil of His love. The obvious analogy is to the death and resurrection of Christ, with whom we are to identify. When we get to the point of that identification, God will give us "the mind of Christ" (1 Cor. 2:16), which will in turn give us the will and the desire to resist the snare of sin and the ability to know what is and isn't sin.

When all is said and done, sin is deception, a mirage in the desert of life. The more our eyes are opened to the truth and the more we nourish ourselves with the "living water" (John 4:10) of Christ, the more clearly we will see it for what it is—a wall that separates us from the joy of truly knowing God. This 20/20 vision is the hope of all believers.

Personal Reflection

1. Have any misconceptions about sin held me back from being who I feel God wants me to be? In what way?
2. In what ways has false guilt been a problem for me?
3. Has God convicted me of a particular sin in my life recently that I now want to set right? What am I going to do about it?
4. In what ways do I bear fruit for God?
5. How will I deal with the next big temptation that comes my way?

Faith: Why Should I Trust God?

No matter how hard we try, we can't see far enough to know God's plan for our life or to understand why certain things happen (although we're reassured in Jer. 29:11, "For I know the plans I have for you, plans to prosper you and not harm you, plans to give you hope and a future"). It takes a lot of faith to entrust everything we are to Him when our natural tendency is to want to see what we can't see.

"Faith" is a word that has become oversimplified in our language today. It's a bit like the word "tolerance," which now means that every belief or behavior is acceptable, whereas it once defined simply being patient with others. Faith, to some, is a catchall word for any belief that works for us. Now, it is even considered fashionable to practice some kind of faith. This is not exactly what our Creator intended.

Faith does not come "off the rack," nor does it come from the fashion centers of the world. It's not something we put on; it's carried inside of us. Faith does not exist in a vacuum. It is a dual concept. It means nothing unless it is both freely given to—and received by—a source that is unshakable and unchangeable under any circumstances. We bring the idea of faith or trust down to our level when we speak of the reliability of a person, an event or a structure, for example. You are being asked to place your faith in a leader when you go to the polls at the age of eighteen and older to vote. You probably never doubt for a moment that you can find fireworks somewhere in America on the Fourth of July. When you or whoever is driving come to a long bridge span over a body of water, you have faith that you can safely cross—even if you have sweaty palms and white knuckles by the time you get across.

The faith that defines our relationship with God may seem like that same kind of everyday faith. Yet, there is one important difference: God is incapable of failing, changing or breaking a promise. He *is* Truth. He *is* Fact. He *is* the Source. Oh, we may *feel* that He has let us down sometimes, but if we look closer at the situation, we will see that it is someone or something else that has failed us. People can and do let us down sometimes. Bridges can and do collapse. Experiencing this misplaced trust enough times can even leave us unable to trust God for a while.

Our Relationships with Others Resemble Our Relationship with God

Probably, we will let others down at some time or another. It's in our human nature. Still, human relationships are to be modeled on our relationship with God. He created us both to know and to love Him on a deeply personal level. When we take our eyes off Him and try to come up with our own solutions or models, we often find that we've taken a wrong turn. We simply cannot plan or invent better than our Creator. If we could do that, we would be on an equal footing with God. If that were the case, where or to whom would we go for help? In whom could we place our faith?

Michelle Nathan, fifteen, knows firsthand what it feels like to be betrayed by a trusted adult and to see her formerly safe world turn into a scary, unpredictable place. Yet, she has known God as her Protector and Heavenly Father. That faith got her through her ordeal and gave her the courage to tell her older sister several years ago that she had been sexually abused beginning at age eight by a close adult friend of her family whom she had even thought of as an uncle. "Looking back now, I can see that God was with me," Michelle remembers. "He made it possible for my family and me to move as far away as I could imagine on the opposite side of the country. When I knew this man couldn't hurt me anymore, I had the strength to bring it out into the open. I even found that my mom had been through something similar when she was young. That meant she could really relate to my pain and confusion."

Michelle is doing well today, thanks to good counseling, a loving family and her faith in God. She knows that learning to forgive the man who abused her may take a very long time, but she is working on it. Fortunately, the legal system came through and he is in prison serving a stiff sentence. She was not his only victim. She still struggles to understand why this happened to her. That is a question to which there are no easy answers. She is aware that the abuse will affect her future relationships with men if she holds onto bitterness and anger. While some people in Michelle's circumstances might turn away from God believing He had deserted them, she sees her problem through different eyes. "Today, I feel even closer to God and to my family," she says. "I know some special people have prayed for me, and that really helps. I think God may have allowed this to happen so that I can help other victims of this kind of abuse when I'm ready."

Growing in Faith:
Why Is Life So Tough?

Some people believe that Christian life is a guarantee that they will be protected from trouble. Look, however, at what Jesus said in John's gospel: "In this world you will have trouble. But take heart! I have overcome the world" (John 16:33). We are not to be surprised when trouble comes, nor are we to expect God to take us out of the situation. Rather, we are to realize that God, in the person of Jesus Christ, has made a way through our troubles. It is going through the valleys of life that teaches us to grow and mature in our faith. This is not always so easy to understand, especially in our teen years, when we are in a hurry to grow up. There are places to go and things to do, and it's all important to us.

God understands our impatience, but He is in no hurry to grow us into fully mature—physically, emotionally and spiritually—individuals. It can take a hundred years to grow a sturdy oak tree. A pumpkin plant is fully grown in a matter of months. Which would you rather be?

Physical growth takes place in spurts, as you know all too well from the pants that got too short overnight or the cramped shoes you just bought. Just as you must eat (healthy foods, hopefully) every day to grow properly or attend school for growth in knowledge, you will also find that faith must grow from the inside out. We exercise our faith each time we face life's challenges: "The testing of your faith develops perseverance. Perseverance must finish its work so that you may be mature and complete, not lacking anything" (James 1:3–4).

Sometimes we will grow rapidly, but at other times it will seem as if nothing is happening. Like that oak tree, some growth rings will show times of *solidifying* rather than increasing current size. This, too, is part of God's plan. It's important to remember that He does allow us to fail sometimes. Without occasional failure, we might come to expect that we could do anything and have no need of God. He must teach us that it is foolish to rely upon ourselves only. As Scottish pastor and teacher Oswald Chambers once said, "God does not give us overcoming life; He gives us life *as we overcome*."

24/7: God Doesn't Want You to "Go It Alone"

We are bombarded with images in movies and on television today of larger-than-life heroes who take matters into their own hands or vaporize the bad guys. While it is reassuring to see evil being handled decisively, we must remember that these lone-wolf tough guys are a Hollywood stunt mirage. They just don't exist in the real world. The Marines may be looking for "a few good men" and women, but they aren't looking for die-hard Rambos. They are looking for team players who know each individual job done well is a brick that forms a solid wall of strength when combined with others. Anyone who has survived real combat will tell you that the training wasn't tough enough to prepare him for all wartime situations. In order to outsmart the enemy, he and those who fought alongside him had to learn to grow stronger and smarter day by day.

In the struggles of real life, we can't always know what we'll have to face, either. We can only store up so much strength, no matter how much we pump iron or work out. It is the daily discipline of faith that gives us fresh strength and brings us God's grace for each new challenge.

<u>F</u>alse <u>E</u>vidence <u>A</u>ppearing <u>R</u>eal: How Do I Know It's Not Real?

If it's true that we are to expect some trouble in our lives from time to time, how do we handle life as usual? Are we to go around waiting for the sky to fall, just because we know it could? No way! The God who is worthy of our faith is the God who is in control 24/7. It is to the enemy's advantage to get us believing that our world is in chaos and that things just happen without rhyme or reason (can anyone say *terrorism*?). One day you're up, the next you're down. That kind of thinking can get you down and keep you down. Where is hope, then?

". . . a Time to Love and a Time to Hate, a Time for War and a Time for Peace . . ."

Ecclesiastes 3:1, 4, 6–8 beautifully reminds us "there is a time for everything, and a season for every activity under heaven: a time to be born and a time to die, a time to plant and a time to uproot . . . a time to weep and a time to laugh, a time to mourn and a time to dance . . . a time to keep and a time to throw away . . . a time to be silent and a time to speak, a time to love and a time to hate, a time for war and a time for peace." God knows the "seasons" and how they affect our lives. That is certainly a boost to our faith. Unshakable faith in the unchangeable God can give us nothing but hope. Constant fear of what's coming around the next curve is the unfortunate result of lies heaped on us by old Slewfoot, the father of lies, himself. Of course, he might instead deceive you into thinking all is well when, in fact, the bridge really is out ahead. Either way, you are sunk if you listen. God wants us to have faith in Him no matter what the situation.

Have you found yourself on that cliff lately? It can seem like a long way down when you're trying to do the balancing act. But do remember this: There are legitimate things to fear in this world. Evil and temptation are not to be taken lying down. Getting out of control through the desire for some thrill—experimenting with alcohol, drugs or sex, even hanging with the cool, tough "alpha" crowd, or as sixteen-year-old Bobbie Burres says her mother often warns, "driving faster than your angels can fly"—is certainly flirting with disaster. God has taught us to run from temptation because He knows our human weaknesses all too well. So does the enemy. The good news is we have weapons that are highly effective if we just remember to use them. One of the most important truths to remember is this: " . . . the one who is in you is greater than the one who is in the world" (1 John 4:4). Faith in God and His Word is our lifeline. Prayer is our communication system. We have superior force.

Do You Doubt That God Can Help You?

Do you still have doubts that real faith in the real God can help get you through these teen years of turmoil? Then welcome to the club. Everybody has doubt from time to time. How could we expect to grow unless we stopped and examined the world around us occasionally? Questioning should strengthen our faith instead of making it shaky. Do you ever question a teacher in school, or do you just accept every word of instruction as absolute truth? A good teacher wants a pupil to question because it means he or she is listening and is thinking. God is no different. Just hold on for the ride and see for yourself.

Perhaps you feel entitled to test the waters or to spread your wings. *Is there really any harm in living a little?* you might wonder. *Isn't that what all teens do?* Ultimately, you will have to look around you and really weigh the consequences of your decisions. If you doubt the reality of those consequences, you are likely to get into trouble. You already know someone who pushed it to the limits and lost it all or suffered terribly. This type of tragedy can be a wake-up call for others. It's one thing to face challenges through no fault of your own or to be blindsided, but quite another to walk head-on into the face of danger. In either case, whether living life as usual or overcoming your own mistakes, your faith will be the key. It's not your own wits, your own strength or luck that will see you through.

Is Faith for Wimps? God's Hall-of-Faith Heroes—And What They Can Teach Me

Is faith for wimps? Don't believe that for one minute. David (yes, the teenager who killed Goliath and later became king of Israel) was anything but a wimp. Oh, he had weaknesses like we all do, and he suffered the earthly consequences for his sins. Yet David was called a man after God's own heart. He made the famous list in the book of Hebrews that is known as God's "Hall of Faith" (Heb. 11). David also wrote many of the psalms that beautifully portray both his sorrow for his sin and his love and gratitude toward God and His awesome creation.

Hebrews 11 begins, "Now faith is being sure of what we hope for and certain of what we do not see." That same book of Hebrews was written specifically to Jewish Christians to remind them of their heritage and the great Jewish heroes of faith, but also to help them understand that God's love even extended beyond the laws and promises of old to include His plan of salvation through Jesus Christ, His Messiah. The Mount of Zion, a reference to heaven, is compared to the mountain on which Moses received the Ten Commandments (Heb. 12:18, 22). Hebrews 12:23 says, "You have come to God, the judge of all men, to the spirits of righteous men made perfect, to Jesus the mediator of a new covenant, and to the sprinkled blood that speaks a better word than the blood of Abel." This is a reference to the shed blood of Jesus, which was a greater sacrifice than that of Cain's murdered brother Abel (the first sons of Adam and Eve), because Jesus was also the son of God.

Because early Christians were subject to horrible persecution or suffering for their faith, the writer of Hebrews felt the need to encourage them. We likewise can feel encouraged when we read it today. He refers to the early heroes "whose weakness was turned to strength" (Heb. 11:34), and says "the world was not worthy of them" (Heb. 11:38). The author of Hebrews also reminds us that hardships are often a form of discipline from God, who treats us as sons and daughters (Heb. 12:7). It is our faith, he concludes, that will help us endure the tough times until we finish the race that we all must run.

If the men and women of old could trust God with their lives and all they possessed, so can we in this day and age. Our faith is the same as theirs because we believe in the same God, the same Messiah.

Personal Reflection

1. Where would I place my faith today on a scale of 1 to 10, with 1 being no faith and 10 being a champion of faith?
2. What has been the biggest test of my faith that I can remember?
3. Who is the best role model for faith that I know today? Why? If I don't have one currently, is there a faith hero from the Bible whom I particularly admire?
4. How am I running my race—with courage and endurance or with fear and doubt?
5. What does the Scripture, "God chose the foolish things of the world to shame the wise and . . . the weak things of the world to shame the strong" (1 Cor. 1:27), mean to me?

Why Didn't Jesus Simply Come to Us as a Superhero? Why Did He Have to Be Crucified?

Although we would much rather think about the beauty of this world God created for us than the bothersome nature of "sin," admitting this truth about mankind's "sinful nature" helps us more fully appreciate the full impact of God's compassion for us. Just as in the early days, sin is still very much with us. Just read any headlines or glimpse any television news at all, and you'll probably agree.

What do you do when you find yourself looking into the eye of the storm—such as the war on terrorism? Do you pretend issues such as these do not relate to you and so avoid discussing them? Or do you consider something of this magnitude to be "between the leaders of nations," and so feel it's irrelevant to you? Or do you just want to crawl into the safety of family and friends and wait things out? As much as we want to, we cannot deceive ourselves into thinking we can make the bad news go away by ignoring it.

What's so great about the good news of the gospel of Christ is that it isn't just a nice view of the world through rose-colored glasses. The gospel message takes in *all* aspects of life—the good, the bad, the beautiful and the ugly. Jesus Christ—the man— recognized the human pain of despair, guilt and loneliness. He particularly knew loneliness all too well. Nevertheless, he went about offering hope and healing to all who believed. He was even tempted by Satan—and withstood that temptation—both at the beginning and at the end of his ministry, and all throughout. As for guilt and despair, those emotions were heaped on him as he transitioned from life on Earth, through the cross, back to the Father. This was part of the penalty he paid for the sins of all mankind—to literally *become* sin and to know the temporary agony of punishment for that sin and separation from God in our place.

Jesus constantly addressed human pain and anxiety when he spoke to his disciples and those who surrounded him in the days of his earthly ministry, saying again and again: "Do not let your hearts be troubled" (John 14:1, 27). Can you imagine how it must have felt to have been handpicked by Jesus Christ to "go and bear fruit—fruit that will last" (John 15:16)? Wow! History bears out to this day that the chosen disciples and other early witnesses did their job well. Every generation since then has borne the same fruit as branches of the living vine, Jesus. That is good news, indeed. We can all use some of that.

Understanding the Real
Significance of the Cross

Have you taken the time to really think about the significance of Christ's life and death? If you're like the average person, it comes to mind mostly at Christmas or Easter. There are some troubling aspects of that whole death scene, aren't there?

Honestly, couldn't Jesus just have appeared in all his heavenly glory with a big "J" on his chest to rain heavenly terror down on his tormentors instead of facing crucifixion on the cross? Why would God choose to do it that way? First, it's important to remember that it is simple, childlike faith that impresses God the most. He wants us to search for the real truth in the cross. That's why youth can actually be an advantage to being a Christian. The older we get, the more complicated our thinking process becomes. It's not brilliant intellect that reasons the answers from God. It's faith.

If Christ had been a superhero, where would that have left us? In constant need of a superhero. Instead, he humbled himself to complete his Father's plan and gave us something we could imitate, without the need for superhuman strength. He died one death to pay the penalty for the sins of all. His words on the cross as he breathed his last—"It is finished"—signaled the end of one age and the beginning of another. The crucifixion and resurrection became the door through which we can all "die" to our old nature and receive new life, forgiven and set right with God, or *justified*. Perhaps you've heard this term before. It's really a simple and beautiful concept.

Christian Life Goes Beyond "Live and Let Live"

For some of your friends (and maybe even you), just getting past the idea that there really is a God will have been a major step. To make the leap to go the whole nine yards and buy into the big picture of sin and Satan and eternal judgment and Jesus as the answer—well, that's asking a lot of anyone. But here's the thing: Christian life goes way beyond "live and let live." We don't just get to do our own thing as long as it doesn't hurt anybody. We are called out to be a light to the world and the salt (preservative) of the Earth. We are to make a difference.

God is the ultimate parent, but a fair one. Here's the real amazing news: He has adopted us into His family along with the ultimate son. There's no sibling rivalry, though. No jealousy. In fact, we are called "fellow heirs" with Christ: "The Spirit Himself bears witness that we are children of God and if children, then heirs—heirs of God and joint heirs with Christ, that we may also be glorified together" (Rom. 8:16–17). We get the same birthright!

Why Were We Born with a "Sinful Nature"?

Why is it so hard for us to accept that we are born with a sinful nature? *A loving God wouldn't really do that to us, would He? What did we do to deserve this?*

It takes some time to learn who we really are in our Heavenly Father's eyes and to mature in our faith. Sinful, yes, but also redeemed and wonderfully, fully acceptable to Him. We have a choice. Those who reject the idea that we're all painted with the original-sin brush want instead to paint God as a wrathful, cruel dictator. They want to believe people are basically good and that we can earn our way into heaven. Along comes Jesus Christ with a 2,000-year-old message that says, "Hold on there, partner. You're leaving out one part of the equation: me. I died for all sins, including yours, so that you might have everlasting life."

That message is spelled out in great detail in God's Word, even in the Old Testament with prophecies of Jesus' arrival. ". . . the Lord has anointed me to preach good news to the poor. He has sent me to bind up the brokenhearted, to proclaim freedom for the captives and release from darkness for the prisoners. . . ." (Isa. 61:1). Yet it still falls on many deaf ears. There have been many scholars and intellectuals through the ages who have tried to convince us how ridiculous Christ's claim is—that he is not the son of God. On exactly whose authority does one dispute God? Our own? Like you and me, the enemy was created by God. Arguing with God is like the moon trying to outdo the sun, whose light it must reflect to be seen at all. C. S. Lewis put it another way: "Man can no more defy God than a stream can rise higher than its source."

We can rest assured that God knows how easy it is for us to be selfish and sinful. He gave us the answer to that little problem—the mind and strength of Christ through the Holy Spirit. Even the apostle Paul, arguably the greatest Christian who ever lived, struggled with his sinful desires: "For what I do is not the good I want to do; no, the evil I do not want to do—this I keep on doing" (Rom. 7:19).

What Is God's "Get-Out-of-Jail" Card?

Since we don't have much of a choice but to accept that we're born with a sinful nature, we might as well get on with accepting the key to making things right—Jesus Christ. Even many Christians go around dragging the chains of a guilty nature behind them when they could be free of them with a simple turn of the key. (There is no freedom like the freedom from our own emotional anguish.) Why is it so hard to turn that key?

We are conditioned so easily into believing certain things about ourselves. Even megadoses of healthy self-esteem or imagined happiness aren't going to replace our need to accept Christ's atoning, sacrificial love. We can attempt to play God, or we can let God be God. God forces us sooner or later to look deep inside ourselves and to see ourselves as we really are. Only by realizing who we are without Him can we then free ourselves to become what He wants us to be. Some of you already have reached that point in your lives. Others have yet to get there.

God wants us to use that key—His get-out-of-jail card. It's accepted more readily than even that well-known credit card. And there's no debt, no balance to pay. Ever. It's paid in full. This is the greatest love imaginable.

Personal Reflection

1. Do I struggle with worry or anxiety? Why is it useless to worry about the future?
2. What does being "justified" through Christ mean to me?
3. Does God allow me to argue with Him sometimes? Why or why not?
4. Can I have too much self-esteem? How does being arrogant or conceited conflict with the nature of God?
5. Is it harder or easier for a Christian to feel free from the past than one who doesn't believe? Why?

Religions of the World: Why Do We Choose to Worship the Same God in So Many Ways?

You've no doubt already encountered friends, neighbors or classmates who practice other faiths, and you may even discuss the differences in your beliefs on occasion. Do you ever wonder why we can't all just believe the same things? In this chapter, we'll briefly review the four major faiths in the world besides the Christian view. These four are divided, for the most part, into two categories—the *mystical* and the *prophetic*—although each shares elements of both of these qualities.

Each major faith has a geographical origin. What are known as the primarily *prophetic* faiths (Judaism, Christianity and Islam) began with the Jews and came out of the ancient Near East. The primarily *mystical* faiths (such as Hinduism) came from India. Buddhism, which came out of China, counts as an independent religious phenomenon that would be placed in the Indian category because this is where it received its greatest influence.

In understanding the similarities and differences of each of the religious faiths, it can be helpful to look at how each teaches and celebrates the following:

- values or the ideal the group is striving to reach;
- ceremonies and practices, which the group uses to help gain these values;
- "worldview," which unites the search for values with the power of the universe around the individuals who practice the faith.

It would be impossible to cover each faith extensively in this book, so we'll try to concentrate primarily on these three factors of each of the four religions.

Understanding the Four
Major Faiths, Besides Christianity

Judaism

Judaism, which is the Jewish faith, holds that the world and all life were created by God, the supreme, all-good, personal Creator. Man, according to Jewish belief, was given free will and was meant to use this freedom to both enjoy life and follow God's guidance. Judaism teaches that God will lead the destiny of the world through historical changes and ups and downs, until finally a Messiah will come to deliver the Jewish people and bring about paradise. The Jewish faith holds that Jesus was a great prophet, but not the Messiah.

The early books of the Old Testament record a great deal of the genealogy of the Jewish race (including the earthly ancestry of Jesus), God's destruction of the world except for one faithful man and his family (Noah) and the story of God's covenant with Abraham which resulted in the twelve tribes of Israel. The Old Testament, in addition to recording the early history of the Jewish nation—particularly the fleeing or exodus of the Israelites from many years of slavery in Egypt and the giving of the Ten

Commandments to their leader, Moses—covers most of the important laws and teachings of this faith. The Torah (what Christians call the Pentateuch or the first five books of the Bible) was given to the Jews by divine revelation in about 1400 B.C. Their rabbis, or religious teachers, explained these sacred Scriptures to the people. Jesus attributed the writing of these Scriptures to Moses. New laws were written in a book called the Talmud (which means "teaching"). These laws, passed on by the rabbis, were thought necessary to protect and maintain the spirit of the Torah. This book wasn't completed until about 500 A.D.

The practices of the Jewish faith include attending a synagogue or temple for worship on the Sabbath. They also honor the Sabbath by refraining from any physical labor during Sabbath hours, which begin at sunset on Friday evening and last until sunset on Saturday. Orthodox Jewish faith embraces a diet that consists of only certain "kosher" foods historically approved by God and observes several holy days that include special ceremonies and observations. The holy days include these "High Holidays":

- Rosh Hashanah, the Jewish New Year, which falls in the Jewish calendar's month of Tishri (between September and October);
- Yom Kippur, the "Day of Atonement," which is observed on the tenth day of the Jewish month Tishri;
- Hanukkah, which is known as "the festival of lights" and "the feast of dedication," observed in December;
- Passover, which commemorates their ancestors' freedom from slavery in Egypt.

Jewish celebrations, ceremonies and traditions are practiced in the home as well as in the synagogue or temple. Judaism teaches that man is to use the Law of Moses to honor and serve God. This faith requires its followers to maintain their identity as a people. It teaches that all must actively strive for world peace, social justice and brotherhood among all men and nations. The first Christians came from among the Jews, as did Jesus.

Islam

The Islamic faith holds that the world and all life was created by God or "Allah," a supreme, personal creator who reveals Himself to man and gives direct guidance. Its followers, known as Muslims, believe the world was created for man but is under Allah's absolute rule. Islam teaches that the destiny of the world is ultimate destruction, which will take place on the Day of Judgment, or the last day. Man will be judged on this day and will either be given rewards or punishment in the second creation. In order to earn the rewards of the second creation—which is a type of paradise—one must adhere to a routine called the "Shari'a," which includes the "Five Pillars":

- A declaration of faith in Allah as the one and only God and in Mohammed as the final prophet;
- Prayer to Allah five times a day;
- Charitable giving of a percentage of all one's possessions to the poor;
- The fast of Ramadan (which is a month of fasting from sunrise to sunset);
- Making a pilgrimage to Mecca at least once in one's lifetime.

Islam began in Arabia during the 600s (A.D.) with Mohammed's teachings. Mohammed was the last, and considered the greatest, of this religion's prophets. (Islam also recognizes the Jewish prophets.) He believed that he was called to be God's prophet to the heathen and less civilized tribes of Arabia. In the beginning, Mohammed taught anywhere he could gather together people to listen. While he lived in Mecca, for many years he was scorned by most of the people in his hometown. Eventually, his critics were so hostile that they forced him to flee to Medina—a neighboring city. Because of the importance of this forced flight, known as "Hegira," the Muslim people date their calendar from this time.

The Islamic faith holds that Jesus was a great prophet. Mohammed is said to have taught the Arabs about Jesus Christ, whom he referred to as the Word and the Spirit of God. He stressed Jesus' teaching of kindness and forgiveness. He also spoke of Abraham, Moses and other Old Testament prophets, saying that all such prophets of God taught the same essential truths. The laws of the Old Testament were the crux of his teaching, as he instructed his followers not to kill, steal, envy others or commit adultery. What's more, he directed them to give to the poor, protect orphans and be honest in business, as well as in all their other words and actions, much as Jesus taught. Mohammed taught the ideal of complete submission of the heart, body and soul to the will of Allah. "Islam" is the Arabic word for submission, and it is the name Mohammed gave his teachings. These revelations are written in the Koran (also spelled Q'ran), the Muslim sacred scriptures. Mohammed taught that respect should be given to those of other faiths who have a holy book, such as Christians and Jews. Since Mohammed believed man's strength came from heaven, he urged his followers to pray five times a day, with their first prayer being recited at dawn.

Long after Mohammed died in 632 A.D., the Muslim world divided into two major sects, and a third sect was formed in the eighteenth century. As a result, there are great rifts in both the religious and political unity of the Islamic people. Some extremists believe that Allah wants them to rid the world of those whom they call infidels, and this includes those of Jewish and Christian faith. They seek to wage jihad or holy war around the world for this purpose. Yet, when it comes to tradition, they still follow the same beliefs.

Hinduism

Hinduism holds that the world experiences continuous cycles of creation and destruction, but has no definite or actual beginning or end. The Hindu faith teaches that the one reality is Brahman, known as the "One Mind" or "Life." Hindus believe this Life expresses itself in all that exists, and they compare this to a flame taking many shapes. Hinduism teaches that, like the world, mankind has no real beginning and that people go through many, many lifetimes (reincarnation) as determined by "karma." Simply put, karma means the continual process of evolving by paying for your wrongs and receiving rewards for your good deeds from God, the supreme, all-good, personal creator. This series of many lifetimes, according to Hinduism, may include episodes of heavens and hells. Finally, Hindus believe the individual will transcend karma through a complete realization of God.

The Hindu faith is exceptionally varied, including a number of views of theology and philosophy, many popular sects and huge temples dedicated to many "gods" symbolizing the many attributes of a single God. The Hindu faith is explained in their sacred scriptures, the Vedas (Veda means wisdom or knowledge), the Upanishads and the Bhagavad-Gita. The Vedic tradition was originally taught by word of mouth and is made up of a number of types or writings, which were completed between 1400 and 400 B.C. Its earliest writings hold that there are many different gods, and are quite different from the later writings which instead teach that one God is in everything. The later scriptures have set the tone for the more recent (although still ancient) development of this religion, which is a highly complex one.

In Hindu homes, devotees begin their day at dawn. After ritually splashing himself with water the moment he arises at dawn, the head of the house goes to his rooftop or porch and says the morning hymn to the sun, which is called the "Gayatri mantrum." He will then go to the shrine in his home and chant the praise and mantra of the deity he worships. After that, he washes the deity, offering it food prepared by his wife. The home is the center of this faith. Many times devout Hindus do not go to a public temple. The life of devoted Hindus may also include "sacred marks" on their bodies, as well as following what is known as "dharma" through rituals, behavior and good deeds.

The Hindu faith claims there are four basic goals that motivate humans: pleasure, gain, righteousness and liberation. The goal of liberation is the highest and can be reached by following the teachings of Krishna, Shiva or Yogis. In India, the endeavor would be undertaken under the guidance of a Guru.

The ultimate goal and value of the Hindu faith is to rise above everything—become as "free as sunlight and clouds." It is then that Hindus believe one knows who he really is. In this freedom, one realizes that there is only One—Brahman or God.

Buddhism

Buddhism holds that humans live in a realm of suffering ruled by karma (as noted previously) that can also be simplistically described as "what goes around comes around." Buddhists also believe that one can and should transcend this suffering existence and achieve a state of illumination in the "void," also known as "Nirvana," by gradually extinguishing the self and the senses. Buddhists teach that God is this ultimate reality beyond all opposites. This faith also teaches that the universe has no beginning or end, but that it goes through world cycles. It claims that each person is a process of cause and effect rather than a self—and there is no beginning to this process. Buddhism teaches that humans will experience countless lifetimes in this and other worlds according to their karma and what they earn, eventually breaking through to achieve the state of Nirvana.

Approximately 2,500 years ago there was a young man named

Gautama, who was the founder and champion of Buddhism. He was given the title Buddha, which means "Enlightened One," and called Gautama Buddha. There are many ancient tales of the teachings and miracles of this man. He was born in northern India around 563 B.C., the son of a chief. When he was still a young man, Gautama desired to help his people and to deliver them from their problems, both physically and emotionally. Giving up his considerable inheritance, he instead sought the truth that would bring peace to his country. One night, after seven years of searching, the truth is said to have come to him as he sat beneath the sacred fig tree, known as a bo tree. He believed all the world's sorrow stemmed from selfishness. His plans for overcoming such selfishness created the basis for the Buddhist religion. To this day, Buddhists still refer to him as master, the Divine Physician and teacher.

Buddhists are called to do good. Their faith teaches that the ultimate secret of all life is brotherly love—and hatred only stops when it is overcome by love's power. It teaches the "Eightfold Path," which can conquer selfishness; this eightfold path includes right ideals, right beliefs, right deeds, right efforts, right words, right thinking, right livelihood and right meditation. According to Buddhism, there are ten sins: Three are of the body (murder, stealing, being sexually impure); four are of speech (lying, verbal abuse, slander, useless conversation); three are of the mind (malice, envy, lack of faith). Buddhists are expected to practice religious and moral works that will assure them a positive rebirth. They are to seek Nirvana by meditation or related spiritual practices. Buddhism teaches that the well-trained mind holds a kind and compassionate view of everyone and every living thing. The pinnacle of devout Buddhist life is to love one's enemies.

The Buddhist's goal is to reach Nirvana—the state of mind that encompasses total peace and love—during one's present lifetime. Nirvana is only achieved if a person has perfect selflessness, self-control, enlightenment, kindness and knowledge. It is believed that all passion, fear, anger and sin must be rejected to attain Nirvana.

Although Buddhism was rooted in China earlier than 100 A.D., in the sixth century it was embraced in Japan. Revitalizing and adding to the teachings of Confucius, it stimulated a new era of art. Near the end of the eighth century, Buddhism came to Tibet and has experienced various influences under the teaching of the Lamas, the leader of these being the Dalai Lama.

Christian Sacraments or Sacred Observances

This discussion is intended only to highlight the main ideologies that characterize what the world acknowledges as major, established religions. While we're on the subject of religious practices or customs, we will also mention here some of the customary observances or "sacraments" of the Christian faith as you may be wondering about these. To Christians, the two most holy days or seasons of the year are those during which we commemorate the birth of Jesus Christ—Christmas—and the time that we remember Jesus' death and resurrection or Easter. Each observance is meaningless without the other. There are no strict ways in which we observe these holy days. Most Christians will attend special church services, read the portions of Scripture that relate these historical events and spend time in prayers of thanksgiving for the gift of Christ's birth and resurrection to everlasting life. Other elements of pagan holidays surrounding Christmas and Easter creep into our celebrations. We put up Christmas trees, exchange gifts (some say to commemorate the gifts of the Magi or wise men to Jesus), sing both hymns and traditional carols and feast. We give Easter baskets and bunnies and have egg hunts. While the real meaning of these celebrations can easily get lost in all the commercialism, Christians strive to keep their observances centered on Christ.

While certain sacraments are observed differently from denomination to denomination or between Catholics and Protestants, the two most important are the sacraments of baptism and the Eucharist, or the Lord's Supper. Water baptism symbolizes the death and resurrection of Christ and our identification with him as believers. Some denominations sprinkle with water while others believe in total immersion. Some believe in the importance of infant baptism while others believe that baptism can only seal the decision of a person who is old enough to decide to accept Christ as personal savior.

The Eucharist or Lord's Supper observance consists of eating a small piece of bread or a wafer that represents the broken body of Christ and drinking a small amount of wine or grape juice that represents the shed blood of Christ or the new covenant. It is this practice that caused some detractors in earlier days to accuse Christians of being cannibals. The Eucharist is modeled after the last supper that Jesus had with his disciples on the eve of his crucifixion. He told them to "do this in remembrance of me" (Luke 22:19). It is considered a mysterious way of identification with Christ and is quite sacred. Protestants usually observe the Lord's Supper en masse as a whole congregation in a special church service. Catholics may offer it in every mass for Catholics who choose to partake. It is also included in many wedding ceremonies.

You may wish to read additional books or material (see Suggested Readings and Resources) if you have a keen interest in comparative religion. It will be helpful to you to have some basic knowledge about other faiths in the world so that you can better understand some of the world events taking place, and so that you might have better relationships with people whose beliefs differ from yours. We are called to "love [our] neighbors as [ourselves]" (Matt. 22:39; Mark 12:31; Gal. 5:14), the second greatest commandment Jesus gave his followers and the summation of the entire law, according to the apostle Paul. You can take this chapter as a starting point. The following chapter will address some questions that this one raises.

Personal Reflection

1. Do I know what my personal faith is? Do I really understand what I believe?
2. What concerns do I have about faiths other than my own? Am I afraid or intolerant of other religions?
3. How do I relate to friends or acquaintances who believe differently than I do?
4. Why do I think that people choose to worship the same God in so many ways?
5. Have I been tempted to use the violence that I see among people of different religions as an excuse not to believe in God?

How Do I Relate to People of Other Faiths?

12

Looking at each of the major religions or faiths we have discussed, you can see there are a number of differences. Yet, most of the major faiths in the world also share some similar, if not identical, principles or values. These are often called "universal truths" and provide at least some common ground for us to comfortably live among people of other faiths. Perhaps the best known of these is what is known as the "Golden Rule" (we will discuss this principle in more detail in chapter 17). As an example, Christianity teaches this by instructing: "Do to others as you would have them do to you, for this is the law and the prophets" (Matt. 7:12; Luke 6:31). Here is how other faiths state that same instruction:

Judaism: "What is hurtful to yourself do not to your fellow man. That is the whole of the Torah and the remainder is but commentary."

Islam: "Do unto all men as you would wish to have done unto you; and reject for others what you would reject for yourselves."

Hinduism: "This the sum of all true righteousness: Treat others as thou wouldst thyself be treated."

Buddhism: "Hurt not others with that which pains yourself."

The other similarities in the basic teachings of these faiths are just too numerous to discuss in this chapter, but include the principles of sowing and reaping, honoring your parents, refusing to judge others, being truthful, living peacefully and giving to help others in need. You can use these principles as a starting point for discussing faith with friends who practice a different religion. You may find, when you start talking with others, that you don't know as much about the faith you may have been brought up to observe as you think. Then, too, you will hear views expressed about your faith with which you will disagree. Remembering that America was founded on the principle that all people could worship (or not worship) as they pleased, can keep us humble and our discussions with others more respectful.

The Unifying Principle of Major Religions: Love and Respect Our Fellow Traveler

As you have seen, all the major faiths claim to share some common ground when it comes to promoting love and seeking to improve the world and those who live in it. While you may not agree with some of the teachings of other faiths or the way in which some of their followers go about practicing them, you can at least respect this common desire for what is good and use it as a starting point to promote greater peace and understanding in the world around you. Realizing this, you can feel more at ease among your friends of different faiths. It is possible that one or more people outside your faith may put you down simply because they don't understand your beliefs or they believe their religion teaches their faith is superior. Having strong faith convictions may be admirable, but again, the unifying principle of all major religions is love and respect for our fellow man. If a friendly discussion turns into an unfriendly or ugly debate, it is best to decline to talk further and simply to wish the person well. There have been enough religious wars fought throughout history, so why start another?

It's hard not to notice the strong feelings and equally strong language that is often exchanged between certain ethnic or religious groups around the world. Because the United States has long been considered the "melting pot" of the world, people of many different nationalities and religions call it their home. Even though our constitution guarantees religious freedom, that doesn't mean you won't hear or see religious intolerance and so-called "hate speech" here and there. The volume of some of this speech was turned up in the months following the 9/11 terrorist attacks. The fear and unrest that have characterized some parts of the world for generations suddenly became apparent within our own shores. Extremists from all sides have chosen to point fingers and cast blame for what happened. Some say God's judgment was evident. Others say their religious views are being misinterpreted. Still others say there are obvious clues to the violence in the scriptures of one faith or the other. What happens when both sides view a war as just and see God as being on their side? There are no easy answers. Only God knows for sure what is going on. You are no more or less confused about this than the average person and must search out the truth in Scripture for yourself. Just knowing God is in charge and that He does have a purpose can make a difference in times like these. He is the ultimate judge, and we can rest assured that He will bring His power to bear when He is ready.

Understanding the Judeo-Christian Heritage

It is helpful for all those who accept Christianity to be especially familiar with the Jewish roots of the Christian faith. History and tradition are sacred to the Jews because they are known as God's chosen people, and indeed, biblical history bears this out. Both Old and New Testament prophecies speak of the promise that God will save a portion of His chosen race. In fact, in what we refer to as the "end times" or the prophesied end of this present age before Jesus returns to the Earth to fulfill the rest of his role as Messiah, the Bible predicts a great spiritual revival that is for Jews and Gentiles alike.

All through Old Testament Scripture, God refers to the Jews as His children. Jesus wept when he looked out over Jerusalem near the end of his ministry and realized that his own people were largely rejecting him as their Messiah: "If you, even you, had only known on this day what would bring you peace—but now it is hidden from your eyes" (Luke 20:42). In Matthew's gospel, Jesus takes on even more of a parental tone when he says, "O Jerusalem, Jerusalem . . . how often I have longed to gather your children together, as a hen gathers her chicks under her wings, but you were not willing. Look, your house is left to you desolate" (Matt. 24:37–38). While orthodox (strictly traditional) Jews still do not accept the divinity of Jesus Christ or that he was and is the true Messiah spoken of in prophecies of old, many Jews over the centuries have chosen to accept Christ as the promised Savior. They are referred to as Messianic or "completed" Jews.

The apostle Paul, who came out of a strict Jewish background to accept Christ as the Messiah and to witness so fervently for him, loved the Jewish nation and prayed for the eyes of his people to be opened to God's truth. What is that truth that Jesus and his followers preached and still preach? It is that no matter how well any of us keeps the old laws God gave to Moses and observes the practices meant to make us righteous (blameless) before God, we can never be righteous on our own because the debt—the weight of our own sin—is too great. It took God's tremendous love through Jesus' atoning death to release us from that burden. *This is the belief that separates Christianity from all other faiths, and it is a substantial difference.* The stubborn confidence of so many of the Jews in Jesus' day that God would grant them salvation through His original covenant with Abraham (which they broke many times in their history, requiring God to make a new covenant) is addressed in a number of Paul's writings in the New Testament and was spoken against by many of the Old Testament prophets. That division still stands. So intertwined are Judaism and Christianity, nevertheless, that many godly truths are referred to as "Judeo-Christian."

What About Other Religions and Cults—Are They Dangerous?

In addition to the major religions we have discussed, lots of variations on religious themes have sprung up over time. There is some kind of religion or system of thought for every letter in the alphabet. People are divided as to which ones we might call cults.

Two of the more widely known and younger religions/ churches that were established in this country in the nineteenth century are the Mormon Church (The Church of Jesus Christ of Latter-Day Saints) and the Christian Science Church (The Church of Christ, Science). Each has its own "sacred" text.

The Mormon Church has one version of the Bible called *The Book of Mormon*, while the Christian Science Church has *Science and Health with Key to the Scriptures*, a book written by its founder, Mary Baker Eddy, to explain her interpretation of healing and spirituality from the Bible. When placed next to the Bible, these two books and the doctrines they represent differ from biblical precepts in significant ways. There are plenty of wonderful people who accept either of these belief systems, but if someone belonging to either church tells you he or she is a Christian, you need to know that their definition of "Christian" is not the same as what we describe in this book or what the Bible expresses. In fact, Mormons often refer to Christians as "Gentiles," which is an interesting historical reference to those who were outside the Jewish faith.

To their credit, Mormons have very strong family values. Both churches revere their respective founders and accept as gospel the "revelations" supposedly made to them, which form the basis of their creeds. Those who adhere to biblical Christianity see these creeds as based on "relative truth," which of course is a contradiction in terms implying that truth changes with varying circumstances, a widely held misconception today, as we have already seen.

The Jehovah's Witnesses are another church that you may know a little about. We see them at work frequently as they go door-to-door "witnessing" their faith to others or us. Many professing Christians politely decline to discuss their doctrines with them, as their interpretation of Scripture is, again, different from that of established Protestant or Catholic churches. Some, however, choose to witness right back to them, as well as to the Mormon missionaries who also show up at their doors on occasion. Whatever you think about the faith of the Jehovah's Witnesses, their enthusiasm for spreading their version of the gospel is admirable.

While we should not seek to cast down those of other faiths—we are all God's children—the Christian faith focuses on the original Holy Bible as its authority. Christians are sometimes accused of not being inclusive enough, but John 3:17 reminds us, "God did not send His son into the world to condemn the world, but to save the world through him." That salvation is for *all* people, regardless of background. Belief in Christ is the great equalizer. You can't get more inclusive than that. It is God who says we can't sit on both sides of the fence. There is a new covenant, period. It rests in Jesus Christ. The apostle Paul advises us all to be careful of any belief that is contrary to Christ's truth: "See to it that no one takes you captive through hollow and deceptive philosophy, which depends on human tradition and the basic principles of this world rather than on Christ" (Col. 2:8). We live in a world today where deception comes in many forms. Satan's best disguise is as an "angel of light" (2 Cor. 11:14). It looks so good, how could it not be true?

New Age Spiritualism: A Class by Itself

What about so-called "New Age" spiritualism? The New Age movement is not a formal religion since it follows no holy text and has no real clergy or geographic center of origin, yet it is considered the third largest system of faith in America. It is a loosely defined spiritual movement, a network of believers who share some similar beliefs and practices. Many people who adhere to an established faith follow some New Age beliefs, nevertheless. Recent surveys indicate that many American adults may hold at least some New Age beliefs:

- 8 percent believe in astrology as a method of foretelling the future;
- 7 percent believe that crystals are a source of healing or energizing power;
- 9 percent believe that tarot cards are a reliable base for life decisions;
- 25 percent believe in a nontraditional concept of the nature of God;
- 11 percent believe that God is "a state of higher consciousness";
- 8 percent define God as "the total realization of personal, human potential";
- 3 percent believe that each person is God.

Source: Ontario Consultants on Religious Tolerance, *www. religioustolerance.org*

Channeling: Is It Possible to Get in Touch with Someone Who Is "on the Other Side"?

You may hear talk of "channeling," which is attempting to get in touch with someone who is no longer living. What is unsettling about both New Age and Christian Science philosophy to Christians is the emphasis that is placed on the self instead of on God. This is known as humanism. It appears to be based on half-truths and a more secular, as opposed to sacred or faith-based, view of the world. New Age and Eastern mystical philosophy permeate much of the media around us today, including many of the television shows and movies we see. It is very "Hollywoodsy," but not exactly biblical.

There are many smaller "religions" being practiced all around us in addition to the major ones. Even occultic practices, witchcraft (Wicca), neopaganism and Satanism (Satan worship) are recognized as legitimate religions in our very open society of worship. While an atheist (one who denies the existence of God) might call all religions or systems of worship "cults," certainly those who adhere to an established world faith have a much more narrow definition of a cult. To most people, *a cult is some extreme or obsessive form of religion or worship that has a rigid set of rules and is unusually exclusive or intolerant of those outside their membership.* Once in, cult members may have a hard time being released should they change their minds.

Cult leaders and the general membership can impose a strong sense of guilt on defectors and even threaten them. The most extreme kinds of cults may attract people who feel they don't belong anywhere else or who are sure there is a shortcut to whatever they view as eternity. They are easily seduced by the charismatic personalities of the leader or leaders and are made to feel special. They may even be promised a special place or position in the "next life" or special rewards in this one. Some cults may appear relatively harmless, and perhaps they are. Others are not. Mass suicides, physical mutilation and sacrificial rituals are not acceptable religious practices in the modern world. Of course, anything that keeps a person from hearing God's real truth is actually helpful to the enemy, and that is not a good thing.

While some people have mislabeled any religion they don't understand as a cult, there are clearly churches or religions that are on the fringes of what we would call normal. Strange rituals and a tendency for members to withdraw from public view or accepted practices (some even refuse medical care) can point to a cultic religion. It may not bother us that our neighbors practice a faith that doesn't allow them to observe holidays or that we have people coming to our doors to "witness" to us with their different version of the Bible. We all have freedom of religion, right? Being forced or coerced into a cult, however, or being abused physically, emotionally or sexually in the name of some religion is another matter. Now we're talking about crossing legal boundaries, and that can't be tolerated in any free society.

The best policy is to treat others with respect unless or until they begin to impose their views on you against your will. Then you must speak up and inform a parent or someone in authority. Such practices are unacceptable, no matter what the motivation. Even people calling themselves Christians can go astray in this way. Just know that God doesn't operate like this. He doesn't need to.

Do All Religious Roads Lead to Heaven?

One of the more divisive questions that confronts us today is "What is the true road to heaven?" Assuming that you possess a faith that accepts life after death, you may ponder this all the time. We can accept that there is one God and one heaven, but what about all those different religious beliefs, even within the major faiths? Perhaps you hear respected people giving their views and wonder why you shouldn't believe them. Still, they can't all be right, can they?

This is a question that we all must answer someday. As you have seen from the previous chapter's discussion about other religions, even the definitions of heaven vary greatly. If we have disagreement on what constitutes heaven, it stands to reason that there would also be a lot of debate on how to get there. The Christian view, based on biblical teaching, is that Jesus, as he said, is "the way and the truth and the life. No one comes to the Father except through me" (John 14:6). It is accepting Jesus as Savior, then, that assures one of knowing God and of spending eternity with Him. *But what about all the good people who believe in God and do good things, but don't accept Jesus as their personal Savior? Won't they go to heaven? How could a loving God banish them for all eternity?* Good question. How does the Bible address it?

As Jesus was on his way to Jerusalem for the last time, someone asked him, "Lord, are only a few people going to be saved?" His reply was, "Make every effort to enter through the narrow door, because many, I tell you, will try to enter and will not be able to" (Luke 13:23–24). Jesus then goes on to relate a story of the owner of a house who, at a certain point, shuts the door in the face of many who are knocking and pleading to come in. "But he will answer, 'I don't know you or where you come from'" (Luke 13:27). In Matthew's gospel, Jesus' teaching on this subject is recorded in even more detail. He refers to the "narrow" gate again and contrasts it to the "broad road" that "leads to destruction" (Matt. 7:13).

Jesus goes on to warn of "false prophets" who come as wolves in sheep's clothing. He says we will know them by the "fruit" they bear, or in other words, by the results of their teaching. "A good tree cannot bear bad fruit, and a bad tree cannot bear good fruit," he said (Matt. 7:18). The crux of Jesus' message is in these words: "Not everyone who says to me 'Lord, Lord' will enter the kingdom of heaven, but only he who does the will of my Father who is in heaven" (Matt. 7:21). He puts the period on that statement in the gospel of John, by following his statement that he is "the way, the truth and the life" with this: "If you really knew me, you would know my Father as well" (John 14:7).

When the Real Truth Becomes
Evident to You, You Will Know It

We don't profess to be prophets who possess godly wisdom or all of the secrets of the universe. Like you, we are just traveling through this life trying to do our best to know God and His will for us. We know we're far from perfect and that people can only attain what we consider to be perfection when God accepts them into His heavenly presence or kingdom after death. Truth, as we have said, ultimately comes from God. When the real truth becomes evident to you, *you will know it*. It is possible that you may accept some half-truths between now and then. But God is patient, loving and kind. He allows us to make course corrections as we come to know Him more and more. Every time you open the Bible to read it for yourself, you give the Holy Spirit an opportunity to preach a sermon directly to your heart. Powerful.

Personal Reflection

1. Do I know why I believe or worship as I do? How would I explain my faith if someone asked me about it?
2. Could I listen patiently if someone wanted to tell me about their faith, even if I felt I must politely decline to believe as they do?
3. Have I been guilty of slandering another person because of their religious beliefs? Do I believe God loves that person just as much as He loves me?
4. Can I really accept that Jesus is "the way, the truth and the life"? Why or why not?
5. Do I spend much time reflecting on heaven and life after death? How do I feel about my eventual death?

Part 3

Life 101–How Is God a Part of My Everyday Life?

Prayer does not change God; it changes me.
—C. S. Lewis

"Life is just too much for me," complained Charlie Brown. "I've been confused from the day I was born. I think the whole trouble is that we're thrown into life too fast. . . . We're not really prepared." Asks Linus, "What did you want, a chance to warm up first?"
—Charles M. Schulz, "Peanuts"

We've always needed God from the very beginning of this nation, but today we need Him especially. We're facing a new kind of enemy. We're involved in a new kind of warfare, and we need the help of the Spirit of God.
—Billy Graham, "National Day of Prayer and Remembrance" (September 14, 2001)

13

Passing "The" Test: The Most Important Question I'll Need to Answer

Some of you reading this book have had the opportunity to learn about God—and more specifically, Jesus Christ—at an early age. Others of you either have come to know Him more recently or still are contemplating what Christian life is all about. Whenever we do come to understand that great truth—that we were created for a personal relationship with God through His son—we then can begin to "work out" our life-changing and life-long relationship with the Father, Son and Holy Spirit. The journey begins with our answer to one very important question: Am I ready to listen to that still, small voice and to allow my old life to "die" so that I can then be *reborn* and *regenerated* to a new life in Him? That's a big deal, regardless of how many years a person has lived or how many experiences they have had. Even a person who thinks he or she has that relationship may realize that is not the case, as was true for some of the teens whose stories you'll read about in part 6 of this book.

Repenting Means More
than Saying "I'm Sorry"

If your parents (or grandparents) are the right age, you might ask them if they remember a movie from 1972 called *Love Story* starring Ryan O'Neal and Ali McGraw that was a big hit. Maybe that's an appropriate period to remember since so many of you are into the retro-'70s look these days: polyester, platform shoes and flares (which your parents call "wannabe" bell-bottoms). That movie spawned the curious line, "Love means never having to say you're sorry." Oh, yeah? Just try that with your special someone . . . or a parent. Get real, Hollywood!

We all mess up from time to time and have to eat that humble pie. "I'm sorry" is one of the most important phrases in any language. While God has incredible patience with us, He still expects us to make some changes if we are to have a relationship with Him. Step one is repentance. Do you really understand what that word means? You may say it means expressing sorrow for your sins or for your old life to God and asking forgiveness, and you would be right—to a point. Feeling sorry or regretting one's mistakes is a nearly universal human occurrence if one has any conscience at all. An accused criminal appearing before a judge or a jury may feel sorry or express regret (sometimes only at being caught) for his or her crime. If this wayward person were truly repenting of that life, it would mean making a commitment to change and refusing to commit further crimes, not just shedding "crocodile tears." Repentance is much more than merely saying you're sorry. It is a door to a new life of change. "Therefore if anyone is in Christ, he is a new creation; the old has gone, the new has come!" (2 Cor. 5:17).

"Reborn": Is That Possible?

Since none of us can escape the human tendency to do bad things from time to time, then it goes without saying that we will all have some areas in our lives that need to be changed. It may take us a while to discover some of them, but God's Holy Spirit is perfectly designed to help us find those areas. When our conscience starts to make us feel uncomfortable, it's best to listen. Change is scary and never easy. It is seldom accomplished all at once, but usually involves some backsliding into old behaviors before we break through into new ones. As Christians, we can collectively pray with the psalmist, "Create in me a pure heart, O God, and renew a steadfast spirit within me" (Ps. 51:10).

The idea of regeneration or rebirth into a new person can be somewhat confusing. If I am capable of being spiritually reborn the instant I give my life to Christ, then am I also expected to change instantly into that entire new creature? Think of the literal process of conception and birth for a moment. You don't quite remember that blessed event when you made the trip down the birth canal or were gently lifted out during a C-section delivery. Neither do we. We know it happened, though, because here we are. While the egg and sperm that caused you to be conceived were joined in a single instant, it took nine months or so for you to grow to the point where you could make your grand entrance into the light of day and survive outside the womb. Voilà! First birth.

The spiritual rebirth process is no less awesome. There is a moment when your new life is conceived, establishing that you are a new person in Christ's eyes. However, you won't emerge from the womb of warmth and comfort as one who is ready to walk with Christ through all circumstances right away anymore than a baby can jump up and care for itself. Even this womb of spiritual development will not necessarily be a tranquil place. You may not receive the nourishment you need; you may be lacking in life support. The world around you may be downright hostile at times. This doesn't mean you are not developing into a baby Christian; it just means you may have to struggle to get there.

It takes the loving support of others who are "older" in their faith to walk alongside you, encouraging and nourishing you, in order for you to safely grow in your own faith. We call these people spiritual mentors. Once you are mature enough in your faith and learn to hear God's voice clearly, you will rely more on your personal relationship with Him through the Holy Spirit. You will still need the encouragement of others at times—that's what the church is for—but you will be strong enough to stand alone with God, if that is necessary.

Why Doesn't God Guarantee
Christians an Easier Life?

The Marines have had some wonderful and memorable recruiting slogans over the years. One of these was "We don't promise you a rose garden." Any Marine can tell you that's a true statement. God tends to make the same promise. Of course, roses also have thorns, you know. The Christian life is for the long haul—roses, thorns and all. Here's an interesting thought: A teenager can become a spiritual "parent" before an older adult can. Is that news to you? We've already pointed out through scriptural and historical evidence that God can and does single out young people for His specific purposes. Others may not really meet Him in a personal way until much later in life. God is gracious in His timetable. He calls, but He doesn't badger us. He waits for us to respond.

Are you familiar with the biblical story of the rich, young ruler from Luke's gospel? Luke tells us this man approached Jesus one day and asked, "What must I do to inherit eternal life?" (Luke 18:18). Even though he had kept all the commandments from his youth, Jesus said this man was still lacking one thing: In order to be "complete," he must sell all that he owned, give to the poor and follow him. The rich ruler was devastated because he knew he had great wealth. Instead of agreeing on the spot with Jesus, he went away, dumbfounded. Now, we are not told that he chose to defy Christ's command. We just know he couldn't find the strength to do it at that moment. Perhaps he eventually did; perhaps not. Here is where Jesus made his famous statement about it being harder for a rich person to enter the kingdom of God than for a camel to go through the eye of a needle (Luke 18:25). Those who heard this thought he must have been referring to something that was impossible. Jesus clarified, however, in his next statement: "What is impossible with men is possible with God" (Luke 18:27). By the way, you do not necessarily have to sell all you have to follow Jesus. As we have already suggested, if your possessions, your relationships or anything keep you chained to the world and prevent you from knowing God, then you may have to "sell out" unless you can reorder your priorities.

While it can *seem* incredibly hard to change, it is never impossible. The variation in time it takes for different people to come to a true relationship with God is based on their ability to accept the truth that God continually puts before them and to decide to make necessary changes. God calls; we choose to respond or not.

How Can I Tell if God Is Speaking to Me?

Have you been uncertain at times if God were really speaking to you or calling you to do a particular thing? How can you get to the point of knowing? Study His truths through His Word. Pray for wisdom in applying those principles. Listen for His voice and let Him open your eyes to the real meaning behind the Scriptures. This is a lifelong quest. God finds ways to confirm that He is speaking to us. You may feel a tug at your heart or a prick of your conscience. He may confirm it through the voice of a friend. Eventually, you will know God's voice, and it will lead you to discover your purpose. If you go off on your own in pursuit of your life's work or consult only with other people, feeling confident that you are heading in the right direction, you may be surprised to find God throwing up a roadblock to your plans.

But it seemed so right, we may say. Yes, in our limited human sight. God-sight is much more focused.

If God should hold up a stop sign, it's best not to run it. He may let you shed some tears. Tears serve a real purpose in real sorrow. Here's a new word to add to your vocabulary: *contrite.* Definition? "Humbled by guilt and *repentant* for one's sins." Ouch. Was that a thorn? Yes, but it's attached to a beautiful rose.

Personal Reflection

1. Do I feel something may be standing in the way of my relationship with God, something I need to confess or repent of?
2. When have I felt that God was speaking to me or calling me to do a particular thing?
3. How has my life already changed since opening up to Christ? Can my friends tell a difference?
4. Have I sought God's answer for what I am to do with my life, or am I not yet ready to look for my life's purpose? Have I received any answers yet?
5. Have I made a real decision to accept Jesus Christ as my savior? If not, am I ready?

Living My Faith: Walking the Talk

To say that the Christian life is easier said than done is an understatement. We are met at every turn by the subtle, confusing influences of the world, not to mention the in-your-face, pulpit-slamming, Bible-toting hypocrites who want to set us on the road to righteousness. Jesus called these kinds of people in his day "vipers," or poisonous snakes. They can poison our walk with God if we let them. One of the most amusing bumper stickers spotted in recent years says, "Lord, Save Me from My Fellow Christians." Sad, but too often true. It's no wonder outsiders looking in—those window-shopping for churches—often shake their heads in disbelief and walk away. Some Christians make the walk easier for us while others seem to make it harder, a fact of life that teens Kelly Chakeen and Lance Waldrop (who write about their experiences in part 6) discovered. We can't pretend this doesn't happen. Is the walk still worth it? If it weren't, God would have let Christianity die long ago.

Good people who may have started out professing their faith from a heart of deep conviction and love for God can become hypocrites. Some take themselves and their brand of faith too seriously. Some of us forget to examine the plank in our own eye before pointing out the speck in another's eye (see Matt. 7:5). Doctrine and legalism (following a strict set of rules) can take the place of the simple Christlike principles upon which the church was first built.

Often, new Christians mistakenly model their own faith after these various misguided and legalistic versions. Even entire church communities can go off on a tangent. The worst cases we know are cults. Any church, however, that is not lined up with biblical principles is likely to find itself stagnant and decaying from within. Churches sometimes split right down the middle with one faction going elsewhere. Why can't all Christians just get along? It's the age-old question. Perhaps the answer is because they don't hang out with Jesus enough. If each professing Christian really had a personal relationship with the Savior, things would be different. It's easy to get caught up in that kind of "churchiness" and to drive people away rather than draw them into a loving fellowship.

The accounts we read in the New Testament of the early church are really no different from what we see today. The same disputes arise today that the early church planters dealt with more than 2,000 years ago. But the church has endured, in spite of itself. God is bigger still than all our petty differences.

I Want to Be a Christian, but I Don't Want to Be Considered a Dork!

Even if some hypocritical "Christian" doesn't run you off, you may still feel uncomfortable with the idea of being a Christian because of someone you knew who gave you the creeps or because you feel you will never be able to have fun again. Obviously, not all Christians are "dorky," even though you're sure to think some are. "When I'm eating lunch at school with my friends," says fourteen-year-old Samantha Nichols, "I always see this weird girl sitting alone at the table reading her Bible. The other kids make fun of her, and she looks so unhappy. She seems nice, but I'm afraid if I try to be nice to her, my friends will think I'm weird, too." Ever feel this way? Some Christian parents (or churches) set very strict rules about how to live in "the world." They are concerned that *any* social contact with folks outside their families or church will have a corrupting influence on their lives. That's a bit extreme and not in keeping with the example Jesus set in the Bible. How can we have a "ministry of reconciliation" (2 Cor. 5:18) or fulfill the Great Commission to those around us if we won't even associate with them?

Okay, that one may be a no-brainer. You can see through that one. Ever heard this one? *My church says that dancing is a sin, and I think they're wrong. I go to a Christian school that doesn't hold a prom or homecoming dance, or any dance. Some of us guys go out with girls from other schools just so we can go to their dances. We get dissed by some of the folks at church who say we're juvenile delinquents. Why can't they get out of the dark ages? We can listen to some music that's not by Christian bands and dance as long as we don't do anything vulgar or improper.* Sound like a recipe for rebellion, or just normal behavior?

Some church youth groups and parents are even opposed to dating. They think teens should just hang out in groups and wait until they're ready to "court" somebody seriously—somebody they would want to marry. You're no doubt wondering how you are supposed to know when that is. *How am I going to learn about love and relationships unless I date?* You might even consider quitting youth group or going to another church if they took this position.

Where does this reasoning come from? Some Christians believe teen dating, especially in a serious way, is opening a door to heartache or encouraging too much intimacy. Maybe you can speak with a voice of experience in this matter. Jeanne Williams, sixteen, went with a guy from her Christian school for nearly two years before they broke up. They attended church youth functions and school events together, and hung out at each other's houses. "At first I thought it was really cool having a boyfriend," she said. "Our parents wouldn't let us go out alone, and we didn't get physical, and that was okay. But the intensity of the relationship actually scared me after a while. We seemed to argue more and more, and I felt like I didn't know who I was anymore."

As you already have figured out, being with others is about learning about them—and ourselves—in relationship to each other. As we do that, there's going to be both good and bad experiences. But it is important that you always watch out for your heart and your well-being, something that teens Jennifer Stripe and Kristen Cartwright (see part 6 for their stories) discovered when the relationships they both were in took a turn in the direction of the "going too far" category.

Not all relationships will be so intense, but it may take getting out of one to know it actually was too overwhelming. Does that make sense? Ultimately, you will have to listen to your own heart—and to your parents—when it comes to dating relationships. Parents still get to make some rules as long as you live at home. The older you get, the more negotiable those rules become and the more freedom you will get.

Does Being a Christian Mean I Have to Behave in a Certain Way?

Here's another one: Sometimes you see a classmate "street witnessing" with his family, and you always go out of your way to avoid him. If that's what it takes to be a Christian, you want no part of it. *Do I have to be a "Jesus freak," always telling people about Jesus?* Naturally, you'd scare a lot of people off if you were constantly witnessing. There is a time and place for everything, just as teen Paul Cattaneo (his story is profiled in part 6) discovered as he sat with fellow teens at a national conference and was led to share his faith with a group of teens who point-blank told him beforehand they had a problem seeing the "relevance" of God. Sharing your faith is something you will do in your own way, when you are ready. Some people are comfortable with street evangelism. It's certainly not for everyone. "I know some teens in my youth group go along with the witnessing part of the ministry program because everybody else is doing it," says fifteen-year-old David Proffitt. "It's fun to put the message into drama or singing or something cool like a karate demonstration, but only some of the kids really have their hearts in it. You can tell by what they do when they're not in church. We have some great youth pastors. I think they know that some of these guys are really witnessing to themselves." We hear you!

Churches and communities are filled with lots of individual people who have a lot more in common than they realize. Each of us carries some part of the responsibility for making a church a safe haven and a place of growth and healing. Each of us has varying personality traits and habits, both good and bad. You look to your leaders, as you should, for guidance and some kind of example worthy of following. Sometimes, it is the youth who set the pace in a movement that can revive a faltering church. (Did you ever hear of the Jesus Movement? If not, ask your parents or grandparents.)

It's not even unusual for a teen to lead his or her parents to a meaningful relationship with God. Certainly this was the case for Martha Haake (whose story is profiled in part 6), whose father continues to marvel at the effects of Martha's faith at work in her life—and his, as well. Likewise, you can and do make an enormous difference in the world around you. Whether we call this "affecting our culture" or "growing our communities," you can and do make a difference. We know you probably get tired of hearing this, but you are the future leaders of all the world's institutions. Today's older generations will be looking to you to clean up some of the messes they have made. Not really fair, when you think of it, but this seems to be true for each generation. The fallout of corporate greed, environmental problems, media bias, entertainment excesses, the failings of the education and political systems, and the disastrous effects of sacrificing long-term goals so as to showcase short-term ones—just to name a few—will be passed along to your generation. How will you handle it? If moral blindness has messed things up, will those future leaders who have a strong moral foundation be able to turn things around? That's a question with which some teens already wrestle, and, of course, many teens are already making a difference in their homes and communities. Many are even making a difference in the world. Are you one of them?

Bad Habits: Why Doesn't Doing What's Right Come Easy?

We create our own reality for better or worse through our habits and the actions they generate. No one likes a person who says one thing and does another. Like it or not, we are creatures of habit—and "slaves" to our habits—which include what we think, say and do. Jesus realized this all too well when he came into his ministry. He understood human nature and the slavery of our sinful habits like no one around him could. "I tell you the truth, everyone who sins is a slave to sin," Jesus said in John's gospel. But he also promised, "If the Son sets you free, you will be free indeed" (John 8:34, 36).

The Roman Empire in Jesus' day was growing more and more corrupt and was on a course bent on destruction, although many of its citizens had no clue. The apostle Paul, who was an infamous persecutor of Christians, became a sold-out follower and preacher of the gospel after experiencing one of the most dramatic conversions in history. He, too, took up the message of overcoming human weakness. Paul knew we are all at war with ourselves over our habits, writing in his letter to the Roman church, "I do not understand what I do. For what I want to do I do not do, but what I hate I do" (Rom. 7:15). Do you feel like that sometimes?

Obviously, bad habits come naturally. We have to work at

changing them, but even then, we can't do it on our own, as Paul said. It is in submitting our self-will and all the bad habits of our nature to Christ that we experience the freedom of becoming a "good slave" to his new life in us. (By the way, scientists say it takes about three weeks to change a habit, in case you plan to work on changing one.) It is in this transformation that we can begin to walk the talk of a Christian and not just speak empty words.

"Cussing" and Other Word Games: Do I Have to Censor What I Say?

Speaking of words, have you noticed how difficult it is to tame the tongue? We can all get into big trouble by opening our mouths before we engage our brains. Of course, we could plead the curse of our human nature, as Paul did. Do we just throw up our hands in defeat, then? Is there any hope for us poor humans? You may not think it at first when you read what James, the brother of Jesus, had to say: "Consider what a great forest is set on fire by a small spark. The tongue is also a fire, a world of evil among the parts of the body. It corrupts the whole person, sets the whole course of his life on fire" (James 2:6). Okay, we're doomed on this one.

The tongue is a tough animal to subdue, but think for a moment about how easily a 1,500-pound horse can be guided with a small bit or how a tiny rudder has the ability to turn a huge ship. This illustration works both ways. It means either we can let the tongue lead us around with no direction, or it can be subdued and we can be guided by someone who knows what he's doing. Someone still has to do the steering, right? As a horse submits to the skilled rider, so we can submit to Christ. With him steering, we don't get into trouble. Given its own choice, a horse will wander back to the barn or the nearest pasture, or it will follow the herd, if there is one nearby. It can then easily get into trouble or become hurt. Are we not the same if left on our own? Have you found yourself following any "herds" lately? They do tend to kick and bite, don't they?

Have You "Had Words" with Your Parents?

It is a virtual guarantee that you will exchange some unpleasant words with your parents from time to time as you become more and more independent. It's part of God's way of beginning to separate you from those apron strings. The tricky part of these "conversations" is for each of you not to be cruel or injure the other with harsh words. A parent's stinging words can echo through your head for a long time, just as your answer to what you perceive as an insult to you can hurt right back. When you lose control, you will feel worlds better if you can apologize. Parents need to do the same. Cutting remarks can damage relationships and emotions faster than anything. "Reckless words pierce like a sword, but the tongue of the wise brings healing" (Prov. 12:18).

The same responsibility for what we say follows us wherever we go. If you have acquired the habit of using four-letter words around your friends because you think it is cool, you may have a hard time breaking that habit. It is almost sure to embarrass you some day. What we think, we generally say sooner or later. It is important, then, that we "take every thought captive to the obedience of Christ" (2 Cor. 10:5) before our thoughts take us captive.

Gossip: If Not Done Maliciously, It's Not as Bad, Right?

Gossip is another destructive form of speech into which we can all fall at times. If you've ever been on the receiving end of someone's gossiping, then you know how much it hurts. Remembering that (and the Golden Rule) should keep us from doing the same to others. Christians face the temptation to spread gossip even in the guise of prayers they offer for others during a church service. Often, when too many details about someone's private situation are shared this way, people begin speculating about why the problem exists or who is at fault. This can lead to some untrue and hurtful things being said. Why would people want to even bother to ask for prayer if they feel they may be "violated" in this way? It is better to offer an unspoken prayer request (God knows the details) than to worry about sharing too much. Our motto, as Billy Graham has been known to say, should be: "May the absent always feel safe with us."

Risky Behavior: Making Choices About the Pressures of Sex, Drugs, "Explicit Lyrics" and Internet Porn

In our youth, it's easy to think of ourselves as practically indestructible, judging by the number of bumps, cuts, bruises and maybe even broken bones we accumulate from the time we're toddlers. It isn't so, however. These bodies of ours need some tender loving care in order to function at their best. Are you surprised to know that teen girls are smoking more now than they did fifteen years ago? Boys, before you lord it over your female friends for being so careless with their health, you need to know that teen guys consume the most alcohol and take the most risks with high-speed driving. And teen sex—those statistics are pretty high, too. It's happening all around you, and possibly even to you. As Kristen Cartwright was told by her girlfriend, *"Everyone's* doing it." Will that make it right for you, or will you ask God about how to handle the pressures you're sure to face?

And speaking of other pressures teens face, how do you handle the pressures of smoking, drinking or doing drugs when your friends expect you to take these risks? Do you know of someone who is facing heartbreak as a result? Using almost always leads to a sobering wake-up call for those involved. Still, it isn't always easy to "just say no," is it? You have to be strong enough to walk away and not to care about the insults or taunts from others when you refuse to join them in substance abuse. Drugs and alcohol impair your judgment and your ability even to know right from wrong. This is where some of your friends are. You can see, and they can't.

Explicit Lyrics: Not All Words Are "Music to Your Ears"

There is no question about the importance of music in our lives. It helps us to unwind and get in touch with our emotions. We can express what otherwise is difficult to put into words through music. Does it seem as if you could have written some of those songs? Of course. Many speak a universal language. Still, as you're all too well aware, there are too many songs that not only are a shock to your ears, but are a jolt to your mind as well. It's doubtful that the music industry will see its responsibility to maintain decency in some of the lyrics that are recorded, so we might as well learn to "police" ourselves.

So how do you know when you're crossing the line of acceptable language and emotional expression with your music? Your conscience ought to tell you when something is too explicit, revolting or violent. Lyrics that degrade us as humans—especially with references to women—or that glorify sex and drugs and incite us to violence are just plain criminal. Those who push these kinds of lyrics know that we deal with more than our share of anger in the teen years. The normal emotional fluctuations we feel can spike to dangerously high levels through words that keep us angry, confused and ready to take our fears out on others. There is a lot of anger and violence in our environment every day; you've probably already heard some music that shocked you. If you listen to a daily dose of this, you are sure to be influenced into thinking it's okay to be angry and violent, and to act out in a negative way. If we want to identify with that kind of pain, perhaps we should find opportunities to reach out and provide a needed service. Give to a ministry, serve food in a soup kitchen or donate clothing. Share the gospel message with someone who is receptive. Anger and violence are not cool. They kill.

The Perils of Pornography

One of the deadliest traps lying in wait for teens today is at their fingertips. We're talking about the lure of Internet pornography, so easily accessed through your personal computer in the privacy of your home or, amazingly, even in many public libraries. What a tangled web to fall into—one that is incredibly sticky and hard to get out of. Parents should know the seriousness of this threat. What is the real harm of merely watching someone else committing sexual acts on a screen or in a magazine? The danger exists in that you may view these graphic images as normal and one day feel that you simply must do what you've been watching.

Pornography dehumanizes those who are involved in it. You may be one of those people who can only satisfy those sexual cravings with porn that has to be hard-core and violent. Psychologists and law officials together say there is no question that viewing these kinds of "images" can lead to committing acts of violence against innocent victims. The most sobering realization that violent porn can transform a person into a monster came from the lips of convicted mass murderer Ted Bundy on the eve of his 1989 execution. In an exclusive interview with Dr. James Dobson, Bundy said his steady diet of hard-core pornography was the catalyst that drove him to commit those murders of women. He had pegged out his thrill meter with just watching those acts in movies and on the Internet. He had to actually go out and commit those hideous crimes in order to satisfy his craving for sexual lust. The most shocking fact in Bundy's case is that he came from a good, Christian home. His addiction began when he discovered porn magazines in a Dumpster as a young teenager. He didn't know then that he was one of those people who would so easily be drawn into that sordid world where there was no escape. If you've fallen into this pit and want to get out, there is help available. We've listed some resources in Suggested Readings and Resources. Talk to a pastor or counselor. You will need someone to hold you accountable, while not judging you.

How many adults today—those lucky enough to still be alive—would love to have the chance to live part of their lives over and undo the serious consequences of risky behavior? Too many to count. When we start to see ourselves as belonging to a loving, personal God (Psalm 139:14 says, "You are fearfully and wonderfully made"), we tend to value our bodies and our minds much more. "Do you not know that your body is a temple of the Holy Spirit? . . . You were bought at a price. Therefore honor God with your body" (1 Cor. 6:20). When we honor and take care of our bodies, we show our glory for God.

Being a Christian Is Not for Wimps!

Walking your faith takes courage. No, it isn't for wimps. You will never win at anything more important than this. You may have to overcome hardship and temptation, but God will honor your continued faith. It's interesting to note that even the apostle Paul had a "thorn in the flesh" that was never identified in the Bible. Though he asked God several times to remove it, God refused. Because we don't really know what it was, we can speculate on many possibilities. Some say it was his poor eyesight. Others say it was a temptation of some kind. The beauty of not knowing is that we can all relate, no matter what our own "thorns" are. Paul said his thorn kept him humble and aware of his need of God. It's the same for us. We need our thorns. Without them, we might never become roses.

Personal Reflection

1. Have you known any Christian "legalists"? In what way have they impacted your walk with the Lord?
2. Have your habits made you more of a good slave or a bad slave?
3. What changes would you make if you were a government leader?
4. How would you rate the purity of your body on a scale of 1 to 10 with 1 being a garbage can and 10 being a holy temple?
5. Do you have a "thorn in the flesh"? If so, how does it affect your relationship with God?

"911—Pick Up, God!"

The psalmist wrote, "God is our refuge and strength, an ever-present help in trouble. . . . Be still and know that I am God" (Ps. 46:1, 10a). Is this just a lovely and comforting thought or a divine promise? To "be still," which also means to cease striving and rely on God for deliverance from tough times, is one of the hardest commands we face. It seems humanly impossible, in fact. Like some teens whose stories appear in part 6, we are tempted to turn our backs on God and His promises whenever we reflect on the times we believe He didn't deliver.

When disaster strikes or we find ourselves in a really bad jam, we may cry out in despair to God, but we tend to swing into action as if everything depends on us. Surely, we can work ourselves out of this, we think. We can and must try to make a difference. We are conditioned to *do something*. It's therapeutic, right?

Are you familiar with the account in John's gospel of the death of Jesus' dear friend Lazarus? You'll find it in John 11. As Jesus was resting near the Jordan River following a brush with death in Jerusalem, messengers came to tell him that Lazarus was very sick. Jesus did not get up and go at once, but he stayed two additional days there before going back to the hostile vicinity of Jerusalem once more where Lazarus and his family lived. Upon Jesus' arrival, he was told that his friend had died and had been in the tomb for four days. "You arrived too late," Lazarus' sisters

145

told him. John then recorded that Jesus performed one of his most spectacular miracles and actually brought Lazarus back to life. He did not rush to his side or heal him from a distance, as he had done in other cases. He ceased striving and let others know who God was and that nothing was too difficult for Him to accomplish.

Surely, we have all observed miracles taking place around us when we were powerless to do anything ourselves. Some things just defy any other explanation. If Jesus were to appear in our midst during these times of crisis, he might say, as he did before he raised Lazarus, that these things happened for "the glory of God" (John 11:4). We hardheads need to be shown once in a while.

That's all well and good, you may be thinking, but what about the awful things that happen anyway when it seems God is nowhere to be found? What about the terrorist attacks of 9/11 that killed some 3,000 innocent people? Where was God then? How could that possibly glorify Him or be of any positive value?

We're Not Unsinkable: Lessons from 9/11 and the *Titanic*

Is it possible that we all believed the mighty and awesome World Trade Center towers were indestructible or the Pentagon was unbreachable? Surely those magnificent, titan towers of 110 floors in Manhattan represented one of man's ultimate achievements. As long as they stood, we could gaze upon them with a sense of pride and self-satisfaction. Perhaps those who had been to the observation decks even felt closer to God as they stood there, drinking in the skyline and peering into the distant horizon on a cloudless day.

No doubt, those who boarded the great ocean liner *Titanic* in 1912 likewise felt the awe of being a part of one of man's greatest achievements of that time. *Titanic* was something to behold with its ornate and richly appointed rooms and decks. What made it most unique, however, was that it was said to be unsinkable. The people who boarded her for her maiden voyage across the cold North Atlantic that fateful April had complete faith that they would arrive safely at their destination—just as all those who worked in the various World Trade Center buildings believed they would go home at the end of that September day as usual. Through no fault of their own, history tells us they were deceived. In a relatively short time, these great landmarks were gone forever.

In both disasters, real heroes emerged, and real prayers were offered to God. Some escaped with their lives, but with the haunting realization of what nearly was and the memories of those who weren't so fortunate. How do you tell someone who was there or who lost loved ones to "be still" and know who God is? It isn't easy. The strains of "Nearer My God to Thee" that came from the deck of the *Titanic* as she was sinking may have made even angels weep, but what an awesome testimony! The words of "The Lord's Prayer" that Todd Beamer asked a telephone operator to recite with him before he led a charge to successfully wrestle control of a doomed airliner from the hands of terrorists bent on destroying yet another landmark no doubt provided a final sense of comfort for him and others near him.

Pain and Sorrow: A Natural Part of the Ebb and Flow of Life

God created us with a unique resilience, but also with the deep need to connect with something greater than ourselves. Is it really that divine power at work in us when we appear to have superhuman strength or defy the odds during moments of crisis? Can we still take a message of hope with us, even when the death toll and suffering are so great?

The answer is, "Yes, we can." We just need to remember who we are and who God is. We get confused when we forget that pain and sorrow are a natural part of the ebb and flow of life. Were we ever promised happiness in this life? The Declaration of Independence might have assured Americans a *right* to "life, liberty and the pursuit of happiness," but did it guarantee us happiness? No, not anymore than all the promises of the God who inspired that great document passed down through the ages. God promises we'll never be alone, not that we won't have problems or trials. "Man is born for trouble, as sparks fly upward," cried Job 5:7 in his affliction. We can't permanently escape it. Sometimes bad things happen for no reason, and we have no choice but to grieve or feel anger. After the time for grieving has passed, we must decide how we are going to respond.

But, wait a minute. Aren't Christians supposed to rejoice in their sorrow? Isn't that one of the fruits of the spirit? Aha! Now we're on to something. What is the difference between joy and happiness? Can a person have joy in his heart and in his relationship with God, while still experiencing the pain of life? Oh yes, it happens every day. In fact, how could we even know joy without first knowing pain and sorrow? Isn't it the rain that makes the sunshine so welcoming? Constant sun creates a desert, you know.

Still not convinced? Happiness is a temporary state of mind that comes and goes with our circumstances. Thinking we have found it is like having a firm grasp on an empty sack. We may think we have something for a moment until we look inside and see only air. That is one of the hardest principles to understand in our youth. All of us, without exception, take the long road to that truth, and sadly, some never get there. The peace and joy that come from a saving knowledge of the Lord Jesus Christ are in us forever. That is our anchor through the storms of life. Romans 8:28 is one of the most quoted, but perhaps least understood verses in the Bible: "And we know that in all things God works for the good of those who love Him, who have been called according to His purpose." That doesn't mean everything that happens is good, but rather that when we love God, He will eventually bring about a good result from whatever our circumstances might be.

This same truth is echoed in the Old Testament story of Joseph, the youngest of Jacob's twelve sons who became the heads of the twelve tribes of Israel. Joseph's older brothers were jealous of his relationship with his father and with God. They plotted to get rid of him by selling him off to a traveling caravan, telling his father that a wild animal had killed him. He endured years of slavery and many other hardships in Egypt before finally being made the second most powerful figure, next to the Pharaoh himself. Joseph had the foresight through a divine vision to store up enough food to save Egypt and the surrounding lands from an extreme drought. He realized God's divine intervention in all of this as he was eventually reunited with his family and forgave them: "You intended to harm me, but God intended it for good to accomplish what is now being done, the saving of many lives" (Gen. 50:20).

If I'm Throwing a Pity Party, Why Will God Be a No-Show?

Okay, you're facing a major challenge in your life. On a scale of 1 to 10, the meter is pegged out at 12. We're talking CRISIS!

You: *Is anyone listening here? I need help, and I need it yesterday! Don't tell me to chill out. This is **real**. Hello, hello! Is this thing on?*

God: *Transmission received. I was there before you even finished talking.*

Does it help the least little bit to know you're not alone? Not only is God aware of the problem, but if you really look around on any given day, you will discover a whole army of people, young and old, who are going down for the third time, too. Good thing God has a lot of life preservers, and He knows just when to throw one out. Hint: He likes to make sure you really can't swim first. If you can swim well enough to make it to shore, you're not getting one. Does that make you upset? For some people, it does. Can you imagine a more ridiculous scene than one in which a struggling swimmer who really can dog-paddle her way to shore gets in such a huff over not being tossed a life ring that she just gives up out of spite and goes to the bottom of the lake? Someone could even be standing on the shore giving her encouragement. A comic tragedy, you say?

Now try this scenario. Your best friend (it's always your best friend, never you, right?) is sitting home, threatening not to eat or ever come to school again because her boyfriend was clowning around while driving with her and hit a telephone pole, causing her to break her leg and miss the rest of volleyball season. No life-and-death matter, right? She'll heal. Oh, did we mention she's in line for a college scholarship and the scouts are coming to the next game only . . . and that her parents can't afford to send her to college without the scholarship . . . and that she wants to be a doctor?

Would you find yourself angry and bitter with God in those circumstances? You might. God, no doubt, hears such angry cries all the time. Like any loving parent who only wants what is best for us, He can put up with that to a point. He is incredibly patient. It's when that kind of anguish turns into real destructive self-pity that He is likely to say, "Talk to the hand." That may sound cruel, but not coming to our pity party is the kindest thing anyone can do for us at that point, and that includes God. It does none of us any good to feel sorry for ourselves and to attempt to drag others along for the ride.

Sometimes an apparent tragedy turns out to be a blessing in disguise (remember Rom. 8:28?). As the saying goes, some of God's greatest gifts are often unanswered prayers. We don't realize He is giving us an opportunity to grow or learn a lesson we might otherwise have missed. "'For I know the plans I have for you,' declares the Lord, 'plans to prosper you and not to harm you, plans to give you hope and a future'" (Jer. 29:11).

What Is "Grace"—And How Does It Show Up in My Life?

When we receive one of those special gifts from God, we call it grace. It is completely undeserved and unexpected, but hopefully we will recognize and appreciate it. God may not choose to remove an obstacle from our path. More often, He gives us the ability to see the obstacle and a way around it. Through the trials and crises of life, we learn what trust is all about and find out what we're made of. We're a lot tougher than we think. Some of you already have experienced more heartache than others will know in a lifetime. You have two basic choices—to become bitter or better. One leads to destruction, the other to healing.

Let's go back for a moment to our volleyball player with the broken leg. Is her life over? Not really. Sure, it's a major bummer, but there are all sorts of possible avenues for her to still achieve her goals if she truly wants to succeed. She could submit a videotape to the scouts and maybe even still win a scholarship. God may open another door to financial aid for her. She may go to a community college for two years, take time off to earn money and apply to another school. She may decide to go in an entirely different direction. She has options . . . but so does God.

"Better Angels": Comforting Others Who Face the Struggles We've Known

What's just as wonderful as receiving it is having the opportunity to recycle God's grace to others. If God didn't allow some of us to suffer and then overcome specific sorrows, we would be unable to help others facing similar struggles. There is no friend truer or more needed than the one who understands you and your pain because he or she has been through that testing fire. This is known as the "ministry of reconciliation" of which we have already spoken. Each of us is a link in a great chain of comfort and understanding. Through that ministry, we get to know the side of ourselves that Abraham Lincoln called "our better angels." Each of us has two sides to show the world, and one of them, we know, always strives to perfect our nature. Our better angel is the one who "comforts those in any trouble with the comfort we ourselves have received from God" (2 Cor. 1:3).

No, we can't expect God to eliminate all the suffering in the world, not the one we're living in now, anyway. Peace is not to be a long-term reality in this world, but God's indescribable peace of mind can come to each and every soul when we accept His grace and choose to learn from the tough times.

Personal Reflection

1. What's the worst crisis I've been through? Can I look back now and see a lesson God was teaching me?
2. Have I thrown any pity parties lately? If so, over what?
3. Do I bring God into the picture right away when I'm in trouble, or does it take a while to remember?
4. How have I had the opportunity to pass grace along to someone in need?
5. What do I think Abraham Lincoln really meant by the phrase "our better angels"?

16

Family Bonds:
God, Family and Me

God's Word has some very specific guidelines for our relationship with our parents and other family members. In fact, one of the Ten Commandments (the fifth) is to "honor your father and mother so that you may live long in the land the Lord your God is giving you" (Exod. 20:12). It is the only one of the Ten Commandments with a promise attached to it. That sets it apart from the others, giving the concept of family a high priority with God.

In case you didn't know it, you get to remind your parents (respectfully, now) of another Christian guideline, if not a commandment directly from the mouth of God. It appears in Ephesians 6 where the apostle Paul is giving instructions to the early church. Right after he reminds children to "obey your parents in the Lord," Paul adds, "And, fathers, do not exasperate your children; instead, bring them up in the training and instruction of the Lord" (Eph. 6:4). Another biblical translation for "exasperate" is "provoke to anger." There, feel better now? Parents have some rules, too.

God Expects Your Parents
to Follow His Rules, Too

That doesn't mean you get to throw out *all* their attempts at discipline because they "provoke" you to anger. Parental correction might tick you off, but that's not the same as angry punishment. You know the difference, don't you?

Proper discipline falls under that "training and instruction" category from the verse above, and is always tempered with love. Parents aren't perfect, so on a bad day they might cross that line. If that happens, a genuine apology to you is in order. God must deal with a parent's heart sometimes, too.

Just as God has expected the basic family unit of father, mother and children to be healthy and loving, He has planned for the overall Christian "family" to be a harmonious extension of this wholeness. He has given us the ideals on which to model our homes and churches, knowing full well that we are human and will mess it up many times over. (Yes, church congregations mess it up, too.) Still, we are expected to do our best, with God's help, to form strong homes and families in accordance with His commandments. Healthy families are the foundation of a healthy society. That's why the concept of family can't be overemphasized.

Does God Have a Rating System for Families—"Perfect"; "Big Problems"; "Really Dysfunctional"?

With our own kids, we have the chance to rewrite history—to parent them as we wish we had been parented. Thus does our own reparenting occur. We release the future as we release the past.
—Marianne Williamson

God designed the family with a specific plan in mind—namely, to model His love for one another and to reproduce in kind. That plan has fallen more and more on deaf ears, however. Why? Well, what does the word "family" mean to you? Back in the early to mid-'70s, when your parents were still likely to be living at home with their parents, the *American Heritage Dictionary* defined family as: "1. The most instinctive, fundamental social or mating group in man and animal, especially the union of man and woman through marriage and their offspring; parents and their children." All the way down in definition number 5 came this: "All the members of a household; those who share one's domestic home."

Today, you are more likely to see something like definition 5 much higher, even on equal footing with the original definition. In fact, the 2000 edition of the *American Heritage Dictionary* now defines family as follows: "1a. A fundamental social group in society typically consisting of one or two parents and their children. b. Two or more people who *share goals and values, have long-term commitments to one another,* and reside usually in the same dwelling place" (italics ours).

As you can see, the fundamental definition of what is accepted as a family today is quite different from what it was a few decades ago. The new definition reflects the crumbling "nuclear" family unit (husband, wife, children) that has fallen victim to rising divorce rates and the changing moral values of a society that has gradually grown further and further from God's truths as laid out in the Bible. Too many of us have tried to replace God with self. Since none of us can claim to have created the universe, this just doesn't work.

The godly blueprint begins in Genesis when God the Father, Son and Holy Spirit say to each other, "Let us make man in our own image, in our likeness. . . . So God created man in His own image . . . male and female He created them" (Gen. 1:26a, 27). Then God said to the first man and woman, "Be fruitful and increase in number" (Gen. 1:28a). In Genesis 2:18, as more of the story of Adam and Eve is filled in, God said, "It is not good for man to be alone. I will make a helper suitable for him." Thus, the foundation of the family was established.

When you look around today, what you see is quite different from that foundation in many homes—possibly even yours. Will you choose to have your family resemble that of Noeli Rios's (see part 6), or will you be pressured by those around you in the coming years to simply set up housekeeping and even to have children with someone without bothering to marry that person just because you appear to "share goals and values" (see definition 1b. previous page)? Of course, these are all things you must answer for yourself. If Hollywood has anything to say about it, we'll get to set our own definitions of family.

We're told to accept this as perfectly normal, yet something deep inside us senses the inappropriateness of it. That's our conscience, the shape of God in our hearts. He said thousands of years ago to the children of Israel, "Love the Lord your God with all your heart and with all your soul and with all your strength. These commandments that I give you today are to be upon your hearts. Write them on the door frames of your houses and on your gates" (Deut. 6:5–6, 8b). If God ever intends to change the rules, He'll tell us. Because we are made in God's image, we have an innate knowledge of what is right and wrong.

What if My Family Isn't Perfect? Is God Judging?

As you will discover one day if you choose to marry and build a family, it is not easy to keep that home together. Many outside pressures, and some from within, will threaten to tear it apart. Your parents or guardians are no exception. They are dealing with life as it comes, and no doubt you feel caught in the middle sometimes. We don't plan for all the twists and turns that come with life. As sincere as most men and women are when they stand before God and witnesses and exchange their wedding vows, it can appear that the world is determined to intrude on that home and break it apart from day one. What started as love can eventually grow cold, and two people who thought they had a lot in common can find themselves drifting apart. Financial burdens are also a major enemy to a happy home life.

Am I Living in a Troubled Home?

Living in a troubled home is a tough place in which to be, especially from your perspective because you seldom get to know all of what's going on. When divorce is looming as a real possibility on the horizon, there is no peace in the home. Are marriage commitments—sacred contracts—to be so easily broken? All this family discord must break God's heart. Does it make you angry or sad, or do you feel you just have to be resigned to the "facts"? Can you ever hope to turn around the failing commitments of your parents' generation or your very own parents? Or will you be expected to carry on the tradition of staying married only if it's convenient or as long as you feel deeply and passionately in love? Real love is a commitment, a decision that says, "I will honor my promises to you even when I don't feel like it." It is not based on the emotions of the moment that change with the wind.

Obviously, it is possible to "love, honor and cherish" another person for a lifetime. Many people have done it and are doing it. What makes the difference in their relationships? Perhaps the key lies in what is known as the "fruit of the Spirit," or the qualities that form the basis for interpersonal relationships and allow us to love one another unconditionally. These are "love, joy, peace, patience, kindness, goodness, faithfulness, gentleness and self-control" (Gal. 5:22). *But how can my family and I live like that all the time?* you may wonder. *That's impossible.* You're right. God knows that. That's why He taught us how to forgive each other, just as He forgives us. It's the glue that helps hold us together.

Is Someone in My Home Stressed-Out, Ill or Disabled?

A sudden, long-term illness or disability in a home can throw it into turmoil because of the extra care required or the possible loss of income and strain from medical bills. Because a significant percentage of the population experiences some form of mental illness, you may live in a home where a parent or sibling suffers from a serious disorder that requires medical treatment such as major depression, bipolar disorder (manic-depression) or schizophrenia. Even ADHD (attention deficit hyperactivity disorder) can turn a household upside down. It's not unusual for family members to become stressed-out so much in these situations that they overlook each other's needs and everyone becomes angry and defensive. You can feel lost in the shuffle or burdened with the need to keep peace. Such circumstances can either draw a family closer together or tear it apart. It takes enormous understanding, love and patience on everyone's part to survive.

If you do live in a stressed-out or even a broken home, does that mean you are less worthy than your friend who lives with two parents who are happily married to each other? Absolutely not. God values you as His precious child, no matter what your origin or family situation. It is your God-given "inalienable right," as our Declaration of Independence says, to share the same status and freedoms as anyone in this country, no matter what your birth. But look at what God does. He takes it one step further and declares you an *adopted fellow heir* with his son, Jesus Christ (Rom. 8:17). You are royalty, whether you know it or not.

No, God is not necessarily judging you or your family for some sin you're not even aware of. He just refuses to bend the rules for marriage and family commitments, even a little. There will be pain from time to time. It's inevitable. But misery is always more easily borne in the company of others who love you. That's the real benefit—and power—of family.

Family Crisis: What if Someone in My Family Is Doing Something Wrong?

A crisis in the home can come from something a parent is doing or something a brother or sister is doing. If one of the parents who brought you into the world and is supposed to nurture, protect and love you becomes involved in an affair or is drinking heavily or even using drugs, the resulting turmoil can leave a huge, gaping hole in your heart. For all practical purposes, it's like being abandoned. When a parent simply takes off and refuses to be your guardian, to give you the love you need, or be there for you and teach you all that you must learn, that creates a huge hole in your heart as well. As you'll read in part 6, such was the case for Justina Jasper whose pain over a father who left her years ago is still raw to this day.

Such pain can even follow you all the way into adulthood if you don't get some help early on. Maybe your parents yell and fight all the time, if they're still together, and that's painful, too. Wouldn't we all be better off, you wonder, if they just got a divorce? That's hard to say because each case is different. If there is violence in the home and you fear for your safety or the safety of one or both parents, perhaps the marriage is beyond saving and everyone would be emotionally healthier if it ended. It is also possible that a family counselor can help you all to work through it. Some situations that have appeared perfectly awful have dramatically turned around after the parties involved took personal responsibility. God is certainly in the business of healing and saving families.

The most severe kind of family crisis imaginable exists when a parent or another relative or close friend is abusing you or a sibling, whether physically, emotionally or sexually. In many cases of sexual abuse (which is also physical and emotional abuse), no one but you and your abuser knows what's going on because you may be embarrassed to tell anyone or you may have been threatened with even greater harm if you reveal the secret. Let's be clear here: *No* kind of sexual contact between you or any family member or relative is appropriate. That means any kind of physical contact, gestures, looks or words that make you feel as if you're being exploited or giving someone else improper pleasure at your expense. Sometimes younger children are innocently curious about each other's bodies, but we're specifically talking about an act that generally occurs between a child under the age of eighteen and an adult—something that you or someone else is asked to do *against your will*. You can even be abused by someone younger than you are.

I Must Never Allow Myself to Be a Victim—In Any Way

If this kind of abuse is happening in your home or within your family, we urge you to go to a safe, trusted adult. Hopefully, this will be a parent. But occasionally, a parent does not believe the abuse is real. Then you must go to a counselor at school or a pastor or a friend's parent whom you can trust. All forms of abuse are criminal. It is confusing to have a love/hate relationship with a parent, grandparent, uncle or aunt or even a sibling who is abusing you—trying to pretend it isn't happening because you love them but hate what they are doing to you. You must realize that your abuser has a serious problem and must get help. Protecting that person is not helping either of you. Good counseling can help you to overcome the pain and anger and even eventually to forgive the person. A victim is *not responsible* in any way for abuse, no matter what you are told.

Other kinds of crises can result from a poor choice that you or a brother or sister make. It's frightening to watch people you love doing something that can threaten to ruin or even destroy their lives, like experimenting with drugs or alcohol, gambling, shoplifting or getting into a dangerous relationship. What do you do? Do you let your parents or someone in authority know before it's too late? If you don't, will you carry the burden of guilt for the rest of your life for not doing something if the worst happens? The bond between siblings is a precious one. For all the fighting and fussing we do with them as we are growing up, they are often our very best friends throughout life. (We know it's hard to imagine this now. You'll just have to trust us.)

Remember, going before God in prayer is always the first line of defense in a family crisis situation. Next is mustering the courage for you or your family members to face the truth or to get help. Again, you or your parents may have to ask for a pastor or an older relative to step in and help make some decisions. The temporary pain of dealing with a crisis situation, no matter what it is jail or detention time, deciding how to handle a teen pregnancy, going into a drug or alcohol rehab program—is far less costly than the long-term pain of helping to cover up the problem. Counselors call this desire to hide someone's problem being "codependent" with that person. It's kind of like being an accessory to a crime. It's an easy trap to fall into when you love someone as much as you do a family member. It is their choice, ultimately, to make the necessary changes and to receive the help being offered. The greatest music to your ears one day may be the thanks you hear from a grateful loved one after you've helped out in a crisis. You know you would feel the same way if someone loved you enough to intervene on your behalf.

Will God Hold Me Accountable for the Choices My Family Makes?

You are approaching, or perhaps already have reached, what is known as "the age of accountability." That is simply the age at which you become responsible for your own actions. It is easy to want to place all the responsibility for who you are on your parents or whoever has raised you thus far—and they do play an important and undeniable role in influencing you, for good or bad. But ultimately you are God's child, and He will also hold you accountable for the choices you make once you are old enough to know the difference between right and wrong. That's the way it is for each and every one of us. (You'll remember this the next time you want to clobber your brother or sister, right?)

The responsibility for unconditional love that rests on the shoulders of your parents also rests on yours. It's so easy for us to forget that love is a two-way street. Yes, the more we know, the more God holds us accountable. "From everyone who has been given much, much will be demanded" (Luke 12:48). God's plan is for children to be considered a blessing in any family. Part of that blessing is the innocent love we all give to our parents when we are young, when we see them as capable of doing no wrong. In fact, our fathers, in particular, are our first role models for God in our lives. If we are blessed with a loving, nurturing father, we tend to have an easier time recognizing God as our loving Heavenly Father. Likewise, a father who abandoned us or is too busy to care about us can make it harder for us to trust God.

Does "Unconditional Love"— No Strings Attached—Really Exist?

When any serious relationship, marriage included, goes sour, it is because one or both parties have fallen down in one of the nine spiritual character traits we spoke of above as the "fruit of the Spirit." Look at your own family for a moment. Remember this principle whether you are considering your own family or someone else's: *A good start is no guarantee of a good finish.* You can turn that statement around, replacing the word "good" with "bad" and it would still be true. It takes constant love and attention to the needs of each family member for any family model to be successful. Sometimes you have to work with what you have.

Look for Unconditional Love in My Life

If you don't know the unconditional love that God intends for everyone in your home to give to each other, you may take comfort in knowing that God finds ways to send that kind of love into your life. You may seek that love in a lot of places—some of them not healthy—until you think you've found it. God has a better plan. He can intervene and send a positive, loving role model into your life when you least expect it. It's as if He's answering the unspoken prayer and longing of your heart. A compassionate teacher, coach, neighbor or church worker often has the privilege of filling this void in your life. When that happens, you can know it is God sending you His own unconditional love.

Families may be facing all sorts of problems and crises today, but that doesn't mean they are still not God's best and safest place for kids to grow up. His plan is fine, even if we tend to mess it up sometimes. "Home is the place where, when you have to go there, they have to take you in," said poet Robert Frost. How right he was. And God is the Father who, when you have to get a hug, has the biggest arms in the world.

Personal Reflection

1. How does my definition of family line up with either of those offered in this chapter?
2. On a scale of 1 to 10, with 10 being the most ideal home, how would I rate my own home? Why?
3. Has God (perhaps in the form of friends, counselors or doctors) helped me or my family through a crisis, or is He helping me through one now? If so, in what ways?
4. Who in my life has best modeled unconditional love? What is my relationship with that person or those persons?
5. How does Robert Frost's statement about home make me feel?

17

Why Is "The Golden Rule" So Important?

"Do to others as you would have them do to you" (Luke 6:31 and Matt. 7:12). Even if you haven't grown up reading the Bible or going to church, you are likely to be familiar with this statement that has been known down through the ages as "The Golden Rule." It came from the lips of Jesus as he was speaking what is called his famous "Sermon on the Mount," which contains many illustrations of life principles. It's a logical rule, right? Why would we expect to be allowed to treat people any way other than the way we want to be treated? It's what makes four-way intersections with no traffic lights generally function smoothly. Everyone knows they have to take their turn or traffic gets snarled and people get angry. It's the same with life.

What Does "What Goes Around Comes Around" Mean to God?

Another way of interpreting The Golden Rule is to realize that it works even turned inside out, meaning that we can expect to have what we do to others generally come back to us, even if it's not so good. "What goes around comes around" then is more of a negative warning than a promise of something good. Here's how Jesus further illustrates it in the Sermon on the Mount: "Do not judge, or you too will be judged. For in the same way you judge others, you will be judged, and with the measures you use, it will be measured back to you" (Matt. 7:1). That was a specific reference to the merchants and shopkeepers who had a habit of using a weighted scale that cheated people out of some of what they paid for. It's an effective word picture. Does that sort of thing still happen today? You bet.

How about this famous lesson immediately following the illustration from above: "Why do you look at the speck of sawdust in your brother's eye and pay no attention to the plank in your own eye? How can you say to your brother, 'Let me take the speck out of your eye,' when all the time there is a plank in your eye?" (Matt. 7:5). You can't miss that picture. Jesus loved to use that sort of ridiculous analogy for emphasis. It makes the point, right?

When someone does us wrong, don't we find ourselves waiting and hoping for that person to get the same treatment from someone else as his or her payback? "The Lord says 'Vengeance is mine. I will repay'" (Rom. 12:19), we remind ourselves, confident that He'll somehow "zap" them to teach them a lesson. And if we don't want to bother God by bringing Him into the picture, we can always take care of the problem ourselves, right? God's pretty busy, you know. He won't mind a little help.

Not so fast. What kind of world would this be if we all had free rein in taking revenge on everyone who did us wrong? In short, it would be chaos. A grand mess. Do you think God might have known this when He had his son stand up and preach that sermon to the multitudes of people who came to listen? *But part of the world is already a mess because so many people don't follow The Golden Rule.* God's got that one covered, too. "'There is no peace,' says my God, 'for the wicked'" (Isa. 57:21). Sooner or later, everyone must face that truth. Selfish, rude, unloving people may sometimes seem to have it made from outward appearances, but inside it's often a different story. Nothing lasting is ever built on self-centered rules. Moral bankruptcy and the lack of love that tends to go with it are the worst kind of poverty in the world.

Can we be patient when every fiber of our being is straining to get back at someone? It's hard, but not impossible. Wait and see how many times God's rebuke of that person is so much better and more creative than anything you could have devised. In truth, though, God doesn't care for us to be on the lookout for His judgment of others. We may never know what their fate is. We just know we can trust Him. He's taking care of it on His timetable, not ours.

Restoring Friendship: When Issues Come Between Me and My Friends

We can accept that we'll have trouble from people who we might call our enemies, but how do we handle it when we're at odds with a friend? Common wisdom says that a friend isn't really a friend unless you fall out with each other occasionally. Did you know that? We're more easily wounded by the people we love the most. That doesn't mean we can constantly be bickering, however. Who needs a friend like that? It's what we have in common that generally draws us to someone, although we may also enjoy being around a person who is a little different or who balances or offsets our own personality in some way.

It's sad to see good friends part company over a dispute and never become reconciled. It happens to family members sometimes, too. Usually, one party feels more angered or deeply wounded than the other, and the wound just seems too deep to heal. Holding onto that pain and bitterness can, indeed, keep the wound open and bleeding for years. Bitterness then may grow into hatred, and that's a dangerous and unhealthy place to live. It can cause sickness and even death in the most extreme cases.

Did you know you can literally grieve yourself to death? Losing a friend is cause for real grief. Part of the pain is justified if you truly have been mistreated or misunderstood, but closing yourself off to the hope of reconciliation with the friend with whom you're angry will only make you more unhappy.

What if My Friend Won't Listen to Me or Doesn't Want to Make Up?

You can't force a friend to either forgive you or accept your forgiveness, even though you can still offer it in your heart and gain some peace. It takes a lot of patience if you truly want to restore a broken relationship. Prayer certainly helps. Even if you're angry with someone, praying for that person has a way of softening your heart and letting you see through their eyes just a little. Try it. It really works. It is God's purpose for us to live in harmony with others, but especially those who share our faith. "Be kind and compassionate to one another, forgiving one another just as in Christ, God forgave you" (Eph. 4:32).

The most difficult kind of wound to heal in a friendship is the one left when someone you really care about betrays you. This is a deliberate and undeserved hurt that seems to have no real cause but the selfishness of the other person. It's tough to be betrayed by someone you formerly trusted. Bryce Stanford, a high-school senior, found this out when his "best" friend showed up at the homecoming dance at school with the girl Bryce was going with until she ditched him at the last minute. This was a double betrayal, as if both friends had ganged up on Bryce to make him even more miserable. Several other friends who saw what was happening cared enough to console Bryce. "I guess you find out who your real friends are during times like this," he points out.

Megan Weise, fourteen, experienced another kind of betrayal at the hands of several of her friends. She had been in a school literary competition with one of the girls. Megan won the contest with a beautiful poem about friendship. The girl who lost began to spread a false rumor that Megan was writing about a gay relationship she had with another girl. This hurt Megan deeply, and she became the butt of some cruel jokes by other students who just wanted to have some fun at her expense. "I nearly left school over this," Megan recalls. "Even now after everything has been cleared up and the girl was made to apologize, some of the kids still look at me funny. You wonder what they're really thinking."

The emotional damage that can be done by such goings-on can be devastating, as you know very well if you've experienced it. It is a small-minded person who seeks to hurt another just to elevate himself or herself. "A friend loves at all times," we are reminded in Proverbs 17:17. Even more convicting are the words Paul writes in 1 Corinthians 13:7: "[Love] always protects, always trusts, always hopes, always perseveres." Forgiveness (keeping "no record of wrongs" in verse 5 of this passage) is the main key to your own sanity in cases when a friend has betrayed you. Even if the relationship is never restored, you still can be at peace.

If a friendship is a worthy one, God will find a way to restore it at the appropriate time. It might be that He wants to teach you and your friend something important in the meantime. It might also be that His desire is for you to part company with that person and wait for another friend to come along. Time has a way of healing wounds. It's just hard for us to see what is right up against our noses. When we back up and get some time and space between us and the problem, we can see more of the whole picture.

Rejection: What if Someone Is Ignoring, Rejecting or "Dissing" Me?

Being rejected or pushed aside by someone is not quite the same as having a disagreement with a true friend or family member. These relationships are well-established. Rejection usually comes early in an attempt to make a friend or perhaps when you want to get to better know someone you may respect. It really stings to have someone ignore or turn away from you, especially if it happens in a public setting where others who know you are looking on. Being made to feel insignificant can be just as bad, if not worse, than falling out with someone you love. Who wants to feel as if they're part of the woodwork? At least anger is some kind of emotion. It keeps the other person thinking about you, even if it's not pretty.

Let's face it: We're all going to have to deal with rejection in life more than once. It's unavoidable. There always will be people who need to make that power play, and we can become their victims if we're not careful. You have several options when you encounter that person: (1) You can harden yourself to the fact of rejection and even go so far as to refuse to get close to anyone for fear of being let down or not accepted into their inner circle; (2) You can believe that being rejected means that something must be wrong with you; or (3) You can step back and see that the other person has the problem because he or she needs to put others down in order to feel more significant.

Love Disarms Enemies—
Still, Never "Throw Pearls to Pigs"

If you choose option three, which is the best and most rational way of thinking, you can go one step further. You can decide to be a positive example to that person or group of people instead of letting them know you crave their attention. Reacting out of love disarms such people and is unsettling to them. In this way, you can model Christ's unconditional love for them. It takes some effort on your part and somewhat thicker skin, but it leaves you feeling at peace with yourself, even if you are dissed again. It puts the ball and the responsibility to change in the other person's court. There is no need, however, to keep going back and being a "glutton for punishment." Jesus warns us in that same Sermon on the Mount, recorded more extensively in Matthew's gospel, "Do not throw your pearls to pigs. If you do, they may trample them under their feet, and then turn and tear you to pieces" (Matt. 7:6). It's another of those graphic illustrations, but it serves to get the point across. Some people will always reject us, no matter what.

One point we must make here, in case you haven't already discovered it, is that becoming a new Christian or making others aware that you are a Christian at this stage in your life might lead to your being rejected by some friends. Did you see the movie *A Walk to Remember*? Mandy Moore plays a straightlaced Christian high-schooler—in fact, the daughter of a minister—who is ridiculed for her beliefs by the cool kids at school. Yet, her quiet, confident devotion to her faith wins over a tough-minded boy who later falls in love with her and accepts her faith. One by one, other friends also come around. (We won't give the plot twists away and spoil the story for you. It's a great one.) It's not the story you usually see on the screen, is it? It can and does happen that way, and it was refreshing to see that candid portrayal of a Christian journey. Being a Christian teen does not automatically make you an outcast, but it does set you against the ways of the world. Those who don't want to go there with you may be afraid of the new you. Don't let that discourage you. God will affirm your decision many times over in the years ahead. Some of your friends may even decide to come along on the road. You never know what God has up His sleeve.

The deeper you walk into the Christian faith, the more you'll appreciate that Sermon on the Mount. It is one of the most memorable passages in the Bible. You can easily find it in a red-letter edition, which sets off the actual words of Christ in red. It's the place where the most red ink appears. It bears reading many times because Jesus teaches so many basic principles of life in it. The Golden Rule is only one aspect of it. You may want to check out the whole passage in Matthew, chapters 5 through 7. A condensed version is in Luke 6.

Personal Reflection

1. How or when did I first hear of "The Golden Rule"? Is it new to me?
2. When have I applied The Golden Rule in my life?
3. Does this chapter give me the courage to try to restore a lost friendship? Am I sure God really wants me to?
4. Have I experienced rejection recently? Was it totally unfair? How am I dealing with it?
5. Do I think the lessons from the Sermon on the Mount are still applicable today?

18

Why Should I Forgive Others?

You can't live long on this Earth without bumping into some poster child for the "Grinches of the World Unite" campaign. You know who we're talking about—the kind of person who would just as soon run over you as look at you. People who can do us wrong without even blinking are on every corner, it seems. They appear to materialize right up out of the pavement when you're on the highway driving somewhere. Ever been almost run down in the school hallway by someone in a big hurry to get to class and found yourself needing to repent of some colorful words or gestures?

Those are the little things that give us headaches on a daily basis. We usually never even know the people involved, so forgiveness doesn't much enter the picture. We just shake our heads, wonder what got into the person and move on. What about the bigger issues involving the people in our lives who matter most? What then?

Am I Expected to Forgive Everyone— Even My Worst Enemy?

There's a difference between the person who is really messed up and the one who is just having a bad day. Both can cause us a lot of grief, nevertheless. Hopefully, the one who offends us on a bad-hair day will realize it and will seek us out and apologize, just as we might do if the situation were reversed and we were the offender. Then there's the typical "drive-by insulter." Let's face it. Some people have real problems. It seems impossible that the same God who created you could have made them, too . . . but He did. If you are a child of God, so is the next person, no matter how despicable he or she may appear. A loving mother may have rocked and sung to even the most hardened of criminals as an infant. There are many reasons why people turn out the way they do.

We automatically assume the worst people are those who were always unloved or cast aside. We must remember there is no one on Earth, no matter how demeaning, mean or useless they appear to be, whom God does not love with all His heart and who is not fully acceptable in His sight. That doesn't mean all people won't be held accountable for their actions, but rather that all are offered forgiveness and a chance at a new, redeemed life through Jesus Christ. "Therefore, if anyone is in Christ, he is a new creation; the old has gone, the new has come!" (2 Cor. 5:17). If you look at the life of Jesus, you see he was always reaching out to the lowest of the low to give them hope and healing because the world rejected them. The only way anyone can exempt himself from that kind of redeeming love is to refuse to accept it for a lifetime, as many who heard the very words of Jesus did. Hearts can become permanently hardened, and that is a sad thing. God continues to love those people to the very end, however. It's a lot harder for us.

Are There Circumstances in Which It's Okay for Me Not to Forgive Someone?

When the word "enemy" is mentioned, there is usually one human face that comes to mind above all others to each of us. (Of course, there is the ultimate spiritual enemy—Satan—who goes around stirring up strife between us and anyone he can tempt.)

There is that one person who did something so awful that we may feel we can never forgive him or her. You may have had the misfortune of being hurt really badly by someone in your life. It may have been a parent, a trusted friend, a relative or a total stranger. How will you choose to respond to the pain that person caused? We're not talking about a provoked response to something you said or did, but an outright, undeserved insult, betrayal or violation of you or your rights as a human being—the toughest case for forgiveness. "Love thy neighbor" is not the first thought that comes to mind in such instances. Even if you do manage to overlook the offense, you're sure you'll never forget it, right?

God wants us to be careful of what we refuse to forget. Holding on to the memory of a wrongdoing, especially when you have thoughts of revenge in mind, can backfire on you. Why? It keeps the offense continually alive in your mind, along with all the pain. That pain can grow bigger and can become a chain of imprisonment to which you add a link every day. Forgiveness is not only God's desire for us, but it is also the best alternative for our health. We can worry ourselves sick over history that is long gone. *The bigger the offense we need to forgive, the more peace we find.* Let God be God. "Do not say 'I'll pay you back for this wrong!' Wait for the Lord, and He will deliver you" (Prov. 20:22).

Does Forgiving Mean Forgetting About It?

Is forgiveness just dismissing the awful thing that happened as if it never happened at all? Of course not. That's next to impossible for any human being to do, and God knows that. Forgiveness is the ability to overlook the offense and the refusal to let it eat away at us forever by putting it into perspective. That perspective is hard to get when we're up close to the event. That's why time tends to aid in the healing and forgiving process. It also helps to try to put ourselves in the other person's shoes. Can we possibly see something in their motives that we couldn't see before?

It helps to remember that at some point in time, we will be on the opposite end of the forgiveness issue, in need of someone else's forgiveness. It's easy to forget that we are all sinners, saved by grace. If we really try, we can even put ourselves in the place of the one who has hurt us. Were it not for the grace of God, we could all be as clueless as that person. There is a whole range of emotions we go through after experiencing something painful at the hand of another person—outrage or angry hatred, a desire for revenge, grief, despair and even disbelief. Just look at some of the Psalms if you want to see how David experienced all these emotions. "Help, Lord, for the godly are no more; the faithful have vanished from among men" (Ps. 12:1); "Break the arm of the wicked and evil man" (Ps. 10:15); "My heart has turned to wax; it has melted away within me" (Ps. 22:14); "Why, O Lord, do you stand far off? Why do You hide Yourself in times of trouble?" (Ps. 10:1). There are many more examples.

Forgiving Others Can Release Me from the Memory and Its Unhealthy Consequences

Despite all David's moaning in the Psalms, he still spends a good deal more time praising God and thanking Him for forgiving his own sins and giving him peace. After we spend more time analyzing our own situation, we can see it more clearly. Perhaps there is an action we will need to take, such as confronting our enemy in a loving way (easier said than done) or reporting the offense or crime to the proper authorities. The offender may have a problem that can be resolved through counseling. If the person you are seeking to forgive is a friend close to your age, inviting that friend to see you in a neutral setting and having a calm talk—if he or she is willing—can disarm the anger and put everything in perspective. That's the best scenario, whenever possible. If that person is older and possibly considered dangerous, you will be wise to keep your distance, no matter how much you want to fight back.

What if the person feels no need to apologize or can't see the wrong in what he or she has done? Then you can choose to be the bigger person and forgive in your heart anyway. Ultimately, you have no choice but to let it go for your own peace of mind. You also can pray for that person to have a change of heart while praying for God to release you from your own anger and hurt. Prayer and forgiveness go hand in hand. Remember, a person doesn't have to acknowledge or accept your forgiveness in order for you to genuinely forgive. He doesn't even have to know you've forgiven at all. The person who hurt you might not even be living any longer. Why bother, then? Simply because forgiveness releases you from the memory and its unhealthy consequences. An effective exercise when you need to forgive someone with whom you can't talk is to write a letter to express your thoughts as if you were speaking to that person. Then tear it up and be done with it.

How Does God Give Us "Beauty for Ashes"?

One of the promises we are given in the Bible is that God will replace the "ashes" of sorrow and destruction in our lives with something beautiful. Isaiah 61 is the foretelling by the Old Testament prophet of Jesus' atoning death and resurrection. It is almost as if Christ himself is speaking: "The Lord has anointed me to preach good news to the poor . . . to bind up the broken-hearted . . . to comfort all who mourn . . . to bestow on them a crown of beauty instead of ashes . . . and a garment of praise instead of a spirit of despair" (Isa. 61:1–3a). Ashes represented mourning for the dead in the Old Testament Jewish custom. A person would literally tear his clothing and put ashes on his forehead and repeat a special prayer for the deceased.

The beauty we are promised for mourning may come in the form of a deeper understanding of God's love or another, more worthy relationship. Have you ever noticed the faces of older people who are totally at peace with themselves? Maybe you've seen this beauty in the face of a grandparent whom you love deeply. We may never know all that's behind that serene and peaceful face. It may be worn and etched with deep lines that represent old pains and heartaches we can't begin to comprehend. Yet, you can instantly distinguish the face of an angry and unforgiving person who has held onto painful memories for many years from the face of the one who has learned how to let it go and has the ability to return good for evil. It can take a lifetime to learn that lesson, but it doesn't have to.

Do I Need to Forgive *Myself* for Things I've Done?

Whom do we often have the most difficulty forgiving? Ourselves. Many people experience the self-torture of continuing to blame themselves for offenses that are in the past. We are powerless to change history. The more we hold on to old guilt already forgotten by God, the more bitter and heartsick we become. We can forgive others much more easily than we can forgive ourselves. If you've made a mistake that has cost you dearly or cost someone else, you may be punishing yourself for that mistake still today. Above all others, you need to love yourself as God loves you. "Love your neighbor as *yourself*," Jesus commanded. If you've checked out of the human race for a while—it could be months or years—because you feel unworthy, you can take great comfort in this beautiful Old Testament promise: "I will repay you for the years the locusts have eaten . . . and you will have plenty to eat, until you are full, and you will praise the name of the Lord your God, who has worked wonders for you; never again will my people be shamed" (Joel 2:25–26).

God does a beautiful thing for us when He forgives us and

casts our sins from us "as far as the east is from the west" (Ps. 103:12), and He promises to "remember [our] sins no more" (Jer. 31:34). *He forgets? God? He knows all and sees all and yet He chooses to forget our sins after He forgives us?* Amazing. The late Corrie ten Boom, a Dutch Christian who, along with some of her family, hid Jews from the Nazis during World War II, had a wonderful way of reminding us of this truth. She used to say that God not only forgets about our sins when He buries them in a deep and bottomless ocean, but He also puts a "No Fishing Allowed" sign there to keep us from going back and dredging them up. Forgiveness was her specialty as she was imprisoned and treated horribly by the Nazis. After the war, she had the opportunity to confront one of her German tormentors. Did she spit in his face? Although she might have been justified in doing just that, she offered her hand in forgiveness instead. Hard as it was, she knew it was what God wanted her to do. Only He could give her the superhuman strength to do it. Later, that officer came to know Jesus Christ as his personal Savior.

What Does "Forgive Seventy Times Seven" Mean?

Jesus used the illustration of forgiving "seventy times seven"—you do the math—to teach us that forgiveness is sometimes an ongoing effort, and there will always be someone to forgive. He also wanted to remind us that we are to do our best to model God's forgiveness, as He is the only one who truly can forgive to that extent. It's hard to imagine someone treating us so badly that we would need to forgive them 490 times! Yet, how many times are we allowed to go to our Heavenly Father and cry out to Him for forgiveness? There is no limit.

Perhaps the clearest illustration of the type of forgiveness we are to have in our hearts for others is in Jesus' parable of the unmerciful servant in Matthew 18:21–35, which Jesus tells after Peter, one of his disciples, asks, "Lord, how many times shall I forgive my brother when he sins against me? Up to seven times?" Jesus answers, "I tell you not seven times, but seventy times seven."* Jesus then proceeds to tell the story of a king who was owed a great deal of money (the equivalent of millions of dollars) by a servant. When he brought the servant before him to settle the account, the man, of course, did not have the money. The king ordered the man and his family to be sold to pay the debt, but the man fell on his knees and begged the king for mercy and more time to repay the debt. The king's heart softened, and he instead canceled the entire debt.

The servant, instead of realizing how grateful he should be, then went out and found a fellow servant who owed him what amounted to a few dollars. He began choking the man and demanded the money. When the man asked the servant to have mercy, he refused and had him thrown into prison. Others watching this went and told the king, who was outraged at the stingy, unforgiving servant. Not only did the king throw the servant he had formerly forgiven into prison, but he ordered that he be tortured as well until he paid back the original debt.

"Turn the Other Cheek": Why Can't I Slap Back?

One of the most difficult and confusing verses in the Bible appears in Jesus' Sermon on the Mount when he says, "Do not resist an evil person. If someone strikes you on the right cheek, turn to him the other also" (Matt. 5:39). *Excuse me, Jesus? Would you care to explain that, please?* Could this be another of Jesus' exaggerations to make a point? Most likely. There is no reason to believe he meant for us to take it literally; otherwise Satan could have a heyday with it, tempting people to "slap us" just for fun

---

*This is from the King James translation. The NIV translation of the Bible says "seventy-seven," which is still quite a large number when it comes to forgiving.

all day long. God doesn't humiliate His children in that way, but He does expect us to stand the world on its head by being different *with a purpose*. And what is that purpose? To demonstrate that love is more powerful than hate. "Loving" our enemies, which Jesus goes on to teach in the verses that follow clearly goes against the world's teaching of getting even with those who have done us wrong.

A favorite game of antiwar activists is to speculate about whether someone like Adolf Hitler or other powermongers of his era (you may substitute other names for today's would-be world dominators) could have been "loved" into submission, thus sparing the world the tragedy of a costly war. What do you think? Is it a valid debate? Missionaries often have laid their lives on the line to test that philosophy over the years. Some lived to tell their stories; others didn't. What does that tell you? Sometimes the cause of peace requires us to turn away an enemy. It's not revenge ("slapping back") for the sake of revenge, but it is maintaining God's laws as He gives us the right to do. Anarchy (chaos) is the result of throwing open the doors for anyone who wants to dominate or be a bully, whether it be in an individual sense or in the case of nation against nation. God's discipline may come in various forms, but there is no reason to believe He may not bring judgment to bear through a righteous action of self-defense. A parent exercises love for a child through discipline sometimes. Some parents take the other extreme and refuse to discipline children in any way. That only allows children to grow up as bullies with no clue about where to draw the line in their own actions.

The Real Meaning of "Forgive Us Our Debts as We Also Have Forgiven Our Debtors"

Jesus' illustration about loving our enemies provides an interesting contrast to the parable of the unmerciful servant cited above. That is also a troubling story in some ways, especially when you read Matt. 18:35: "This is how my Heavenly Father will treat each of you unless you forgive your brother from your heart." *Do the prison and the torture chamber of the story equal eternal damnation and my worst nightmare?* you may be wondering. Or is the torture really referring to the guilt and anguish someone feels when he or she has an unforgiving spirit? The answer is a little of both, and here's what we mean. Jesus used the ridiculously large amount of money the first servant owed the king to make the point that the original debt of sin we all owed God was so great, we could never repay it. That is precisely why He sent His son into the world to suffer and die in our place, effectively canceling the debt for us. It is a simple, beautiful truth that gives the believer the assurance of being spared from the "prison" and the "torture" of eternal separation from God, but also from the earthly guilt and emotional torment we would bear if we had to face the enormous burden of our sins on our own.

Is forgiveness, then, of the utmost importance to God? You'd better believe it. Remember the Lord's Prayer? "Forgive us our debts as we also have forgiven our debtors" (Matt. 5:12), Jesus teaches. Jesus had related this model prayer to his disciples in Matthew a few chapters prior to the parable of the unmerciful servant. He put an exclamation point on that teaching with the story as only he could do. Imagine it. The very payment for all sins—the sacrificial Lamb of God—teaching everyone to be grateful for his own sacrificial death that was to come.

Does it make it any easier to forgive when you consider this story? Maybe, maybe not. It does drive home to us that God takes forgiveness very seriously, and so should we, no matter how hard it is. Most of us, thankfully, will never have to go to the lengths Corrie ten Boom did to forgive an extreme enemy when she may have wanted to "slap back." Think of her encouraging story the next time you're struggling to forgive someone.

Personal Reflection

1. Do I have a hard time forgiving others, no matter what the size of the offense? Why might that be?
2. Have I ever said, "I'll forgive, but I won't forget!"? Can I feel differently now?
3. Has anyone ever forgiven me, even when I knew I was wrong? How did that make me feel?
4. Have I ever "fished the forbidden waters" of my forgiven and forgotten sins? Why doesn't God want me to do that?
5. Who do I need to forgive right now? Can I do it with God's help?

Part 4

Maturing in My Faith—Letting God "Grow Me Up"

*God is able to make a way out of no way and
transform dark yesterdays into bright tomorrows.
This is our hope for becoming better men and women.
This is our mandate for seeking to make a better world.*
—Martin Luther King Jr.

*I have held many things in my hands,
and I have lost them all; but whatever
I have placed in God's hands, that I still possess.*
—Corrie ten Boom

*It takes courage to keep in sync with God.
It takes grit to be an ambassador for Christ
and go beyond the limits to carry out His will.
Yes, Christianity is about being kind, considerate,
compassionate and loving. But there's also a bold side
to our faith. . . . It can take more guts than facing
mortar bombs.*
—Franklin Graham
Living Beyond the Limits

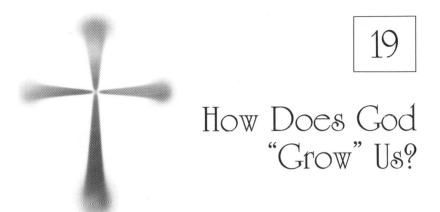

19

How Does God "Grow" Us?

Do you ever have the job of doing yard work to earn some money or to help out at home? Maybe it's only mowing, pulling weeds or raking leaves—and that's hard enough. If you've ever had to help with adding fertilizer to a yard, garden or pasture, you know it's important to use the right formula and to spread the right amount. Too little and the growth won't be sustained; too much and you can burn or kill off grass or plants. Fertilization also works best when you do it at the right time of the year, usually spring or fall. Then you must have adequate water or rainfall.

How does this relate to Christian growth? Some comparisons are obvious. We can't expect to grow in our faith and our knowledge of God without doing something to help stimulate that growth from time to time. Study of God's Word, prayer and spending time with other believers are the regular maintenance routine for steady growth. Periodically, we may have to do something on a deeper level, something that will penetrate to the roots of our being and rejuvenate and feed us for the hot summers and cold winters of life. This "fertilizing" for you may come in the form of a youth camp or conference or a more comprehensive Bible study class or growth group. It may even come in the form of counseling from a pastor or older friend or a parent or grandparent.

Certainly, we can live in our current "soil" with just the sunshine and rain God is bound to send along, right? He cares for the tiniest of sparrows and the lilies of the field, so why can't He care for us in the same way? Does our soil really need fertilizing? It's true, we can all get along to an extent like the wildflowers we see growing alongside the road. But have you noticed how even they seem to lift their heads up to heaven as if to thank God for their growth? What happens to our yards or gardens, and yes, even some of those hardy wildflowers when a drought comes along? If there's been no fertilizer applied, it's much harder to keep them green and growing.

Does God Send Angels to Help Us?

We've talked about God's help to us in the form of the Holy Spirit or as an answer to prayer. What about other forms of help such as angels? Angels are fascinating to contemplate, aren't they? Have you ever wondered if you have encountered one or whether you have one or more guardian angels? Perhaps you think of a deceased loved one, like a grandparent, as being an angel. Angel lore has been with us since the beginning of time, but what is real and what is fantasy?

Looking at the authoritative source, we see in the Bible many descriptions of angels and their various duties. Angels are very powerful spiritual beings created by God, and man was created to be "for a little while" (the literal translation of "a little") lower than the angels (Ps. 8:5). That is to change in what is known as the "Kingdom Age" or the world that will exist after Christ returns. At that time, *humans who have inherited salvation will be elevated to a position higher than the angels.* Angels are sometimes referred to in the Bible as "the heavenly host" who worship and serve God in heaven. The word "host" implies that they exist in vast numbers.

Angels are messengers of God who deliver news to people on Earth, as in the case of the visitation to Mary by the angel Gabriel announcing that she was to be the mother of Jesus (Luke 1:26–38). *And, yes, angels have the power to assume bodily form.* The biblical phrase "angel of the Lord" is believed to refer to God or

Jesus Christ appearing in angelic form. Angels are assigned the role of "reapers" or "harvesters" by God at the end of the age, meaning they will seek out and find those who have rejected God and will cast them into eternal punishment (Matt. 13:39, 41). Angels will accompany Jesus when he returns to the Earth (Matt. 25:31).

The primary role of angels is to administer aid and comfort to people in times of need, as in the case of Elijah when he was exhausted while trying to run away from the queen Jezebel (I Kings 19:5), or Jesus after his forty days of fasting and temptation by Satan in the desert prior to his formal ministry (Matt. 4:11), and when he prayed in Gethsemane before he was arrested and crucified. There is no reason to believe that angels do not fulfill this role today. Many stories testify to the fact that angelic beings have rescued people from imminent danger. Perhaps you or a family member have even experienced similar caring that cannot be explained any other way. Can someone who has died and gone to heaven become an angel? Not according to the Bible. Angels and humans always are to remain separate entities, created by God for different purposes. Who can say, however, that a loved one who has gone on before us might not have some influence in angelic help sent to us? It just might be possible. It is certainly a comforting thought while we wait to join our loved ones in eternity. With everything God already has provided for us, do we really need that kind of extra help? Apparently not. He has us covered from every angle, including angelic help. How can we not grow in the right direction with all that?

Am I Expected to Witness (to Pass On What I Receive)?

As you do what is needed to take care of your own spiritual growth, you will find that God has given you an abundance to share with others. As others have come alongside you and have fed you, encouraging you to grow, so you will nurture those who are not as mature and healthy as you are. Some call this *discipling;* others call it *mentoring.* It simply means you are unselfishly sharing the same lessons and encouragement that have helped you. You almost can't help yourself. It's natural to feel that grateful.

There are many ways we have the opportunity to help others. We may have younger brothers or sisters who will need some encouragement or advice from us. It's touching to see grown children lovingly caring for their elderly, disabled parents just as the parents once cared for them. One day, that may be your role. Wouldn't we all want our future children, if we should have them, to do the same for us if we need that care down the road? You see friends and classmates around you all the time who appear to have lost their way. Have you wondered what you might do to lend a hand? As a successful businesswoman once said, it seems as if half the world is waiting for the other half to say, "Hello." Which half are you in?

Our much-quoted church father, Paul, wrote to the early Christian church in Thessalonica these words, which he repeated to every church: "We urge you, brothers, warn those who are idle, encourage the timid, help the weak, be patient with everyone" (1 Thess. 5:15). One of the cornerstones of Christian living is building up and encouraging those around us, especially struggling believers. You will know you have achieved some significant spiritual growth when you find yourself automatically doing that.

One thing we must look out for is the tendency to try to do God's job for Him. As you are learning and growing in your own Christian walk, you may encounter someone who is playing such a large role in helping you that he or she interferes with God's presence in your life. You may find yourself repeating this pattern as you reach out to someone else later on. How easy it is to make a god of someone who we love and respect as a Christian leader or friend. Influential preachers and teachers tend to amass quite a following. Their words can become the gospel to hungry and needy ears, and there's genuine help in that.

Sometimes, however, we are led astray by ideas that contain partial truths or are outright lies. Remember, Satan can appear as an angel of light. How else could Adolf Hitler so readily have captivated the minds and hearts of the people who allowed him to rise to power in the years preceding World War II? Hitler is an extreme example, but one that shows how easily persuasive and charismatic personalities can sweep large groups of unsuspecting people into their influence. It has happened all throughout church history, and it's happening today.

Strong, godly leaders are very important, make no mistake. It's only when their voices drown out the voice of God in our lives that we get into trouble. Then we must go back to the Word of God to retrace our steps and pick up His truth again. Only that truth keeps us free and our vision unclouded. Incidentally, one of the most beloved and effective evangelists preaching today is a southern pastor by the name of David Ring. He has a unique gift of touching hearts and opening minds when he speaks. Is he a talented orator with a commanding presence or musical voice? Quite the opposite. He has suffered from childhood with cerebral palsy, which affects both his speech and his movements. His pastor father abandoned the family and his mother, his greatest cheerleader, died when he was fourteen. His enthusiasm and love for God and his perseverance in the face of his disability hold his audiences in rapt attention wherever he speaks. God's warriors come in all kinds of packages.

Remember, you will naturally be more of a student at this stage in your life. You may be bright and a quick study, but the road still stretches far ahead of you, and many lessons are waiting for you, requiring new teachers. An Eastern proverb says, "When the student is ready, the teacher will appear." Someday, you may be that teacher. Even now, you can share and support at your level.

Teen enthusiasm for God is an awesome thing to behold. When God gets into a life, look out! Miraculous things happen.

Why Does God Allow Bad Things to Happen to Good People?

This is one of the most troubling questions any of us inevitably must face. It is an accepted principle that God will sometimes bring about some significant growth in us through tragic circumstances or a loss of some kind. We still can't answer the question "Why?" In Proverbs 25:2, Solomon writes, "It is the glory of God to conceal a matter. . . ." The apostle Paul reminds us in 1 Corinthians 2:11, "No one knows the thoughts of God except the Spirit of God." We read in Isaiah 55:8–9, "'For My thoughts are not your thoughts, neither are My ways your ways,' declares the Lord." Unfortunately, some of you, even at your tender age, have been through difficult times. Even though some of you may even believe you are immune to such troubles, one day life will open you to the reality of pain and hardship, and you will find yourself asking that troubling question, "Why, God?" Some things are just not meant to be understood in this life. We simply must trust that God has a purpose, even when we can't see it.

Gianna Jessen, today in her mid-twenties, is a walking miracle. She lived through a failed saline abortion attempt in a southern California clinic when her biological mother was seven months pregnant. Hers is a voice that speaks for those who can't speak for themselves—the unborn, whether alive or dead. Testifying before a special congressional committee hearing for the "Born-Alive Infants Protection Act of 2000," Gianna said:

> A saline abortion is a solution of salt saline that is injected into the mother's womb. The baby then gulps the solution, it burns the baby inside and out, and then

the mother is to deliver a dead baby within twenty-four hours. This happened to me! I remained in the solution for approximately eighteen hours and was delivered ALIVE on April 6, 1977 at 6 A.M. . . . I weighed a mere two pounds. I was saved by the sheer power of Jesus Christ.

Ladies and gentleman, I should be blind, burned . . . I should be dead! And yet, I live! Due to a lack of oxygen supply during the abortion, I live with cerebral palsy. When I was diagnosed with this, all I could do was lie there. "They" said that was all I would ever do! Through prayer and hard work by my foster mother, I was walking at age three-and-a-half with the help of a walker and leg braces. At that time I was also adopted into my wonderful family. Today I am left only with a slight limp. I no longer have need of a walker or leg braces.

I am so thankful for my cerebral palsy. It allows me to really depend on Jesus for everything.

Gianna's story is truly amazing. What faith she lives by! Is there any doubt that God has a purpose for this young lady?

Life is full of choices, big and little. Tough times can come from our own choices, as well as from circumstances we can't explain. How do we make decisions when the stakes are fairly high and we're afraid of blowing it? It's easy to block God's working in our lives by charging ahead and doing it our way. Yet, isn't that pretty ridiculous when you think about it? If we don't give Him some room to work, He may just let us botch it up, to our own shame and disappointment. It's called a learning experience.

Pain, Sorrow and Heartache Can
Teach Us to Turn Our Eyes Heavenward

Sometimes growth and wisdom come through trial and error. It's the same for all of us. Other times, we'll do our best to bring

God into the picture and still things will appear to fall apart. What can look like a disaster or a big "No" on God's part may really be His way of leading you in another direction, stretching your faith. Instead of saying "No," God may be saying, "Not that way, this way. I have something better for you." God will gladly prune you in this way because He knows you will branch out and grow even stronger and lovelier and bear more fruit. He must also let you experience some rain because He knows it will send your roots deeper into the soil and make you better able to withstand the weather extremes. Remember that fertilizer you've been spreading? Without rain or water, you're only wasting your time.

You are "a planting of the Lord" (Isa. 61:3), intended to grow and blossom in His time. He wants you to have the soil-enriching nutrients in the proper amounts and on schedule so you won't be undernourished or overwhelmed with too much, too soon. The Master Gardener always knows what He's doing, even when He gets out the pruning shears.

What Do I Do if I'm Caught in a "Storm"—The "Crazy Stuff" of Life?

Some of what we come up against does not exactly fit into the category of unexplained tragedy or poor choices. Nevertheless, it can send us into an emotional tailspin or leave us wondering who we are and where God is. One example is coping with divorced parents, which is more and more common. If you're in this situation, you may be in the custody of one parent, or you may go back and forth between households, possibly even learning to get along with stepsiblings. It seldom runs smoothly and can feel like it never will. You naturally will grieve for what is no more. That is understandable. Still, you will have little choice but to accept what is, fair or not. Perhaps you think your parents are being selfish and childish or just downright mean. You may end up hating the parent whom you see as being most responsible. In time, God can help these emotional wounds heal. You may feel as if you're being asked to grow up faster, and you probably will. Somewhere in the back of your mind may be Romans 8:28: "And we know that all things work together for good to those who love God, to those who are the called according to His purpose." In time, you may recall that verse and realize God really has been working to bring some good out of a bad situation.

Coping with a Chronic Illness, Handicap or Confusion About Sexual Identity

How about dealing with a chronic illness or a handicap, whether physical or mental? These are life-changing events certainly not of your own choosing. And yet, the more you have to rely on Him, the more He can be glorified through your life. What happens when you put a lighted candle into an earthen pot and put the lid on? You don't see any light, do you? In fact, the candle will go out if it doesn't have enough oxygen. Put that same candle into a pot with a crack or a hole in it, and what do you see? Jesus said we are to be the "light of the world" (Matt. 5:14). Sometimes we need "holes" in order to be whole or to share our light with others.

Another tough issue you or someone you know may come up against is confusion about your sexual identity. You may worry about possibly being gay because you have conflicting feelings. It is not unusual to have some of this confusion as you are going through the various stages of your sexual and emotional development. It's growing pains in many cases. You may develop an emotional attachment to someone of your own sex, which sometimes also feels like a physical one. You may even fantasize about that person. Some of us are more needy in an emotional sense than others, especially if we've had strained relations with our parents or have been through traumatic events. Sexual abuse by someone of either sex can certainly make us question our own sexuality.

It is also possible that you may feel excessive guilt. If you have serious questions, you may want to see a pastor or Christian counselor. Many people who have experienced such feelings go on to realize that they are indeed heterosexual, and they have fulfilling relationships with the opposite sex. You may be vulnerable to suggestion if you talk to someone who is gay and wants to convince you that you must be, too. Don't jump to hasty conclusions. Remember, all sex outside of marriage is forbidden by God. Homosexuality is a complex subject. Should you be genuinely struggling with it, there is help available. (See the resources in the back of this book.) God loves you, no matter what you think of yourself. He doesn't create us with problems that can't be overcome.

If I Bail Out on God, Will He Bail Out on Me?

What if you temporarily bail out on God in a time of emotional chaos? Will He bail out on you, too? Never. Jesus tells us in Matthew 5:3, "Blessed are the poor in spirit, for theirs is the kingdom of heaven." The next verse says, "Blessed are those who mourn, for they will be comforted." These are the first two of what we know as the Beatitudes in which Jesus gives a series of promises to those who are in a tough place. In Psalm 139, we are reminded that we can never get away from God's love: "Where can I flee from Your presence? If I go up to the heavens, You are there; if I make my bed in the depths, You are there. If I rise on the wings of the dawn, if I settle on the far side of the sea, even there Your hand will guide me . . . " (verses 7–10a). We can try to run away from God, but His love will follow us to the ends of the Earth.

We don't get to see how our entire lives will unfold. We probably couldn't handle knowing. Life comes to us a day at a time, and that's how we must live it. It's only in looking back that we can see how much we've grown from all we've gone through, good and bad. The road, as you look back one day, will have many twists and turns, ups and downs, and some pretty major holes and bumps. You'll wonder how you ever made it. Then you'll remember: "Your word is a lamp to my feet and a light for my path" (Ps. 119:105). We can see any obstacle if God shines His light on it.

Spiritual growth, then, results from trusting Jesus Christ. "The just shall live by faith" (Gal. 3:11). A life of faith will enable you to trust God increasingly with every detail of your life and to practice what New Life Ministries calls the ABCs of Christian G-R-O-W-T-H, which include:

Go to God in prayer daily. *But if you stay joined to me and my words remain in you, you may ask any request you like, and it will be granted.*

—John 15:7

Read God's Word daily. *And the people of Berea were more open-minded than those in Thessalonica, and they listened eagerly to Paul's message. They searched the Scriptures day after day to check up on Paul and Silas, to see if they were really teaching the truth.*

—Acts 17:11

Obey God, moment by moment. *Those who obey my commandments are the ones who love me. And because they love me, my Father will love them, and I will love them. And I will reveal myself to each one of them.*

—John 14:21

Witness for Christ by your life and words. *My true disciples produce much fruit. This brings great glory to my Father.*

—John 15:8

Trust God for every detail of your life. *Give all your worries and cares to God, for He cares about what happens to you.*

—1 Peter 5:7

Holy Spirit—allow Him to empower your daily life. *So I advise you to live according to your new life in the Holy Spirit. Then you won't be doing what your sinful nature craves. . . . These two forces are constantly fighting each other, and your choices are never free from this conflict.*

—Galatians 5:16–17

But when the Holy Spirit has come upon you, you will receive power and will tell people about me—everywhere . . . to the ends of the Earth.
—Acts 1:8

Personal Reflection

1. Have I experienced a shot of spiritual "fertilizer" in my life—an event or an experience that helped me to grow in my faith or knowledge? How did it change me?
2. Do I think I've ever encountered an angel in my life? If so, how do I think this "person" helped me?
3. Have I found myself either playing God's role in helping someone else or realizing another mentor was doing that for me?
4. Have I struggled to understand something in my life that makes no sense whatsoever? Did it (or does it) make me angry with God?
5. Has God "pruned" me in some way so He could lead me in another direction or deepen my faith? How did I figure that out?

20

God's Providence: What Does "God Helps Those Who Help Themselves" Mean?

Believing in God and trying to live your life according to The Golden Rule and the Ten Commandments is one thing. Trusting Him to provide for what you truly need—in *every* area of your life—is a big leap of faith for most of us. *He doesn't really mean for us to do that, does He?* Well, yeah. He does. *But what about my responsibility—you know, "God helps those who help themselves"?* It's true that God expects us to take some initiative and to have a good work ethic. Laziness ("slothfulness") is known as one of the "Seven Deadly Sins" and is covered many times in the book of Proverbs and elsewhere in the Bible. Old Testament Jewish law said basically, if you don't work, you don't eat. That's fair, right? None of us likes to provide for the welfare of any individual who is capable of working for himself. Still, Jesus tells us that God feeds the birds and clothes the lilies of the field; therefore, we are not to worry about our own daily needs. "Are you not much more valuable than they?" (Matt. 6:26b).

If God "Feeds the Sparrows," Why Can't He "Feed" Me?

So what is the difference between trusting in God's providence and living up to one's responsibilities? Good question, and one this chapter will answer. First, we must remember that the word "need" refers to something basic and common to us all—something we can't do without. We all need food, clothing, shelter, medical care, income and a way to get around. These days, we have extended that definition quite a bit to include items we think we can't live without. It's not just what is adequate for our needs, but too often what gives us the most status that we are busy pursuing. We feel we must "keep up with the Joneses"—or at least their hip sons and daughters—who have the best of everything. That's not need, that's greed, and it's another of those deadly sins we are to avoid. God is not impressed with that attitude; in fact, He detests it. "The righteousness of the upright will deliver them, but the treacherous will be caught by their own greed" (Prov. 11:6, New American Standard).

Does God Watch What I Do with My Money?

It's not exactly treacherous to desire nice things if one can afford them, but to place an emphasis on money or material possessions in a way that causes you to overlook the needs of others or to become consumed with your own greed is a sin. It is better to live beneath your means than to overextend your finances in pursuit of more and more "stuff." At this stage in life, you are working with a limited budget. Some of you have part-time jobs and earn some income, but many of you don't. Maybe you figure it's not important what you do with your money and that you should be able to spend it any way you please. You have figured out, we hope, that your parents are not an unlimited supply of money, and one day you will have to manage for yourself. Much as we all would like to have the proverbial money tree in our backyards, it takes hard work, a careful budget and self-discipline to handle our finances properly. You might as well know it now. The time is coming sooner than you think when you will be on your own.

Did you know the Bible has more to say about the subject of money than any other topic? Surprised? God takes our handling of money quite seriously. You may have heard the well-known verse from 1 Timothy 6:10 (King James Version) misquoted, omitting the word "love." With the right words, it reads, "The *love* of money is the root of all evil." Remember Jesus' parable of the rich young ruler of which we spoke earlier? We may think that illustration is meant to cast judgment against wealth, but what Jesus is really saying is that money or material possessions should never stand between God and us. When he says it is easier for a camel to go through the eye of a needle than for a rich man to get into heaven, he is referring to the vast numbers of people whose wealth corrupts them. Greed and lust for money and power can really mess us up, and Jesus wants us to know that, "for where your treasure is, there your heart will be also" (Matt. 6:21).

If God chooses to bless you or your family with a more comfortable lifestyle than your neighbor, He is giving you the opportunity to demonstrate that you can handle it responsibly. As Dr. James Dobson says, "It takes a steady hand to hold a full cup." Give God thanks always for what He provides, but don't take it for granted. He can just as easily "unprovide." If you are near the other end of the spectrum and must struggle just to make ends meet, you may feel as if God has forgotten about you. That's an easy trap to fall into. "He causes His sun to rise on the evil and the good, and sends rain on the righteous and the unrighteous," Jesus reminds us in his Sermon on the Mount (Matt. 5:45). Nobody gets to have perfect prosperity all the time, no matter how it looks to us from the outside. No, God certainly has not forgotten you, no matter what your circumstances. People who are born into privileged lives often miss the opportunity to grow by learning the value of hard work and tough times.

The worst kind of bankruptcy is the spiritual or moral kind. It is a human desire to "covet" or be jealous of what our neighbor may have, but God put that no-no in one of the Ten Commandments. The apostle Paul knew what it was like to have plenty and to do without. He said, "I have learned to be content whatever the circumstances. . . . I can do everything through him who gives me strength" (Phil. 4:11,13). Paul learned to be humble and thankful when he was blessed, and not to complain when he was lacking. We can do the same.

What Does "Little Is Much in God's Hands" Mean?

It's natural for us to feel pressured to work as hard as we can and to feel that we must plan for the future. Wisdom says to be prepared. Since the beginning of time, people have celebrated the fruits of their labor and God's blessing when the annual harvest is gathered and they have stored up food for the barren winter months. Because we can anticipate some barren, wintry times in our lives, we've been taught to manage our resources and to save what we can. But just as it is with grace that comes to us when we need it, we don't necessarily get to save for all our needs or to borrow against future assets. Sometimes, there is nothing extra, or circumstances beyond our control consume it. Farmers who endure droughts or destructive storms or waves of pests know this truth better than anyone. It's in those times that we have no choice but to rely on God for providing what we need.

Have you ever noticed what looked like a small amount of something appear to stretch and grow beyond what you thought possible? Or have you ever had some money turn up just when you needed it? Coincidental? Don't be so sure. These can be acts of divine providence. Who is to say? Rick, Tim and Curt Goad were just teenagers when they lost both parents in separate tragic accidents. They struggled along with their younger sister Carolyn and with some help from older siblings in the early days to carry on the family ministry. Often, they weren't sure where the next meal was coming from. "One day," relates Carolyn, "we were so desperate we went around the house looking under sofa cushions and everywhere we could to find enough change to buy some food. We found just what we needed. We trusted God to take care of us in other ways, too." Today the Goads have an international ministry, reaching out to those in the same position they once were in. They sing and reach out to others all around the world with the message of hope because they know "there but for the grace of God go I."

God can intervene in small ways or in powerful ways in our lives. Jesus performed one of his most dramatic miracles by taking a boy's lunch of five small loaves of bread and two fish and multiplying the food to feed a crowd of 5,000 people—and there were leftovers! This was not a parable or an abstract illustration used to teach a principle, but it is presented in the Bible as an actual, historical event. It isn't the only such event. Numerous miracles are recorded in both the Old and New Testaments. These events speak of God's divine providence and remind us that He controls the universe. Is such divine intervention still happening? If you were to put on a reporter's hat and go out into the world, you would find more recipients of divine miracles than you ever could interview in a lifetime.

Tithing: Does Sharing
My Time and Talent Count?

The concept of tithing, or of giving one-tenth of all you earn to God or the church, is closely related to God's divine protection of His people. Although there is no specific place in the Old Testament where God actually commands "Thus saith the Lord: thou shalt give a tenth portion of your increase to the Lord your God," scholars have pointed out the clear implication that such a command was given since there are several references to the giving of the one-tenth tithe from the time of Abraham on. Tithing was not just an arbitrary concept, then. It has become known as a spiritual law that is linked with God's blessing.

For historical purposes, tithing was first mentioned in Genesis 14:20 when Abraham (then still referred to as Abram) received a special blessing from a high priest of God after he had defeated a Babylonian army and rescued his nephew Lot, who they had kidnapped. Following the priest's blessing, "Abram gave him a tenth of everything," referring to the spoils of war he had recovered. Again, in Genesis 28, we find Jacob, Abraham's grandson, pledging to God, "Of all that You give me, I will give You a tenth" in exchange for God's blessing and protection. During the days of Moses, tithing was clearly emphasized in the Bible. "A tithe of everything from the land . . . belongs to the Lord; it is holy to the Lord. . . . Every tenth animal that passes under the shepherd's rod will be holy to the Lord" (Lev. 27:30, 32). The reference to the tithe as holy to God reminds us that everything we have ultimately comes from God, and He is worthy of our praise and honor.

Are we expected to tithe only money or material gain to God? What about our time and our talent? If God created all things, does our time really belong to us or to Him? The answer is both. God gives us the free will to spend our time as we choose, but in the beginning, He did set aside one day out of seven—the

Sabbath—for us to give back to Him. This, then, can be considered our time tithe to God. Our service to God or in the church is both a time and a talent tithe. God expects us to use whatever He has given us—blessings, gifts, time—to do His work in addition to our own because "faith without deeds is useless" (James 2:20).

But I'm Only a Teenager:
What Does God Expect of Me?

Is tithing, or the way we do it, optional? You may wonder if God will accept less than ten percent from you. *I can't give that much. I can barely afford the basics,* you might argue. Anything that we give freely and with a cheerful attitude pleases God, *but there is nothing in the Scriptures that makes us believe tithing is optional.* God's people failed miserably over many generations at keeping this covenant with Him. The Bible records wars and judgments from God against His chosen people because of this lapse and the failure to keep other commandments. He must take it pretty seriously, then. It is also interesting to note that in every case where the children of Israel repented and resumed following God's commandments—especially concerning tithing—He restored them to prosperity and peace.

The Bible's teaching establishes that God's blessings with regard to prosperity and peace go hand in hand with tithing. Near the end of the Old Testament, God is warning His people through the prophet Malachi and reminding them of the laws given to Moses, from which they have repeatedly fallen away. He speaks specifically of tithing in Malachi 3:8–10: "'Will a man rob God? Yet you rob Me. But you ask, 'How do we rob You?' 'In tithes and offerings. You are under a curse—the whole nation of you—because you are robbing Me. Bring the whole tithe into the storehouse, that there may be food in My house. Test Me in this,' says the Lord Almighty, 'and see if I will not throw open the floodgates of heaven and pour out so much blessing that you will not have room for it.'"

Did these words echo through the minds of the Jewish nation for the hundreds of years that God was silent up until the birth of Christ? Perhaps. Or maybe the words of God were forgotten until the birth of the new church. The early Christians, a number of whom were Jews, were especially generous in giving large portions—much more than a tenth—of their possessions and income for the building of the church just as the Jews had earlier been generous in giving to the building of the Temple. Remember Jesus' words in Luke 12:48, "From everyone who has been given much, much will be demanded." When Jesus came, he only underscored the requirement to tithe.

Tithing Is Our Guarantee for God's Blessings

In a practical sense, tithing is a cure for greed, which can tempt us all. It can also test our faith. Many, many testimonials from individuals and churches attest to the financial blessings that God has heaped on them through tithing. It represents His guarantee for our blessings. The sooner in life one learns the principles of tithing, the stronger will be that person's faith. Is that you? You don't have to take our word for it. Take God's. Go ahead and test Him, as He said to, and see if it is true.

In fact, seventeen-year-old Carl Harper did just that. "I'd heard about tithing since I was a little kid, and my parents helped me put my nickels and pennies into an envelope to give to church," he said. "I never thought much about it then, but later on I started having a hard time taking out that money to give as a tithe. I always managed to find a reason to keep it— something I really needed. Then I heard a sermon from a youth pastor who was visiting our church. He got me thinking about how I really was stealing from God. I was trying to save up for a car I planned to help my parents buy for my sixteenth birthday, so I was desperate to hang onto every cent I had." Something began tugging at Carl on the inside. "I took out 10 percent of what I had saved one Sunday and put it into the offering plate with shaky hands. It felt good, even though I knew I'd have to work extra hard to replace it or wait longer for my car. You know what? I found an even better car than the one I'd been looking at for less than I'd expected to pay. Was God blessing me for giving that money? You can't convince me He wasn't. Do I still tithe? You bet."

Do you have the answer to the question we posed at the beginning of this chapter concerning the relationship between our responsibility and trusting God to provide? It is our responsibility to give Him what is His—and that includes all our faith, along with our tithe—and His to bless us accordingly. We are invited to "taste and see that the Lord is good; blessed is the man who takes refuge in Him" (Ps. 34:8)

Personal Reflection

1. What kind of work ethic do I have? Do I believe every capable person should have to work or contribute to a family or society to eat?
2. Do I struggle with the "need" to keep pace with others around me in my material possessions?
3. What does "I can do all things through him who strengthens me" mean to me?
4. Have I ever been on the receiving end of what I would call a miracle? If so, how do I know?
5. Do I still question the spiritual law of tithing? Am I willing to try it and see how God might bless me?

Part 5

Godly Discipline and Christian Service

*To show great love for God and our neighbor,
we need not do great things. It is how much love
we put in the doing that makes our offering
something beautiful for God.*
—Mother Teresa

*Heavenly Father, use me as an instrument to do
your work and in accordance with your will, that
I may listen to your truth as it speaks
to me in all the ways of this world.*
—Jennifer Leigh Youngs

*Our greatest opportunity to positively
affect another person's life is to accept God's
love into our own. By being the light,
we shine the light, on everyone
and everything.*
—Marianne Williamson

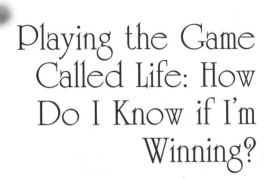

Playing the Game Called Life: How Do I Know if I'm Winning?

Why do we tend to love healthy competition so much? As a society, we are sports nuts, to say the least. It appears as if we were born to wage contests, whether they are athletic events or games—card, board, electronic—depending on our age. We idolize our sports figures, some of whom in today's self-centered, commercial, dog-eat-dog arena are not very worthy heroes. Still, we love a good matchup, and we'll yell until we lose our voices cheering our team on to hopeful victory.

Then there's the big game, the one known as Life. We play this one for keeps. We tend to think of our younger years as our practice sessions, believing that the game doesn't turn serious until later. Besides, don't we have some time-outs we can use to get things back on track if the game plan is falling apart or our opponent's strategy is working better than ours is? Most of us tend to figure out what matters as we are growing older, but we delude ourselves if we believe that all of what we try in the big Game of Life amounts to playing and that there will always be another chance or another game. Sometimes we don't get another chance. We've all seen someone lose big. It has a way of sobering us and jarring us back into reality.

So what does this mean for the Christian? Are there different rules for those who are supposed to be *in* the world, but not *of* the world? How do we play this game?

"Taste Berries" for the Soul: Love, Joy, Peace, Patience, Kindness, Goodness, Faithfulness, Gentleness and Self-Control

Obviously, the Christian character model is supposed to be vastly different from worldly models. It comes from the Holy Spirit, and not from any inclination or effort from within us. Sometimes in looking around, it's hard to tell the rules are any different. How can professing Christians have the same problems to practically the same degree that others who profess no faith have? Divorce statistics and other social problems are no better within the Christian community. Life in the fast lane takes its toll, and Christians are no exception. We all need help.

We can't help but fall short when we make our own rules because we are naturally self-centered. We speak of good, moral people, but upon what is that moral code based? How good can it be if it does not originate with God? When we accept Christ and put him at the center of our lives, he pushes out the selfish desires of our human nature (called "the flesh" in biblical terms) and requests on our behalf for the Holy Spirit be sent to fill that space. The presence of the Holy Spirit, as we discussed earlier, can be confirmed by what we call the "fruit of the Spirit." Those of you who have read any of the *Taste Berries for Teens* books by Bettie and Jennifer Youngs already know about the totally cool "taste berry" (also know as the *Richardella dulcisica*), a little fruit that coaxes the taste buds into believing that any food eaten along with it is pleasant-tasting. Like that berry, we can enhance the more distasteful aspects of life for ourselves and others if we have the fruit of the Spirit.

The apostle Paul listed these spiritual qualities in his letter of encouragement and instruction to the early Galatian church, contrasting these attributes to the "deeds of the flesh" or our selfish desires: "But the fruit of the Spirit is love, joy, peace, patience, kindness, goodness, faithfulness, gentleness and self-control. Against such things there is no law" (Gal. 5:22–23). That's a tall order, isn't it? Yet, the Holy Spirit has no trouble filling it. It's us weak human beings who can't seem to hold all that fruit in our leaky containers. God is perfectly willing to give us the fruit; we have to be willing to hold on to it so we have enough to share with others. It's our gift back to Him. Of course, our fellow human beings benefit from that gift, too.

So here's the object of the game, sports fans: Whoever can gather the most fruit and pass it down the line to his teammates wins. There's an interesting twist to this game, however. You score points for passing it to your opponents, too. Pass attempts count whether they're caught or not, but a completed pass will bring wild cheers from the Coach and all the fans. While you're not likely to see this fruity sport in the X-Games anytime soon, it is the game of true champions.

When you consider how we're really put together—in God's image, that is—you have an easier time of understanding that we're also made for winning. God makes available to all of us the stuff of champions, whether we recognize it or not. You may struggle with your self-worth for many reasons, but God sees your true worth.

We don't have to be alive on this Earth very long to realize there's a "pecking order" for acceptance and popularity that the illusive "they" have established. (Who are *they*? We want names.) "They" are all around us. So what? They are not going away. Do you dare to rank yourself on the social scale of importance? It matters to us, doesn't it? Yes, God knows about those who would try to make us believe we are geeks, nerds or worse. Check out the Psalms sometime to see how this has always been a human problem. (Psalms 12, 22, 31, 35, 41, 56, 70, 89, 109 and

140 are just a few examples.) God cares. Jesus cared during his earthly ministry, too. Why else did he give the hyperreligious sects and self-serving hypocrites who preyed on the powerless among the people such a hard time? He called them a "brood of vipers"—a snake pit.

Self-Importance Can Be a Trap

The challenge to us is in rising above feelings of inferiority, bitterness, anger and all those worldly traps that tend to keep us from experiencing the fruit of the Spirit. Self-importance can be just as big a trap. Regardless of what is holding us back, anything related to self-will must be replaced with Christ's will for us. It takes understanding something called *submission,* a prickly word from which we tend to shy away. While this godly principle has people mistakenly thinking they are doormats, it really means learning to place the needs of others above our own and God above all else. Only then can we know the freedom and the strength that come with the fruit of the Spirit. This is a process that takes time and discipline on our part. Know that you will stumble and fall over and over as you make choices every day. You don't get thrown out of the game; you can only choose to take yourself out. Jesus drove people crazy with his talk of "the least among you" becoming first in the kingdom of heaven. It's not natural to us, but do we really want to argue that point with God? If He didn't think we were worth it, He would have quit on us a long time ago.

Our job is not to quit on God. Oh, we want to sometimes. In fact, if the truth were known, we would all have to say we have quit on Him, more than once. As sixteen-year-old Rachelle Rodrigues says, "I had committed my life to Christ when I was younger, but as a hip teen, well, I had a busy schedule, too busy to spend much time with God. It wasn't long before I got caught up in some pretty terrible things with my friends. I pretty much bailed on my parents as well. I'd go out when I wasn't supposed to and lie to my parents about where I was going. I'd also come home late and lie about where I'd been. But I did miss the me I knew when I walked with God. Without my daily talk with Him, I didn't feel that I was whole. Then I looked around and noticed how those who stayed close to the Heavenly Father were truly happy. I could see the light in their eyes and feel their happiness. All that had once been true for me. The good news is that my friends continued their gentle encouraging to once again embrace God as the center, the core, of my life. I've done that. I've recommitted my life to Christ. I feel so free as a result. I no longer tell lies just to get to do what I want. The light in my soul has been rekindled, now that my Lord has come back to His rightful place in my heart. The friends I've had for a long time notice a definite change in my attitude also. My non-Christian friends notice the difference. They ask me, 'You look different. What'd ya do?' But my Christian friends instantly recognize the change for what it is. They just hug me and say, 'We lafa you!' which I know translates: 'We are happy that you are with Him.'"

Lucky for us, God is far more patient than we are. When we know all eyes are upon us and we're out on the playing field, it's only natural that we expect to give it our best shot. What about the rest of the time when we think we're on our own? Are we allowed to lighten up and forget about the rules of the game . . . or just not play? We can and will do anything our self-will urges us to do. There is, however, a price to pay for doing it our way or for slacking off. Don't expect to get the ball much in that case. God just may put you on the bench until you're ready to be a team player and listen to His coaching.

How do we know what the Coach wants in the game of life? It helps to look at the playbook from time to time—God's Big Rule Book. Funny, but even though it's as old as dirt, we still forget some of those time-tested plays. Showing up for practice and team instruction helps, too. We need to meet with "Coach J" often enough to get familiar with his style.

"Coach J": Why Do I Need to Have the "Mind of Christ"?

In order to perform at our peak in the Big Game, there is one secret weapon we will need to possess. It's not one hotshot play, but it gives us the ability to figure out the opponent's moves and strategies so we can stay one step ahead. Along with knowing the playbook, showing up for practice and being ready to give our all in the game, we will be expected to know the Coach's signals. He wants us to learn to communicate with him, to speak his language so well that we don't have to waste precious time-outs coming to the bench to ask questions. He wants us to be prepared to make the right calls on our own. How do we do that? Through changing our thinking until it closely matches that of Jesus Christ. It's what we call "having the mind of Christ."

"Do not conform any longer to the pattern of this world," wrote Paul to the Roman church, "but be transformed by the renewing of your mind. Then you will be able to test and approve what God's will is—His good, pleasing and perfect will" (Rom. 12:2). Paul drives this point home many times in his letters to the early churches, and they form the basis for much of our church instruction today.

How awesome it would be if we could somehow have our Savior share his infinite wisdom with us as the intriguing Spock of *Star Trek* fame could do through the Vulcan mind-meld technique. In reality, we learn to align our thinking with Christ's wisdom gradually with the help of the Holy Spirit. That's why the Game of Life is so long. It can take pretty much the whole game to learn to master the secret weapon. It's the final score that counts, after all.

Even in this first quarter of the Big Game, you will face some important plays. Don't fret when you drop the ball. Hang in there until you begin to understand the playbook. Pace yourself because you're in it for the long haul. Your teammates will encourage you. And the fans? Well, we hear the angels are pretty good at whooping it up when you score!

Persecution: What if I'm Discriminated Against or Singled Out for My Faith?

You are more likely to think of religious persecution—being singled out for discrimination or oppression for your faith—as something that happens in third-world countries or those far-off lands where we send missionaries to preach the gospel to those entrenched in other beliefs. Maybe you rarely or never think about it at all since it doesn't much affect you. It only takes one incident right here at home to change our minds, however.

Suppose you attend school where a group of students wants to start a Bible study or a Bible club on campus after school hours, but find they are prohibited by the school board because of the so-called separation of church and state. Would you consider that to be unfair discrimination? You may not go so far as to call it persecution since the point could be made that the Christian students were not attacked without provocation, but put themselves on the skyline with their request. Nevertheless, that situation could progress to one of persecution depending on how other students, parents or school officials then treated those Christian students. If they were to be watched closely and harassed for their beliefs or put down for carrying Bibles on school property, that would indeed be persecution of sorts. Some say the trend toward multiculturalism in today's society has begun to influence our public schools in ways that appear unfair to traditional faiths. You will have to make up your mind about that for yourself. It is a debate that isn't going away anytime soon.

Have I Ever Been Out of the Country on a "Mission"?

You may have had the experience of going on a mission trip to another country with a youth group. Many teens have, and they have come away from their trips with some truly awesome experiences (as you'll read in part 6 of this book). Still, other groups have actually found themselves in harm's way, caught in the deadly crossfire of religious or cultural wars. There's no better way to understand the risks that full-time missionaries face every day in some foreign countries. If you've been on the receiving end of insults (or flying objects) hurled at you because you were a Christian, then you have faced persecution such as the early church fathers faced in their day. The apostle Paul encouraged those early Christians in his letters to the churches: "We are hard pressed on every side, but not crushed; perplexed, but not in despair; persecuted, but not abandoned; struck down, but not destroyed" (2 Cor. 4:8–9).

Living in an Age Where Religious Extremists Are Operating as Terrorists

We are living in an age where religious extremists are operating as terrorists, and where both Christians and Jews are targeted for persecution and death by those zealots who believe their God is commanding them to stamp out these two faiths. It is important, then, that we learn who we are and who we are not. Some Christians may even feel persecuted, or at the very least, ridiculed by their Jewish brothers and sisters while Jews may feel the same treatment by some Christians. This is a shame since we really are one family.

Those who really want to understand the biblical position on both Christian and Jewish faith can read Romans 9–11, in which Paul gives a scriptural and historical account of God's judgment of the Jews and the spreading of His message of salvation by accepting Christ to all non-Jews or Gentiles *because* of the Israelites' disobedience. He warns Christians not to be proud in their faith because the "root" of their faith is still good. Were it not for the Jews, there would be no Christians. He compares Gentile Christians to a wild olive branch that has been grafted onto another tree (the Jewish nation), some of whose branches have fallen off. "Do not boast over those branches. If you do, consider this: You do not support the root, but the root supports you" (Rom. 11:18).

This passage is often overlooked in Scripture. There is a lot of misunderstanding among Christians and Jews with respect for each other's position. Paul makes it very clear: "Israel has expe rienced a hardening in part until the full number of the Gentiles has come in. And so all Israel will be saved, as it is written: 'The deliverer will come from Zion: He will turn godlessness away from Jacob. And this is my covenant with them when I take away their sins'" (Rom. 11:25–27). Anyone claiming to be a Christian who doesn't understand their Jewish heritage is missing out on some important truths. Paul was highly qualified to speak that truth since he was a Jew of deep faith whom God appointed to begin taking Jesus' gospel message to the Gentiles.

Why do missionaries go out into the world and work to fulfill the Great Commission, risking persecution and even their lives? The answer is so they can do their part in bringing about God's promise to save His chosen people, the Jewish nation, as well as to bring the Good News to as many Gentiles as possible. Doing our best, as followers of Christ and believers in his gospel message of salvation, really means carrying the fruit of the Spirit with us wherever we go so we can be prepared to do our part. This is the bigger picture.

Personal Reflection

1. What does it mean to me to be *in* the world, but not *of* the world?
2. How have I been responding to God's "coaching"?
3. Have I ever faced a situation in which I chose to do the right thing, even though I feared it would affect my popularity? If so, did I grow from it?
4. Which of the spiritual fruits mentioned in Galatians 5 do I feel I possess?
5. Does reading Romans 9–11 change my perspective of where the Christian faith comes from and perhaps my views of God's chosen people?

22

Fellow Warriors: Fighting the Battles of Life

Deciding to commit to Christian principles doesn't mean that all our troubles are over and Jesus will get us through everything untouched, as if he were our heavenly bodyguard. That assumption goes out the window the first time we find ourselves lost in unfamiliar territory with night closing in around us. But how do we "walk in the light" when—yes, even for Christians—the battery in our flashlight keeps running down? Isn't God the ultimate Energizer?

Why does it seem to get darker sometimes when we carry the light of the universe with us? Like Elijah, the prophet of old, we are most vulnerable soon after we come down off the mountaintop of victory and walk in the real world of petty backbiters and unbelievers. Have you ever been to a youth camp or conference, after which you came home with your feet barely touching the ground? We often experience some emotional highs at such events. Then comes Monday: the real world. The light in the eyes of a new believer can set him or her apart from the rest of the world; after all, the look of love and light threatens the selfish, worldly way of life. The result is that we can become temporarily confused or even depressed. The enemies of our soul can get us on the run before we know it, and soon we're sitting under Elijah's juniper tree, exhausted and asking God to take us out of the world.

An Inevitable Lesson of Life: The Highs of Life Often Have Corresponding Lows

Elijah's story is told in 1 Kings. He has been sent to confront the wickedness of King Ahab and Queen Jezebel, who have turned the people away from God and are worshipping idols. He takes on the prophets of the false god, Baal, challenging them to call on their god to make fire rain down on Mount Carmel, while he asks God to do the same. Of course, they fail and God's fireworks prove He is the true God of Israel. Elijah then has to run for his life as the angry Jezebel threatens to kill him. Finally, when his strength is gone, he collapses under a juniper tree and says to God, "I have had enough, Lord. Take my life; I am no better than my ancestors" (1 Kings 19:4b). Amazing, considering the incredible victory God had just given him!

One of the inevitable lessons we all learn sooner or later is this: The highs of life often have corresponding lows. We aren't made to live on the mountaintop at all times. God may come to us there, but more often, He takes us into the valleys where we have to face our enemies—and ourselves—and He sustains us until we regain our strength and our vision. Elijah did recover from his depression, and God even sent a special friend to walk alongside him and encourage him.

Have you been there yet? Have you ever felt sorry for yourself and ready to quit because the enemy had you on the run and God seemed nowhere to be found? Relax. You're in good company.

The *Real* Star Wars: What I Should Know About Spiritual Warfare

Pitting good against evil and giving each side equal strength makes for great Hollywood entertainment, but it denies one essential truth: Satan is a fallen angel, not a fallen god. The enemy of our souls comes under the authority of God Almighty who created everything. The rebel and his forces are no match for God and his legions of angels. Oh, we can get into some devilish skirmishes down here on Earth. A yapping, heel-nipping little dog can be a major nuisance, but we have to lie down on the ground and give in to be hurt significantly. The truth is his bark is generally worse than his bite. Get enough of these demon dogs coming after you, however, and you may be in trouble. Together, they can be the "roaring lion" that is looking for a meal.

It's the enemy's bark that so often deceives us, echoing throughout the empty chambers of our heads when we have invited one or more of those dogs in after sending God away. Fido goes from room to room, sniffing out the former guest and making quite a ruckus. How can we hear ourselves think or hear God's gentle, reassuring voice with all that noise?

There is a war of confusion being waged all around us, make no mistake. The enemy has learned where our weaknesses are, and he clamps down on our Achilles' heel whenever he sees the opportunity. Most of the time, we never see him coming. It's not the dramatic battle we think we are prepared to fight. It's a cowardly sneak attack, and when we've had enough such attacks, we can become exasperated. Welcome to spiritual warfare.

The Subtle Ways We Are Lured into Accepting "Good" over "Best"

A little-understood fact of spiritual warfare is the cunning weapon of mind games. Knowing that we are conditioned to fight once we finally locate the enemy and figure out his tactics, Old Slewfoot has invented another tactic that works much better than traditional warfare. It's similar to the "bait and switch" routine that an underhanded salesman uses. It works like this: God may be showing us a goal or a blessing He has in mind for us. The sly enemy picks up on this heavenly transmission and jams the radio signal. He doesn't just leave us scratching our heads and wondering where the blessing went, however. He replaces the transmission with his propaganda. He knows he can't make us buy what he really wants to sell us as long as we realize we're being deceived. So he sells us something instead that appears just as good as or maybe even better than the original. The result? We go off on a rabbit trail in pursuit of what we think is God's will for us. It looks like the right path until we either come to a dead end or find another connecting trail, and off we go again until God, the "Hound of Heaven," comes after us and chases us back to the right path.

We don't like to think of ourselves as a bunch of rabbits running aimlessly around in the woods, do we? It's not a flattering thought. *We're "fearfully and wonderfully made"* (Ps. 139:14). *God wouldn't let that happen to His kids, would He? Wouldn't He want us to stand and fight? What about the "armor of God"?* Remember, this is no head-on battle. It's a fight initiated by a coward who cuts and runs after each guerilla strike. We have not been commanded to go after the enemy and attempt to beat him at his own game. Our strength lies in the armament at our disposal, but also in the heavenly "air strikes" we can call in as needed. We have the Big Gun on our side. It's equipped with night vision because our enemy loves darkness.

Peace, Love and the "Great Lie"

All this battlefield imagery serves a purpose, even though it may not be pleasant. While we're told we can love our enemies into submission by those who believe that all the world needs is a little more love, the real world doesn't generally work that way. We are at war with our great spiritual enemy; we are at war among ourselves and, yes, even *within* ourselves. Satan wants to get us believing there is no war. Yes, "Peace on Earth, goodwill toward men" is the gold standard for which we still strive, but it only comes through submission to Jesus Christ. Jesus said, "By this all men will know that you are my disciples, if you love one another" (John 13:35). Yet, Paul also said near the end of his life, "I have fought the good fight, I have finished the race, I have kept the faith" (2 Tim. 4:7). We are never to forget that there is a war to fight. Despite all the forces of evil, our thirst is too strong to quench. Even when forced underground, Christianity finds a way to thrive. No one can deny that.

Christ said he came not to abolish the old Jewish law, but to fulfill it. His death shook to the core even his own chosen disciples, those who believed he would assume the throne of an earthly king and defeat the enemies of the Jewish nation. We already know that Jesus stood the world on its head with his illogical, but never-ending church. He's still doing it, still shaking up us fearfully and wonderfully made, but human nature–flawed people. The victory, it turns out, is a spiritual one with Christ symbolically leading us into the battle. An army of changed hearts is invincible. So is a government made up of such people. That's the goal.

Culture Wars: Fighting Among Ourselves

Another of Satan's weapons comes in the form of what we call the "culture wars." This is one way in which the enemy can get us fighting among ourselves. He even divides churches and families with this one. In short, culture wars are the result of sharp divisions in public opinion about certain social or moral issues in the world such as abortion, the death penalty, gay rights, gun rights, gambling, education and so on. "If a house is divided against itself, that house cannot stand," said Jesus in Mark 3:25. A generation or two ago, this country had more unified views on major social and moral issues. Many believe the erosion of our Judeo-Christian values has led to confusion in our core values and beliefs as a nation. You may decide that for yourself. What is clear is that a war of words and values is being waged among the people of America. An examination of our national and corporate leadership shows many chinks in its armor. Integrity is not what it used to be. Greed is the defining value for many of us. Has the fruit of the Spirit largely been forgotten? It would appear so.

What is our human status these days? You stand on one side of a great divide while your neighbor stands on the other. The two of you cannot meet under your own power. On the one hand, we all still have Adam's flawed human nature, but on the other, we have the new covenant sealed by the blood of Jesus, who is called the second Adam. He came to be the bridge across that wide canyon. Free will is still there, nonetheless. You have the choice of accepting all this as truth or of knowing only, for example, that you'll get a good grade one day if you study *Paradise Lost* in English literature.

We go through life wrestling with the truth, perpetually at war. Some days, we think we have it wired. Others, we feel defeated. We retreat on the bad days and stand with the world. *It's not so bad,* we reassure ourselves. *Our friends are good people. We just want to have a little fun, stretch our wings, find out what life is all about. We're not lost. We know who we are and where we are.* Been to any dead ends lately? Had any "grenades" blow up around you?

Try as we might, we don't get to make the rules of engagement for spiritual warfare. The other side will always be the other side. We can get whiplash going back and forth, trying to be a double agent, playing both ends against the middle. We can think we're pretty smart tiptoeing around all the land mines that lie in no-man's-land, but it's only a matter of time before we step on one. The only way to successfully navigate a minefield is to walk directly in the footprints of the one who is safely going ahead of us. Thankfully, God's footprints are unmistakable. What a relief!

We understand the pressures you're up against. We've been

there, too. We just want you to see the cunning traps that are so easy to fall into. One of them is believing we're all entitled to bend the rules; that bad things only happen to other people. That, too, is part of the Big Lie. If you're not really sure who you are or *whose* you are, you are more apt to fall into the clutches of whoever or whatever gives you the greatest feeling of significance and belonging. That feeling is here today and gone tomorrow, however. Street gangs survive because of the negative concept of brotherhood. The flip side is even stronger. God intended for his people to band together and to set themselves apart from the influences of the world. We are to build each other up and take care of each other's needs while reaching out to a sometimes hostile world to bind the wounds of those who are veterans of the same war. Sometimes we will need to get out of the trenches and go retrieve a fallen brother or sister.

We Are All Fellow Warriors

World War I was known as the Great War or "the war to end all wars." We know that it was far from the last war. The battles were largely fought from long trenches in great, desolate European forests like France's Belleau Wood. Those who fought there endured unspeakable hardships.

One day during some heavy fighting, an Allied soldier was hunkered down in his trench while heavy barrages from the enemy's weapons thundered over his head. His best friend had been ordered with his team to charge out of the trench a few minutes earlier and had been hit. He lay a hundred feet or so out, severely wounded and crying out for help. The soldier in the trench begged his sergeant to let him go and bring his buddy back to safety. The sergeant didn't want to risk losing another man. Besides, he knew the soldier was dying from his wounds. The wounded soldier's friend waited until he could bear it no longer, and finally convinced the sergeant to let him make a run for the dying man. He bolted out of the trench like a deer and made it to his friend in a flash. Somehow, he managed to hoist him over his shoulder and make it safely back to their entrenched unit. When the wounded soldier was handed down to waiting arms, he was already dead. "I told you he wouldn't make it," said the sergeant, shaking his head. The friend said, "That may be, but when I got there, he was still alive and I got to hear him say, 'I knew you would come.'"

That kind of love and courage is what separates the men from the boys and the women from the girls. We are fellow warriors, like it or not. We grow up on the battlefield. Some of us don't make it off; others distinguish themselves as heroes. Most of us just feel honored to be veterans and are grateful to be here to share our war stories and pass on the torch of hope and freedom to others who will come after us.

Personal Reflection

1. Have I had any "mountaintop" experiences? If so, what happened when I came down off the mountain?
2. What are some weapons that I can use in spiritual warfare?
3. In what way do I think I may have settled for the good masquerading as the best?
4. Do I know what my Achilles' heel is? How can I keep from being "bitten" there?
5. Do I know any fallen soldiers? What can I do to help carry them off life's battlefield?

23

Making a Difference: What Does It Mean to Be "in God's Service"?

Remember that Golden Rule? If we are truly children of God, shouldn't we desire to pass along to others what we ourselves have received through our faith? Further, shouldn't it please God to see us serving others and following the example Jesus set for us when he walked the Earth? Not only does this make God happy, but it also makes us feel better about ourselves. Did you know that one of the best prescriptions for feeling down is to go out and help someone else who is worse off? Your generation has already earned a reputation for being concerned about others and for wanting to make a difference in the world. It is only natural, then, that you will find ways to take your faith out into the world and show those who don't know what you know about the wonders of the God whom you are learning to serve. You can do this in any number of ways.

How Can I "Season" the World with Love?

Do you have to be in formal ministry or do mission work to make an impact on the world? Not at all. Look in any direction and you will see someone who is in need of a helping hand or the comforting peace of the Lord. Some of the most fruitful work done in Christian ministry is accomplished by a quiet and powerful army of average people who become involved in the lives of the people they encounter in day-to-day living—in school, on the job or in their neighborhoods. Just being willing to reach out to someone in need puts you in God's service. You don't have to do any more than to "give even a cup of cold water" in Jesus' name (Matt. 10:42) to be of service. Of course, you may pursue some specialized training or even use your educational background in some ministry capacity, but you can have a meaningful impact on the lives of others without going that formal route.

In the New Testament, the apostle Paul writes, "We are God's fellow workers; you are God's field, God's building. By the grace God has given me, I laid a foundation as an expert builder and someone else is building on it. But each one should be careful how he builds. For no one can lay any foundation other than the one already laid, which is Christ Jesus" (1 Cor. 3:9–11). What does this mean? Simply, that we each have a part to play in building the church and spreading the "Good News" for those who come behind us. The foundation may be solid, but we have to make sure we lay the right kind of bricks on top of it or the building will be weak. Every word or action that we speak or do forms one of those bricks. If we look around us today, we can see that some churches are building with solid bricks while others are laying weak or cracked bricks, which make their part of the overall structure unstable. When half-truths or outright lies become part of any church's teaching—meaning that teaching is not based on the Living Word of God—the result is confused and misled people who, in turn, continue confusing those they touch.

The real work of God begins close to home, within the body of each individual church family. There is no need to go abroad and spread the gospel unless you really know what the true gospel is.

How Will I Know if God Is Calling on Me to Do Something?

What if you are "called" to ministry in a significant way? How will you know if that is God's desire for you? You may feel a tugging at your heart that won't go away or realize that you have extraordinary compassion for people in need. This may be as you're going about your day, or maybe—as was the case for several of the teens you'll meet in part 6—while attending a special activity. Or maybe you've set out to do something for God, and then learn that His plans are a little different from what you had in mind, as was the case for Danielle Platt, whose story is also profiled in part 6.

Do you want to do God's work full-time? Maybe. But maybe not. Some people decide at an early age that they want to do God's work full-time; others come to that realization much later. Still others come to this realization after having a traumatic experience, such as a being a victim, or from surviving alcohol or drug abuse. It is amazing to see some of the stories of dramatic U-turns people have made after getting a rough and uncertain start in life. The most effective witness of the power of Christ in a life comes from those who once wanted nothing to do with him and who appeared bound for destruction. God works in some awesome ways. He is certainly never to be underestimated.

Have you ever been afraid that, if you truly commit your life to God, He might call you to be a missionary in some foreign country? This fear is real for many. Those who do find themselves in this position have spoken of the fear and doubt beforehand that were transformed instead into excitement and anticipation of what they would accomplish with God's help. Taleen Kullukian was part of a 2000 youth mission trip to Armenia. "I was really excited to be traveling with everyone for this trip and nervous at the same time," she said. "The group all lived in the same area and had the opportunity to study and learn together. I felt like a bit of an outsider and didn't really know how I'd fit in. There were quite a few times when I wondered, *What am I doing here? How can I help? Is there really any way for me to be effective here?* Spiritually, I had a lot to learn. Not having been involved with a church for a while, and not having been involved in Bible study, this experience opened my eyes to how truly important it is. The realization that I needed to find the right church and the right study group to be involved in was great. I always think I can do it on my own, but the truth is that as a Christian, we do need to surround ourselves with people who believe the same way if we don't want to stray from the path."

Rest assured if you ever end up in any foreign country as a full-time missionary, God will give you the grace to feel that same excitement and sense of purpose and growth. If you doubt this, don't miss reading Franklin Graham's books, most especially *Rebel with a Cause*. It's one of the most exciting accounts of someone who rebelled against listening to God's voice and "hearing" God's intentions for his life. You might be interested in knowing that Franklin is the son of the great evangelist Billy Graham. Most of us will never be sent into the foreign mission field (although more and more teens go abroad on behalf of their churches' youth missions). If you aren't one of them, don't worry. There is no end to the everyday needs that are all around us. As Jesus said in Mark 14:7, "The poor you will always have with you." Missionaries, however, are extraordinary people who deserve the utmost respect for the sacrifices they make.

What Does It Mean to "Witness"? Am I Expected To (or Is Just Being a Friend to Others Enough)?

The concept of "witnessing," which is simply sharing your faith or the Good News of the gospel of Christ with others, has frightened many a person right out of the church. Truly. Why are we so terrified of opening our mouths or of setting a Christian example for others to see? Is it because we worry about what they will think? Hmmm. Might it be a tad more important to concern ourselves with what God thinks? It's true, we want to be liked and respected, to fit in—that's a pretty basic human need—especially when we're younger and so subject to peer pressure. God knows that putting our egos on the line by revealing that we are "one of those" Christians can be a little scary for us all. *Why did God ever have to put that Great Commission thing in the Bible?* we moan. Part of the answer is because He understood the mathematical concept of exponential growth. Any algebra students out there? Start with a few who talk to a few who talk to a few more . . . and before long, you have a worldwide church which even "the gates of Hades [hell] will not overcome" (Matt. 16:18b).

Why Do We Need to Witness?

We need to witness first, to carry out Jesus' Great Commission (see Matt. 28:19–20) and, more down-to-earth, to improve the lives of those who are unhappy or unfulfilled or who can't find their way in the world. When a person has a deep need and is searching for the answer to his or her problems, the door is already open to hear the Good News of the gospel. Let's face it, we need a compelling reason to come to Christ. You may have heard the word "testimony," which refers to a personal story of overcoming or of accepting Jesus Christ as Savior. Our own personal experiences encourage others and point the way to the source of our overcoming.

While it is sometimes enough just to demonstrate God's love to others through the way you live your life, at other times it may be necessary to go a little deeper and share some of your life story and the story of God's great redeeming love for the world with a person who is looking for meaningful truth. It's as if you are giving them a road map. What if you knew of a cool clothing store where there were bargains galore? Would you keep it a secret? Not likely! If we can get excited about the routine things of life, why not become more enthusiastic about the most important area of all—the God who gives life its meaning and helps us to cope with its ups and downs?

We all sometimes miss opportunities to share our faith with someone who is hurting or confused. Don't be surprised at how many people will secretly watch you and how you live, however, just as you may be watching the lives of others to whom you look up. You never know where you will make an impact just by doing some little thing that sets you apart from the masses, or by just being a friend. Of course, the converse is also true. You can have a negative impact by behaving as if you didn't have Christ in your life and by turning your back on others. We don't get to see all the seeds that we plant or know what the eventual harvest will be. We are still expected to unselfishly plant them. You may have questions like twelve-year-old Cassie, who upon seeing her very old neighbor planting a tiny fruit tree asked, "Why are you planting something that you will never get to enjoy?" Her neighbor replied, "Because it gives me great pleasure to know that someday somebody else will."

Although you may not fully understand it right now, there is no feeling to compare with knowing you have made a difference in someone's life. You may only be one person, but you are not alone. You are part of a team, a large family of believers who collectively makes a huge impact on the world. Each member of that team has slightly different talents or gifts, and when they are all linked, the team is equipped to handle any situation. The hand is useless without the arm. The head needs the neck to support it, turn it and link it to the rest of the body.

What Are "Spiritual Gifts"?
Do We All Have Them?

In order for you to understand how to be most effective in Christian service—and even in a career—you will need to know what your unique abilities and "gifts" are. Maybe you already have a clue or two, and that is a start. Some of us, however, have no idea what our real talents are, especially in the area of serving or helping others. Many of us, if we were really truthful, would have to admit that we expect others to step up and do most of the work. It is usually true that 20 percent of the people in any body or organization tend to do 80 percent of the work. While God does expect us to place our relationship with Him first, above all others in our lives, He never meant for us to focus on His work to the exclusion of all else, especially our own families. We all know those people who are so "heavenly-minded" they're no "earthly good." If you've grown up in a family where you saw one or both parents make this mistake, you are understandably turned off to church or ministry work. It is one of the real dangers of Christian service.

How Can I Discover My Own Individual
Spiritual Gifts and Talents?

Spiritual gifts are unique talents and abilities given to each Christian believer by the Holy Spirit. Can you have more than one? Yes. Each of us has at least one primary gift, but we may also have several secondary ones. They are not given according to how special God thinks we are, but simply by His grace and according to the particular purpose He has chosen for us. Our gifts are meant to blend in one harmonious accord when we put them all together, just as various musical instruments, regardless of size or sound, make up the blended melody of an orchestra. Is the tuba player more important than the flute player? They are both necessary. The apostle Paul illustrates this blending concept by speaking of the various parts of the body which must work together to make us whole and fully functioning: "If the whole body were an eye, where would the sense of hearing be? If the whole body were an ear, where would the sense of smell be?" (1 Cor. 12:17).

In two separate letters, the one mentioned above to the Corinthian church, and one to the Ephesian church, Paul writes in detail about the importance of each individual discovering his or her spiritual gifts and using them as God intends for them to be used. He says, while there is one Spirit and one Lord, there are different gifts and different kinds of service. "To one there is given through the Spirit the message of wisdom, to another the message of knowledge by means of the same Spirit, to another faith . . . to another gifts of healing . . ." and so on; the list can go with many possibilities (1 Cor. 12:8–9). The reason we must blend our gifts and talents together, says Paul, is "so that the body of Christ might be built up until we all reach unity in the faith and in the knowledge of the Son of God and become mature . . ." (Eph. 4:12b–13a).

Some gifts are more obvious than others. If you are musically inclined, you generally know it. If you like to talk, that is pretty obvious, too. But what if you are quiet and reserved and feel you have no particular standout talent? There is something at which everyone is good. You just need to discover what it is. Do you like to cook? How about building or making things? Perhaps you like baby-sitting or working with children. You might even prefer to spend time with senior citizens. Maybe you are really good at doing research on the Internet. You may be a good encourager or a good listener. All of these talents are important ones and can be used in service to others.

A good way of finding out what you're gifted in is to take a spiritual gifts survey. Check with your youth pastor. There are lots of variations on this basic questionnaire that ask you to rate your desires or abilities in a number of areas. (You will find one in our book *12 Months of Faith: A Devotional Journal for Teens.* See Suggested Readings and Resources near the end of this book.) You may be surprised at the gifts you discover. It can be a start to finding ways in which you can contribute your time and talent in serving your church or community. Just your technical abilities alone can move the world ahead by leaps and bounds. Take the time to think about who you are. God surely knows.

Personal Reflection

1. Do I really understand now what the Good News of the true gospel of Christ is? Do I see it reflected it my own church, if I attend one?
2. Have I ever felt I may be "called" to a particular ministry? If so, what?
3. In what ways have I been an example of God's love or perhaps even shared my faith with someone else? If an opportunity to witness comes along, do I know what I will say?
4. What is my primary gift, and how might I use it?
5. How would I compare my generation with my parents' generation in terms of making a difference in the world?

24

The Great Homecoming: When I Die . . . Then What?

We have discussed some compelling, practical reasons for living a God-centered life. A barrage of research in recent years confirms that people of faith tend to be happier and healthier, have better relationships and have a deeper sense of purpose in their lives than those who keep God at arm's length or deny His existence. So here we are, down to where the "rubber meets the road," where it all counts. The stakes for turning our backs on God are high, as we have already seen: misery in this life and abandonment in the next. What is the ultimate reward, then, for the person who chooses Jesus Christ as "the way, the truth and the life"? Nothing short of *eternity in his presence.* It's so easy to utter that simple phrase, but it is a deeply profound and joyous reality.

Each day—even each hour—can seem like an eternity to us in our youth. It seems as if we'll never grow to adulthood. Yet, contemplate for just a moment what *forever* really means. Can you even grasp the concept of a never-ending span of time? We are all here on Earth for just a little while in God's grand scheme of things. David writes in Psalm 39: "The span of my years is as nothing before You. Each man's life is but a breath" (verse 5b). Over and over in the Bible, we are reminded of just how brief and fragile our lives are. Are we to "eat, drink and be merry" then? Are we to fret and become depressed because we are so insignificant in the universe? Are our lives really worthwhile? You'd better believe it, young friends! God has something incredibly awesome in store for those who know Him and His son in this life. To receive that prize requires running the race He has set before us all the way to the finish line. No, we don't have to finish first; we just have to finish.

Staying on Course: Pointing My Compass Heavenward to True North

Have you ever heard of the sport of orienteering? It's not for the faint of heart. Basically, it requires a compass and a good pair of running shoes. Competitors are required to "run" a rugged course in all kinds of terrain against the clock, finding checkpoints or "objectives" along the way. Some of these markers are pretty well concealed in heavily wooded areas. How do you find them? That's where the compass comes in. If you are lost or disoriented out in the wild, the first thing you do is "zero" your compass by finding a true north heading. Every compass may deviate slightly from this heading, but you can adjust your direction when you know your own compass. Then you "shoot an azimuth" or get a compass heading toward the object you are seeking, keying off of intermediate objects, such as trees, along the way until finally you arrive at your destination.

Fortunately, we don't have to run at breakneck speed as we navigate our way through the maze we call life. It's far less stressful to make sure we have our bearings and know our compass really is pointed toward our Heavenly Father before we strike out toward the far horizon. In this book, you have been given the map for the course you must navigate. You won't always take the most direct route to your destination. We all get off course from time to time. Sometimes, we're deceived and wind up lost, and sometimes we take what we think will be a shortcut. But there are no shortcuts on the "narrow way" to eternal life. Without the compass of God's Holy Spirit pointing the way of salvation for us, we won't make it. We won't even desire it. And that's the sobering truth.

Why Doesn't God Reveal to Us— Ahead of Time—When We Will Die?

Why doesn't God reveal to us when we will die? Even the psalmist David appears to be asking that question in Psalm 39: "Show me, O Lord, my life's end and the number of my days" (Ps. 39:4). If God wouldn't let David know, surely He isn't going to tell us when we will die either. We only know the finish line is out there somewhere and that the race is worth running, no matter how many times we might fall down or run off course. Life comes to us a day, an hour, a moment at a time. We can't speed it up or slow it down. God expects us to live it just as it comes, but promises us His peace if we choose to "be anxious for nothing" and to "lift up [our] eyes to the hills" where He is waiting to help and to guide us (Phil. 4:6; Ps. 121:1).

As we mature in our faith (and in years) and grow closer to God's ultimate purpose for our lives, we will find that He is asking us to gradually give up more and more of our self-will and replace it with His will. Does this mean we have to stop being the unique individuals that we are? No. God made us to be who we are, and He wants us to always use those gifts for Him. It does mean that we cannot allow our human willfulness and pride to interfere with God's possession of our souls. If we are to "be like Him" (1 John 3:2) as promised when we come into His presence following our death, we must begin putting on that likeness during our living moments. It is the continuing process of being made in His image.

When we face a situation or crisis that causes us to question God's purpose, we can choose to go our own way in that moment or we can step back and give God the opportunity to lead us by prayerfully seeking Him and waiting for His direction. The great pastor and teacher Oswald Chambers spoke of this conflict frequently as the crisis of "giving up my right to myself." Even mature Christians face these moments in their lives. Each time we come to one of these places and patiently wait on the Lord, He gives us a deeper knowledge of who He is and we grow more like Him.

Self-Worth and Self-Esteem: Whose Definition Counts?

One of the barriers that often stands in the way of God's will for our lives is what we call "self-esteem." Self-esteem is what we think of ourselves, right? When we speak of having "low self-esteem" we are generally referring to what we consider to be an unhealthy or false picture of ourselves that keeps us from living up to our potential. Are you with us so far? Now, let's take it one step further. With whose opinion are we really concerned when we refer to our self-esteem—ours or everyone else's? Hmmm. Think about it. It's not so clear now, is it?

We base our worth as individuals on several things—our performance, our looks, our popularity and our intelligence, for instance. But who "evaluates" these things? What is the standard against which we are measured? It's what the world says, right? Our friends can make or break us with one word, look or gesture. How can that be when we are "fearfully and wonderfully made"? Who are they to tell us what our real worth is? Who are we to do the same for them? Yet, this is how we live our lives and make many of our decisions. It's a distorted picture that can be highly damaging to us. Some people never recover from the cruel judgments of those whose opinions they value most. A parent or a teacher can do this kind of harm, sometimes without even knowing it. Did you ever go into a hall of mirrors at an amusement park and laugh at the way your reflection appeared in the different-shaped mirrors? It's fun when it's a game, but not when it's the painful reality of life.

Our Worth to God Is Priceless

God's picture is never distorted or cruel. Our worth to Him is priceless. The apostle Paul wrote in Romans 8, "If God is for us, who can be against us? . . . Who shall separate us from the love of Christ? . . . For I am convinced that neither death nor life, neither angels nor demons, neither the present nor the future, nor any powers, neither height nor depth, nor anything else in all creation, will be able to separate us from the love of God that is in Christ Jesus our Lord" (verses 31, 35, 38–39).

The longer we live, the more opportunities God has to show us this truth. The farther we run in the race of life, the closer we draw to God. Paul said, "There is no condemnation for those who are in Christ Jesus, because through Christ Jesus the law of the Spirit of life set me free from the law of sin and death" (Rom. 8:1–2).

A Home in Heaven: What Will That Be Like?

We have taken the time to painstakingly point out in this book that all spiritual roads don't lead to heaven. Now you have to make a choice to accept that truth or reject it. The stakes are high, but the ultimate reward of accepting Jesus Christ as personal Savior is greater than anything you can even imagine. "Do not let your hearts be troubled. Trust in God; trust also in me. In my Father's house are many rooms. . . . I am going there to prepare a place for you," Jesus told his disciples before he left them to ascend back to heaven (John 14:1–2).

By now, you should have some sense of what that means.

Jesus always existed, along with God the Father. His former existence was one of glory at the Father's right hand in heaven. That is where he resides today. He willingly chose to leave that glory and to come to Earth in the humble form of a human being. Not reincarnation, but *incarnation*. He fulfilled the divine mission of redeeming mankind, after which he returned to his former glory.

The glory of heaven—eternity with the Father, Son and Holy Spirit—is an overwhelming thing to contemplate. Heaven is real. Hell is real. No one can prove otherwise. The closest proof we have is what happens in the final moments before a person dies. If you have had the experience of being with a loved one—perhaps a grandparent or other family member—in the final stages of death, then you may have observed with your own eyes the indescribable peace of one who knows Christ and is about to slip into eternity with him. Doctors, nurses and those doing research on "near-death" or death experiences have observed both extremes—utter peace and joy and terrifying fear—in those who are dying or who come close. Descriptions that sound like both heaven and hell have come back with those who are revived. That should be enough to convince us.

If you really want to read more of what the Bible has to say about heaven, you can look at parts of the book of Revelation. It is helpful to use a reference Bible with a concordance as Revelation, a prophetic book written by Jesus' disciple John, following a divine vision, can be hard to understand. It gives some amazing descriptions of what heaven is supposed to be like and, of course, refers to the "End Times" when Jesus will return to the Earth to judge it (and Satan) and establish his 1,000-year reign as the ultimate King and Messiah in a newly created world.

Revelation contains the final appeal in the Bible to those who do not believe in Jesus. "Those whom I love I rebuke and discipline. So be earnest and repent. Here I am! I stand at the door and knock. If anyone hears my voice, I will come in and eat with him and he with me. To him who overcomes, I will give the right to sit with me on my throne just as I overcame and sat down with my Father on His throne" (Rev. 3:19–21). Near the end of the Bible, Jesus says, "Behold, I am coming soon! Blessed is he who keeps the words of the prophecy in this book" (Rev. 22:7). Those words represent the "free gift of the water of life" that is offered to us by Jesus Christ (Rev. 22:17).

Knowing God: To Know That I Know That I Know

Have you ever heard people who were sharing their personal testimonies about Christ in their lives speak of coming to accept him when they were small children? You might even be one of those people. It does happen. More of us come to know Jesus and his saving grace for us nearer to adulthood. It is not always innocent, childlike faith that compels us to know Christ, but it might instead be a crisis that we believe only he can solve. It doesn't matter what drives us to seek him out. All that matters is that we do it. Once that decision is made, it covers us for life. Salvation is once and for all time. If that were not the case, we would live in constant fear of an arbitrary God striking our names out of the "Book of Life" because we can't live up to His impossibly perfect standards. By now, it should be clear just how ridiculous such thoughts are. Jesus is precisely the answer for our inability to save ourselves and to follow the "law." A person who tries to go it alone is like a dog who is forever chasing his tail, or is "chasing the wind," as Tom Reiner so aptly tells us in his story in part 6. (This phrase, by the way, is also used in the Bible in Ecclesiastes 2.)

The peace of God that comes with accepting His truths and His son as personal Savior simply cannot be explained to one who hasn't made that leap of faith for himself. We can share our experiences with others and tell them how awesome God is to us, but we cannot put that knowledge into their heads. That's

God's job through the Holy Spirit. He can prepare us in different ways and soften our hearts so we can long for the good news of salvation almost as much as we long to breathe. That's a beautiful divine mystery.

When you *know that you know that you know* what you believe, it means that you have what is called the "peace of God which transcends all understanding" (Phil. 4:7a). It is something that is reserved only for those who truly have met Christ face-to-face and have chosen to follow him for the rest of their lives. When you have this peace, you know it, and no one can take it away from you. The one who tries the hardest is Satan, but he is powerless against the truth of Jesus Christ. Satan knows that true salvation is forever, but he wants to weaken your effectiveness as a Christian by tripping you up and making you doubt your salvation if he can. (He also loves to make you doubt his very existence.) Remember the armor we talked about? You have the victory, hands down.

Life throws a lot of stuff at us, day in and day out. We can be up one day and feel we have it wired, and the next find ourselves wondering who we are and how God could possibly love us. Don't feel you have to walk away from being a Christian during these tough times. Your faith is what will get you through it. God actually gives you the freedom to come to Him and pour out your doubts to Him. Sometimes keeping a journal is a good way to express your fears and questions. Faith is always strengthened by working through those doubts. You may wake up one day and say, "I've had it! I'm not going to do this Christian thing anymore." God is the parent who will love you and wait for you to come back to Him, no matter what your feelings are at any given moment.

Never forget that "He who began a good work in you will carry it on to completion until the day of Christ Jesus" (Phil. 1:6). God builds our lives one block at a time. You are not complete until he lays the last one in place. His promise to you is a profound one: "I am the resurrection and the life. He who believes in Me, though he may die, he shall live" (1 Cor. 9:24–17).

Personal Reflection

1. What does "finishing the race" mean to me?
2. Where do I live my life the most—in the past, the present or the future?
3. On what do I base my self-worth—on God or on the opinions of others?
4. Have I faced a crisis that caused me to want to bail out on God? If so, how did I reconnect with Him?
5. Do I truly know that I have eternal salvation? If I'm in doubt, am I ready to ask Jesus Christ into my heart to seal the deal right now?

Part 6

Teen Talk–Real Talk About God in Real Life

Set yourself earnestly to discover
what you are made to do, and then give
yourself passionately to the doing of it.
—Martin Luther King Jr.

God hasn't changed His tune from Bible times. He's
still looking for courageous teens who are not afraid of
being singled out for being godly; are tired of being
hypocrites and willing to stand up against pressure to
follow the crowd; want to develop and use their
spiritual gifts to the level of God's expectation; have a
sincere desire to see miracles happen in their lives. Are
you loyal to the Lord? If not, what's holding you back?
—Miles McPherson
former NFL player, founder and president,
Miles Ahead Youth Ministries
author, *Bad to the Bone*

25

Teens Talk About God—And How They See Faith at Work in the Ups and Downs of Life

The Wind Symphony Audition

My school is known for its outstanding band program. Since most people in my school are involved in band, we aren't considered "band nerds" or anything. There are three bands: Varsity, Symphonic and Wind Symphony, with Wind Symphony being at the top. Making it into Wind Symphony is a great accomplishment because those who make it are considered "the best of the best." I didn't even bother trying out for Wind Symphony my freshman year because I knew I had absolutely no chance of making it, but it was a goal I set for myself for my sophomore year. Absolutely intent on "making the grade," I practiced the remaining part of that year and all that summer. When my sophomore year rolled around, I was ready!

Even though the band director said I was "better than ready," the competition was really tough. It didn't help that my best friend, Christine, was also trying out. We had sat next to each other in band since middle school, so if one of us made Wind Symphony and the other didn't, then we'd feel bad for each other. Even so, I had to just focus on doing well for myself. I started out with all twelve major scales, then played the etude, my solo, and finally sight-reading.

Having done my best, I left thinking it went really well. Since all the other girls thought their auditions "went horrible," I had even more confidence about my placement. Now all I had to do was wait a week for the results.

The results were posted at the end of the day on Wednesday, which couldn't have gone by any slower. My last class took twice as long, and when the bell rang half the school ran down the hallways to the band room. I got up to the Wind Symphony postings and scanned the list.

My name was not on the list!

I thought it was a mistake. I mean, there were only five flutes on the list, so obviously my name not being on the list was a simple error, an oversight. But then I saw my name listed as first chair for Symphonic band, with my friend Christine listed as second chair.

I was simply devastated. I stood there looking at the list, reading it again and again—but even so, my name did not shift places. Seeing that I'd failed to make Wind Symphony was like getting the wind knocked out of me. I'd worked so hard, and now I was stuck in Symphonic band for another whole year! I went home and just cried.

I thought about how my life would be affected by this. Not playing in Wind Symphony meant that I would be hanging out with different people, have a different schedule, and I would play at different events. Tallying up all the "negatives" made me really mad at God; I'd wanted this so much and worked so hard to make it happen. I was really upset at my band director, too. After all, he'd said he was going to pick six flutes, but then he selected only five!

The next day the band director asked me to come and talk with him. When I walked into his office, he offered me a chair and then said, "I wanted to have the chance to talk to you about my decision to have five flutes rather than six in Wind Symphony." He then explained, "I know I'd told you I'd be having six, but I realized that five flutes would actually balance the band better." I remained silent, trying not to act as hurt as I felt as he went on, "I'm sorry that I didn't think of that before the auditions. I just wanted you to know that it had nothing to do with your abilities because if I had wanted six flutes you would be in Wind Symphony."

"I understand—it's all right," I lied, gathering my books to leave. "Sarah," he said, "I wanted to also tell you that you will have *all* the solos next year." I froze—I had totally forgotten about that! I would rather be first chair with solos than to be last chair with none *any* day! "Oh my gosh, that is totally cool! Totally awesome! Really totally awesome! Thank you so much!" I'm sure I sounded like a total dork but I was ecstatic.

The moment I left his office, I said, "Thank you, God!" That's when I realized how foolish it had been to be "mad" at God when I'd learned I hadn't made Wind Symphony. And then I thought about why I'd said, "Thank you, God" and realized it was for His making my win as perfect as it was—which is promised: "'For I know the plans I have for you,' declares the Lord, 'plans to prosper you and not harm you, plans to give you hope and a future'" (Jer. 29:11).

"I'm sorry about losing sight of this, God," I said. "Please just help me trust you like I know I should."

"Do your best and leave the rest up to God," my mother is fond of saying. What important advice. Because of my losing sight of why I'd asked God into my life in the first place, I saw my loss as defeat when in fact God had a plan for me: "No to Wind Symphony for this year—yes to something better."

I know God has plans for my life. I also know they are

divinely orchestrated—and they're all in concert with what's best for me. The God I love and honor—and promise to have heart-to-hearts with on a *daily basis* from here on out—is that all-knowing and so all-loving.

Sarah Erdman, 16

Wounded Angels

Still in bed—and thinking it must be very late—I flopped on my side to get a glimpse of my alarm clock. What I saw—much to my surprise, or should I say, shock—was a girl sitting erect in a bed next to mine, reading the Bible. Startled and more awake now, I asked her, "Who are you, where am I, and how did I get here?"

"My name is Laura, and you're in the lockdown unit of a psych hospital, "she replied, adding, "I don't know why you're here. You were here when I got here, which was a couple of hours ago." Alarmed and completely disoriented, I sat up and looked around, and then at my body—which felt like a semi-truck had run over it. My wrists were sore, and I had a big bruise on my foot—one I had no idea how I got—and my body ached even when I yawned. That's when I noticed a huge clock on the wall; it was four-thirty in the afternoon.

Waking up in a nut ward was cause for a lot of serious reflection! Trying to recall the events of the prior evening, I remembered drinking a lot and having a huge fight with my boyfriend—one that got really out of hand. I remembered two policemen coming, who handcuffed me and made me sit on the side of the curb. I then remembered being taken away by the ambulance, and how irritated I was to be restrained on a stretcher. This was followed by a hazy and monotonously long stay at the hospital emergency room, where I was asked to explain how I'd injured my foot, as well as some other scratches and bruises. I recalled telling the doctor that I just had too much to drink, and I didn't know how I got "scratched up." Then I remembered him saying, "I'm going to give you something to calm you down." I couldn't recall anything from that point on. But here I was, hours later, in a place filled with very weird—and I do mean, weird—people. The good news is that the girl in the bed next to me, reading her Bible, seemed—at least in the first moments of assessment—harmless enough.

Most of the people who I saw later looked as though they had serious problems. One girl wore her sweater wrapped around her head like a turban. Another girl who made quite an impression (and who I made a point of never turning my back on) wore a strange-looking garment that was totally food-stained. Still another would not stop chanting and babbling unintelligibly. Later I would learn that many of them were here because their family members couldn't handle them. Others, such as myself, were there because the state said I was a threat to myself, as well as to others. And some, such as Laura, were here by choice.

Needing to know more, I asked the girl reading the Bible why she'd checked herself in. In a calm and friendly way she told me she'd come here because she had been depressed and couldn't get the notion of suicide out of her head. She said she was frightened that, in fact, she might end her life. Feeling suicidal just hours before she checked herself in, she had called around to the local hospitals asking what she should do. She was encouraged to call a cab and go directly to this hospital, which was exactly what she had done.

She admitted she was scared and uncertain what being here meant in terms of care and treatment for dealing with her feelings—although she was told that later in the day she would be seeing a psychiatrist (as would I) and a treatment plan would be determined by the outcome of the psychiatrist's recommendations. She wanted to be here; I just wanted out of this place—and pronto. But since I was now at the mercy of waiting for that to happen, Laura and I talked. I learned we were about the same age and that we were both pretty scared girls. When she asked why I was here, I couldn't bring myself to tell her that I drank, and when I did, I became completely uncontrollable.

The "behavioral health facility" became my home for the next eleven days. Aside from meeting with the medical staff, I slept a lot. Laura read a lot. When I was awake, Laura and I talked—and talked. She was a gentle person and a good listener. I found myself being "totally myself" with her. Eventually, I did tell her about how terrible drinking had made my life (from parents to school, friends to boyfriend), and how unhappy and depressed I had become. I also told her I thought I must be a terrible, terrible person—and, of course, "a loser."

Without passing any judgment, she just listened and was very accepting. I was a little confused by this—maybe because she didn't see any of these traits in me, or maybe it was her compassion and acceptance of me. And, of course, it seemed out of sync with her own problems: How could a wonderful person so capable of making someone else see their good qualities totally ignore her own? With so much to offer another person, how could she possibly be considering suicide? And, she had said she was a Christian.

I never thought of Christians as having many problems—especially wanting to end their lives. I told her what I was thinking and asked her why, when she had God to turn to, she still felt worthless and very lonely. I mean, I felt worthless and lonely, but God wasn't walking with me. I'd abandoned him a couple of years ago. And, of course, I never wanted anyone to see that I was vulnerable to being unhappy or "un-cool." To make sure they didn't, I covered myself with a blanket of "hard-as-nails attitude"—wanting everyone to believe that my life was just fine. The truth is, I didn't feel comfortable in my own skin unless I had a drink or two—or more.

Days passed. Laura was completely dedicated to reading her Bible each and every day, first thing in the morning and last thing every night. I admired that, and I thought she was gutsy and cool for professing her faith so openly. It wasn't like she had an easy go of it: One woman on the ward told her to "shut up!" while another called her a "Bible thumper." She was unfazed by their razzing. To tell you the truth, I didn't think of her as depressed at all. In fact, I thought she was quite optimistic. For sure, she was optimistic about God and believed with all her heart that He had a plan for her and her life—even though she was completely baffled by what it was or when it was going to be revealed.

One night, as she was deep in thought while reading, I asked her if she could read out loud. She gladly obliged, saying, "I've just opened to James 1:3–4. It says, 'The testing of your faith develops perseverance. Perseverance must finish its work so that you may be mature and complete, not lacking anything.'" Somehow, the words seemed to really hit home: Could it mean that the ways my life looked like a mess didn't have to mean that I was doomed to failure? Or, could it mean I could use these tough times, and what felt like awful experiences, to deepen my faith, to mature, to regroup, get it together and make something out of myself—still? Whatever the answers to these questions, I found the reading meaningful, soothing and something that left me feeling peaceful. And so her reading to me from the Bible became a daily ritual. Each day she read to me, then she and I would discuss what we each felt was the meaning behind the words. Then we would pray and talk about how the reading applied to each of us in our lives now.

I was so thirsty for hope.

By the fourth day, I no longer felt that my first need was to "get out of this place" but rather to "get well"—or at least to get honest with myself. While Laura had described her life as having little, if any, real significance, the truth was, I also knew the feeling all too well. I, too, had contemplated ending my life—and in fact was killing myself slowly every day with my drinking as well as jeopardizing my life by driving under the influence.

One night, I said I would pick a part and read to her. I flipped open the Bible and read from Philippians 1:20–24, "For I live in eager expectation and hope that I will never do anything that causes me shame, but that I will always be bold for Christ, as I have been in the past, and that my life will always honor Christ, whether I live or die. For to me living is for Christ. I really don't know which is better. I'm torn between two desires: Sometimes I long to go and be with Christ. That would be far better for me, but it is better for you that I live."

Upon hearing these words, Laura began sobbing uncontrollably. I went to her and just hugged her, not knowing what on Earth could have just happened! Finally, she told me her tears were because these words found her heart and had ministered to her "crying soul." Because of the words I had read, Laura said she realized that she could not end her life—and then she vowed to God she never would. After all, if she loved God, then she must choose to live. I was so moved by her realization, and by the fact that it was from the words in the Bible that she had found the answer to address what she was feeling. She was to live. She was to focus on life. "To live" must be her goal.

Luckily, I was beginning to do the same.

Laura's ability to use her faith to touch and heal pain that nothing else could mend or cure was its own "message" and ministered to me. I realized that even though I had considered myself a Christian, I really hadn't been acting like one. Then I met Laura. The Holy Spirit had been with us both during the time we spent together, and for the first time I could feel it. That's when I asked Laura to help me renew my relationship with Christ. With tears of joy, she held my hands and together we asked God to come into my life and make me new. I had found a teacher, willing to help me learn of God's love for me. In her hands, I renewed my faith in God and promised again to walk a Christian life. And so in that moment, I became a born-again Christian.

* * *

Nearly two years have passed. Following my eleven-day stay in the behavioral health-care hospital, I voluntarily entered an in-house, twenty-eight-day, residential drug- and alcohol-treatment program. Following this, I went to live (for eight months) in a women's sober living environment so I could learn new habits to once again live a sober life.

Today, I remain active in working and living a twelve-step program, which includes going to meetings for support from other people who have had drug and alcohol problems, and living my life according to spiritual principles, such as "rigorous honesty," hope, faith, love and courage. For me, this includes staying close to God—praying and meditating and doing what it takes to live in a way that is pleasing to Him and healthy for me. And yes, I am still with my boyfriend, but our relationship, too, has been totally transformed. Actually, I should say that God has transformed our relationship. My boyfriend, too, has accepted Christ into his life. We pray together, attend church together and have a truly magnificent relationship—now that we both serve God before all else.

Several weeks ago, I was attending a church service with Laura, who is now a very dear friend. Upon seeing the two of us laughing and chatting, one person in her congregation remarked, "You two seem like such good friends. How did you meet?" I looked at Laura, and Laura looked at me, and neither of us knew quite what to say! I mean, what would it sound like to say we'd met while sharing a room in a psychiatric ward? After all, the reasons why we ended up there still held some shame for both of us—we were still learning to heal some things. And yet, the hospital had been a turning point for both of us. That's where we'd found each other and helped each other heal some very painful wounds of the heart and soul. And now we felt great depth and admiration for each other.

We didn't want to deny the power of our experience, nor what it had meant and led to—a fuller understanding of God's plan for us—so we were momentarily at a loss for words. Then, as with our instant friendship and with God's "instant" love, we looked at one another and as naturally as if it had been planned,

Laura and I replied in unison, "The Lord introduced us." Smiling at each other, we just left it at that.

And we both knew it was true. God had brought us together. He often sends angels to guide and protect, and to carry His message of love—and sometimes those angels are human: Laura credits me with saving her life! And, of course, she helped me save my own. We are so grateful to and for each other—two friends who believe it is because of the other that God's love became abundant for us once again. And we had each found this love and faith in the arms of a human, albeit a "wounded" angel.

Genta Tyla Murray, 18

A Game of Darts

Dear Grandpa,

Your house is still full of your belongings,
Yet every room just seems cold and bare.
Everything is getting dusty,
It's sad, and it all seems so unfair.

Did you really want to leave here?
It's left this huge, empty hole within in my heart,
Do you still remember all our walks and talks,
And all the times that we played darts?

On those days when I miss you most,
I see you in your house, "putzing" here and there,
Watching TV and eating dinner,
Sitting in your big, old, bad wheelchair.

I prayed to God and told Him,
"God, without him, I just feel so forlorn . . ."
To which He gently answered,
"Blessed are they who mourn" (Matt. 5:4).

But you're gone; I feel lost, not blessed,
So I asked the Lord how this could be,
And God replied so clearly,
"Accept it" and reminded He will comfort me.

And so I sought out His love and comfort,
And saw the blessing in plain sight,
As I saw you now with Jesus,
Full of joy and standing there upright!

I love you so very much,
In fact, with all my heart,
And I wish you were still here,
To talk to and play a game of darts.

Yet, I know you are in heaven,
Movin' around just as you please,
Just knowing that you're happy,
Puts me so much at ease.

So I decided to be grateful
For the awesome memories in my heart,
'Cause now, of course, I know that
You can stand as you play darts!

Jenna Peterson, 14

The "D" Word

I signed out on God when I realized He wasn't going to bail me out of a broken heart. It didn't make much sense for me to suddenly "sign out" right when I needed Him most. But sometimes when you get angry, you get rebellious and do things that don't make sense. That's how I look back on things now.

My rebellion took root one fall night when my parents announced we'd be having a "family meeting" after dinner. When I asked my dad what the meeting was about, he told me it was "to discuss the direction our family was headed." Well, you can see how that only raised more questions for me: Had our parents decided on new responsibilities—chores—for each of us kids? Or had one of them lost their job? Were we going to be moving? I had no idea what to expect out of this mysterious family meeting.

We gathered in the living room—my parents, my little sister and me. I noticed right off that my parents looked uncomfortable. They spoke in strained voices, obviously trying to sound calm—while I tried to figure out just what was going on. Then it came—the "D" word—right from their mouths: DIVORCE. They told us they both loved us very much and not to worry, but that the "D" was "best" for the family. Caught totally unprepared— you might say "blindsided"—my sister burst into tears and ran to her room. As my parents both stared after her, looking torn and hurt, I stood up and, without saying anything, headed to my room as well.

Totally confused, I wondered what would happen to our family now that this "best" decision had been made. I mean, a family was meant to stay together—right? Feeling both dazed and angry, I didn't know what to do. And I wanted to know where God was in all this: I mean, why was He letting our family get torn apart this way? He has the power to do anything—why was He letting this happen to us? Mad and confused, I decided that if God wasn't going to keep us together, then I was going to abandon Him as well.

I certainly knew better than to turn God into my scapegoat. I grew up in a Christian home. My parents took my sister and me to church every Sunday. I was taught that God is always there for us—to comfort and protect. But even though I had all this religious background, suddenly I didn't see God as relevant in changing the crisis going on in my family.

Feeling this way was unsettling, and I began to question things. Had I been taking some things for granted? Maybe the relationship my parents had with God had little to do with me, their son. Maybe *I* didn't really know God on a personal level. I mean, my parents believed in God, and so I found it natural that I did, too. And my parents believed they were going to heaven, so I did as well. But maybe I'd been thinking like a child, and now it was time to grow up—to toughen up.

Grown-up thinking aside, I couldn't fathom having my parents living in separate places. I felt like there was a hole in my life— and in my heart. However, I woke up the next morning— and each morning after that—to discover that the world still kept turning. And so my life went on: I kept up with my schoolwork, played sports, mowed the neighbors' lawns for extra money and spent time in other out-of-school activities. I still went to church—because my parents made me go.

Nearly two years after my parents divorced, I was fairly happy. I was getting decent grades and had great friends. I finally accepted the fact that my life had changed, and that it was okay. My father and mother were each remarried and looked much happier than they'd been when they were together. I was living with my dad, and my mom lived about five minutes away. Whenever I wanted to see my mom or my sister, I would just go over to their house.

But then came the dreadful day when I had to make the decision: My father was moving to another city. This time I had to choose who I would live with on a full-time basis. It was an awful "no-win for anyone" decision.

I chose to live with my dad—which devastated my mom. She was crushed that she didn't get to see me on a daily basis. It was frustrating to realize that there was no way I could make everyone happy—myself included. As I struggled with these feelings, once again I saw little to no evidence that God was there to make things any easier for me.

About a year later, my dad said he and I were going to attend a Christian camp in the mountains. I thought it would be fun, hanging out with my dad, and I was looking forward to sharing "camp life" with him. Little did I know it would be a time when I would finally end my standoff with God.

Talking with a youth counselor one night led to prayer. The result was sudden insight about my struggle over my parents' divorce—and clarity about how wrong I'd been about God abandoning me during this painful time. In fact, God had been there with me through it all. I'd just never asked Him to comfort me and to guide me in the decisions I had to confront. He was with me on those days when I felt angry, lost and confused.

I thought of my favorite story, "Footprints," in which a person who is struggling with a difficult time tells God that he knows God walked with him in daily life (as he could tell by noting that there were two sets of footprints in the sand), but saw only one set of footprints during his times of greatest heartache and pain. So he asks God why He wasn't there for him during these hard times. To this, God replies that the reason he finds only one set of footprints in the difficult times is that at such a time, the Lord was *carrying* him. In that moment, I realized God's "carrying me" is a promise: "I have made you, and I will carry you; I will sustain you, and I will rescue you" (Isa. 46:4). All I had to do was seek Him out.

I recommitted my life to Christ that evening. As a result, the hole I'd felt in my heart is now filled with love and forgiveness, and the relationship I have with God is a personal one. I can trust that God is with me every step of the way—in good times and in tough times. Now when I confront a problem or challenge that seems big or overwhelming, I don't turn from God, but rather to Him.

Kyle Leroux, 17

What's the Worst Name You Were Ever Called?

What's the worse name you've ever been called? For me, of all things, it was "little Christian girl." It wasn't really the words themselves that hurt; it was the intention of the person saying them. I worked at a frozen yogurt shop after school. I liked working there. The people who came in were really nice, and it was a cool place: The shop had a little reading corner so people could come to hang out for a while. And I made some pretty good tips. There was one problem, though: Blaine, who happened to be the "twenty-something" manager.

For some reason, Blaine really seemed to get satisfaction out of making fun of my being a Christian. "Hey, little Christian girl, anything exciting going on in your life?" was one of his standard greetings, always asked in a mocking sort of way. Always it was, "little Christian girl" this or "little Christian girl" that. I found it insulting and upsetting.

The shop was usually very busy, and this one day was no different. "I think I'll have a strawberry smoothie," the nice, attractive guy ordered with a smile. "Okay," I said. He was a regular customer, and something about him always just seemed to shine. As I made his smoothie, we were hit with a whirl of customers. Noticing, Blaine looked around and in a really loud voice blurted, "Where's God when you *really* need Him?"

On this day, the comment was just too much. Nearly in tears, I silently prayed, *God, please tell me the right words to say to get this guy to back down, cause I'm about ready to quit, and I really need this job.* Going about helping customers, I wondered why I let the manager's words get to me. Solutions came to mind: I could do everything from politely asking him to knock it off to asking him why he felt so threatened by my faith. I could even simply decide it wasn't so awful to be called a "little Christian girl."

It was also the moment I remembered that Jesus promises us

the right words when we are being persecuted because of our faith: "Do not worry about what to say or how to say it. At that time you will be given what to say, for it will not be you speaking, but the Spirit of your Father speaking through you" (Matt. 10:19–20). And that's what seemed to happen in that moment. Sounding pretty cool and collected, I retorted, "Well, sometimes God gets real busy, and you just have to depend on one of His 'little Christian girls'!" Looking shocked that I'd have a comeback—my first to him—Blaine said nothing.

It's been three months since I issued that little retort and you know, he hasn't bugged me since! It just goes to show you that God answers prayers and even shows us the way to the right words at the right time.

Samantha Long, 16

Dropping the Act

When a person goes to a Christian school, there is a tendency to automatically think of that person in a certain way—for example, that each and every student is a born-again Christian. This assumption is followed by then scrutinizing each student's every move, as though to catch them doing something that somehow is less than "Christian"—which then is followed by the typical, "So you think you're a Christian. Well, you sure don't act like one!" I think it's really unfair to label each other, because I firmly believe it's each person's job to seek out and find his or her way to a personal relationship with God. One of the reasons I'm so adamant about this is, first, because I see it happening all the time, and second, because it recently happened to me.

Only I was the one who had judged myself!

I attend a Christian school and was open and accepting of the importance of God in our lives. I did all of the things I was supposed to do. During chapel I closed my eyes during worship, and sometimes I even prayed in class. I talked about my "relationship" with God at Bible study and went to youth group on a regular basis. By all appearances, I was a "Christian."

But I was leading a double life. Inside I felt mass confusion. I mean, what did I believe, really? I was so filled with questions and doubts, so churning with emotions. Unfortunately, because I'd set myself up as someone who was "mature" in her faith, I didn't think that I could turn to anyone for help in sorting out my doubts and ambivalence—feelings that were beginning to come at me in giant waves.

I had no idea what to do, so I just tried to accept these conflicting sides—the "already a Christian" with the real fear of turning over my will to God. I thought that if I could just keep up "the act," eventually I'd get things figured out. *You're in control; it'll be okay,* I kept saying to myself. Of course, it's completely exhausting to worry constantly about keeping everything in check. It wears you down emotionally. Still, I was doing pretty well at it (or so I thought!).

You know, sometimes it takes being completely ripped from your comfort zone to realize you are utterly lost.

This stark realization hit me when I attended a Christian youth camp. At first I thought attending was yet another obligatory thing to do—although I was looking forward to checking out the guys! I was quite sure I'd be hearing the same things I had heard a thousand times in chapel, so I wasn't about to make any changes. I mean, my life was good: I was in control! And besides, whenever I heard a youth counselor say, "Just give it all to God," well, that completely terrified me. Letting go of my control over the situation could only mean disaster. Relinquishing my power to God would only mean I'd no longer be in control of my life, right? It was up to me to keep it all together; this was my job, not God's.

So I entered chapel intent on checking out the guys. Wouldn't you know the topic was on my biggest fear: control! The speaker was wonderful, and the presentation was powerful, one that zeroed right in on my fears and spoke to my heart. Paying attention and "getting the message," I realized my life wasn't all that great, and that I really wasn't in control no matter how much I tried to kid myself into thinking I was. I was holding on to negative emotions: I was angry. I was bitter. I was way too young to be as tired as I was. I put way too much pressure on myself, and no, I couldn't fix it all myself. I did need to let God take some of my burdens. I did need His help.

When the speaker read 2 Chron. 20:20: "Have faith in the Lord your God and you will be upheld," I knew it was time to turn my life over to God for real.

Those who wanted to rededicate their lives to Christ were called to stand up. With my heart racing, palms sweating and tears streaming down my face, I stood. My confidence wavered for a moment, and a panic swept over me. For the first time, I had put down the mask. I needed Him in my life. This time I sincerely wanted God to walk with me and to guide me. I wanted a real "walk" with Him.

Now with God in my life, my life is more real. I feel at peace. I'm no longer living a double life, no longer doing my balancing act. I don't pretend to be. By allowing God to reign first and foremost in my life, the choices and decisions I need to make are easy. I now know that God is in control, and everything is part of *His* divine balancing act. Now, for real, I stand firmly rooted in my faith, feeling and reflecting the perfect will of God. There are no longer two of me. Feeling in harmony with my life and the "who I am" is a most loving and peaceful feeling. And that's what it feels like to "walk" with God—loving, peaceful, being whole.

Kelly Chakeen, 16

An Ice Cube Sits Home Alone on Saturday Nights

"I'm so tired of not having a boyfriend!" I told my best friend Mariah when we were hanging out at my house on a Saturday afternoon. As usual, she had a date for Saturday night—and for the upcoming school dance, and for the prom—although it was over three months away. Not me: I'd be sitting home this Saturday night. As for the dance in a couple of weeks, well, no doubt I'd be going with friends who themselves didn't have a date—translated: couldn't find a date! Once there, I'd be standing with the group also without dates, just hoping someone (but not a nerd!) would ask me to dance so I didn't look like the wall-flower I was. As for the prom, well, if things kept going as they had been like last year, I'd be stressing over it for months, and then, the actual week of the prom, go into the usual panic of hoping and praying I'd be asked. If this year were a repeat performance of last year, then there was the chance of being asked at the last minute by one of the few guys in the school who couldn't get a date with anyone else. Can you relate? Well, I'm a junior, and I'm pretty tired of things being this way. "Why doesn't anyone cool want to date me, Mariah? What's so *wrong* with me?"

"Easy to answer, my friend," Mariah replied. "It's because you look too conservative, you know, like you're not much fun. You're really nice, smart and pretty and all, but you need to send some signals that you're interested and available. The way you dress, for example, says 'I'm untouchable.'" Then Mariah added, "An ice cube sits home alone on Saturday nights."

"Do you mean to tell me you're having sex with Scott?"

"Mmmm."

"I'm totally shocked! I guess I always thought it was a big deal, something special to save for the guy I marry. Am I that out of it?"

Casually, my friend replied, "C'mon, Kristen. Everyone is doing it; you know they are."

I was shocked at my friend having sex with a guy she'd been dating for less than a month. The next week at school, I looked around more closely and watched the other girls and guys interact. It was true—most of the girls did dress in much more revealing clothes than me. And the guys did seem to give those girls the most attention. Maybe some change was in order. So the next weekend, I went through some old clothes and found some tops that I had thought were too tight and decided to change my looks. The following school day, I wore my new "getup," applying more mascara and eye shadow than I usually wear. Looking in the mirror, I thought, *Good-bye, ice cube! Hello, boyfriend!*

My new look didn't go unnoticed. For months, I'd had a crush on Kyle, who sat next to me in algebra, but he never seemed to notice me. That morning, when I sat down next to him, he took one look and said, "Hey, looking *goooood* today!" All during class, I could see out of the corner of my eye that he kept looking at me. When the bell rang, he made a point of catching up with me, then walked me halfway down the hall to my next class. To make a long story short, by Thursday we had a date for the upcoming dance!

Once at the dance, held in the gym at our school, we danced, dropped by the snack table and danced some more. As the evening progressed, Kyle was holding me closer and closer. I wrapped my arms around him and placed my face up against his neck. I could tell he liked it. Finally, he said, "Let's go out for some fresh air." I followed as he held my hand and led the way out the door, through the parking lot to his car. "Are we leaving so soon?" I asked, to which he said nothing, pulled me close and kissed me—again and again. Within minutes, Kyle was getting carried away, and I could tell he thought that having sex was inevitable!

I was scared, not only because I'd never had sex, but because I truly did want to save it for the man I married. But here I was struggling with Kyle as he tried to unzip my dress. It was a panicky moment, and I wondered what I should do. I mean, I did want Kyle for a boyfriend, and I remembered Mariah's words, ". . . an ice cube sits home . . ." And then I remembered our youth pastor who had cautioned "not to give away in the backseat of a car what God intended to be beautiful and special, an act of love between a husband and wife," and his question, "What do you want—sex, or love?" To this he had followed up with the Scripture: "Serve him with all faithfulness. . . . Choose this day who you will serve" (Josh. 24: 14–15).

"Kyle, stop," I said firmly. When he didn't, I pushed him off.

"You can't stop now!" he said, obviously irritated with me.

"I can't do this," I said. "I thought I could, but I just can't. I'm sorry." I felt embarrassed and guilty, and I was starting to cry.

Kyle was clearly surprised. "Okay, Snow White. If that's what you want, I'm taking you home." With these words, he started the car. When he pulled up in front of my house, I reached for the door and started to get out. "Kristen, wait," Kyle said as he gently took hold of my arm. "I've been thinking about what you said on the way here, especially about my not being interested in you as a person, and that sex was all I wanted. I *am* interested in you. I've liked you for a long time. I was so happy that we went out tonight, and I guess my expectations were way off base, but the way you were dressing this week and acting tonight, well, I thought you expected me to make a move on you."

His words caught me by surprise, so I admitted that I'd taken some very bad advice and tried to be something I'm not. "Can we start all over?" he asked.

"I'd really like that," I told him, feeling so relieved. "But, Kyle, you need to know right up front that I want to do what I believe is right. I'm not ready for sex. I mean, I could give you a lot of reasons: I'm not going to be used, and I'm not going to risk getting pregnant or being exposed to AIDS and other diseases, but quite honestly, my first reason is that I want to save sex for someone I love and wish to marry. If that sounds old-fashioned or prudish, then that's the way it has to be."

"I'm sorry for the way I behaved tonight," Kyle said, adding, "What do you say we go to church together in the morning and start this relationship again—and invite God to be in it with us?"

"That would be so perfect," I said, feeling like a ton of bricks had been lifted from my shoulders. Kyle walked me to the door, and we wrapped our arms around each other and hugged for a very long time. It was very special, and it wasn't about sex! It was an important date; I learned so much. I made a decision never again to compromise what I knew to be right for the sake of impressing someone. What could be emptier?

That was over a year ago, and Kyle and I still have something beautiful together. We hold hands as we walk to class together. We go to school games together, to an occasional movie on Saturday night and, of course, to church. Kyle is not only my boyfriend; he's my best friend. When we're together, we talk about things that are important, and share our dreams as well as our fears. I can tell him anything, and he understands. I try to understand him as well. I love him with all my heart.

Will we get married? Maybe. Maybe not. I hope so—but it's not something I know for certain. We have high school to finish and four years of college ahead, so who knows? What I do know for certain is that whether we marry each other or someone else, I intend to make sex as special and sacred as God intended it to be.

Kristen Cartwright, 17

Her Diary . . . My Diary

I was sitting at my computer, busy typing away to my "instant message buddies," something I love to do, when the phone rang. "Mandy . . ." my dad said, his voice shaking. I intuitively knew something was wrong. He continued, "Honey, I need you to be strong . . . Mom's been in a car accident. . . ." Now crying, he added, "Honey, we've lost her."

I was stunned. I was just with her . . . only moments ago.

I totally freaked out. "It's NOT TRUE!" I screamed, my heart exploding in pain. "She left this house just minutes ago—just minutes ago I was with her!" I dropped the phone and sobbed, remembering how she had asked me if I wanted to ride along to go pick my brother up from school. *I should have gone,* I thought. *I could have watched out for her.* But instead, I had told her "no" so that I could go on-line.

My mother gone? How could that be? I walked around the house, just numb. It all seemed surreal—and there was absolutely NOTHING I could do to change her fate. I yelled at God for *what He had done.* "WHY, GOD?" I screamed as loud as I could. "WHY? WHY?" Filled with rage, I opened the door to the hallway and at the top of my lungs yelled, "I HATE YOU SO MUCH, GOD! I HATE YOU!" The silence following my screams was huge and offered no consolation, so I went back inside to sit alone with my shattered heart.

Restless and aching, I went to the kitchen. She'd just taken things out for dinner. Her raspberry shake was right where she just left it. My mother: She was never coming home. She'd just turned out of our driveway on her way to the middle school to get my little brother. It was all routine, something she did every day. But this day, an eighteen-wheeler clipped her. How scared she must have been. The last things she must have seen were those lights. Her last thought had to be "I love my kids." She was such a mother. She wanted everything for us. "You're going to miss my sister's wedding," I said crying, and then thought of the million other things she would miss . . . like us and her grandchildren. She loved us kids and was really looking forward to, as she said, "getting old with dad and being a grandma." She'll never have that.

And we'll never have her.

My mother died eight days ago in a fatal car crash.

When people say your life can change in a second, they're right. Nothing is the same without her. At school I keep thinking, *Oh, I have to call Mom and tell her about this, or tell her about that.* But as soon as the thought appears, it's shadowed by the memory that I can never again call her cell phone and just blab about my day. I always told her, "I'm your diary, and you're mine." Our relationship was that close. We told each other everything. We were so much alike. We had the same personality. She was forty-six and so young at heart. She was just amazing. And now she's gone. I feel so sorry for everyone who knew her and now will be without her. But mostly I feel sorry for myself. I ache for her.

Sometimes I think this cannot be real. I go over things a hundred times—especially the day she was killed. She'd picked me up early that day from school for an eye doctor's appointment. She ordered glasses for me. We'd stopped for a hamburger on the way home. When I got out of the car, she told me she loved me. I said I loved her, too, and she said, "I'll be back soon." Those words keep running through my head, *I'll be back soon.* Then she left to pick up my little brother.

I spoke at her memorial service. I know she would have wanted that. I shared a poem that I had read to her on a family trip. She had told me, "If I ever go, I want that read." She liked it because I told her it reminded me of her. It was called a "Clown's Prayer." Tears fell the whole time.

I'm sure Mom gives God a lot of smiles. She made you laugh when your day was bad; she always had a positive word to say.

I think my older brother Robert said it best: "She made miracles happen." She was just so amazing; I'm so sad she's not here. My heart will always cry for her. She was my momma.

That I have to live my life without her seems so unfair. Even so, I'm not mad at God anymore. I can't afford to be. Without His comfort—and knowing that my mother is with Him now—I wouldn't even get out of bed in the morning. In 2 Corinthians 1:3–4 it says God is, "The Father of compassion and the God of all comfort, who comforts us in all our troubles, so that we can comfort those in any trouble with the comfort we ourselves have received from God."

God has been all this for me, comforting me and reassuring me. Right after the funeral, sitting in a daze on the couch at my grandma's house, I felt something in my pocket poking me. I reached in and pulled out a handful of stickers—the ones my mother and I had fished from the bowl at the eye doctor's office. We kept looking for a hippo sticker, since her favorite animal was the hippo. So I sat there again going through all the stickers, and I found one with a hippo on it. I smiled, because right at that moment I felt she was there. It might not be a billboard of a sign, but to me it was a sticker of a sign—sort of a quick mental e-mail from her and God. It gave me great comfort. God and Mom were telling me she was all right.

I don't fear death as much anymore. I know that Mom is in heaven and that when I get there, she'll be standing with her arms open to me. I can just see it now as she says, "It's Mandy, my Moony." (Moony is her special nickname for me.)

The other night I prayed to God, telling Him I was sorry for saying I hated Him. I take some comfort in thinking that Mom died because in God's eyes, her duties on Earth were finished, and it's now her time to start her new life in heaven. My dad says, "One day, we'll all be together again." God allows me to find great comfort in that thought, too. My goal is to write a book and name it after her. It will be my special tribute to her.

Oh, but Mom, I just miss you so much! I'm so thankful that we loved and enjoyed each other so much. I promise to love God the way you loved Him; and I promise to make you proud of me. You were such a loving woman; you were so loving to me, and I adored you. It's going to be hard without you, Mom, but I will do the best I can. I won't give up. I know how to do things because you did. You lived and loved every day. And so I will try to do the same. I love you, Mom.

Your Moony
—Mandy Martinez, 18

Clown's Prayer

Dear Lord, as I stumble through this life
help me to create more laughter than tears,
Dispense more happiness than gloom,
Spread more cheer than despair.
Never let me become so blasé that
I fail to see the wonder in the eyes of a child,
Or a twinkle in the eyes of the aged.

Never let me forget my work
Is to cheer people,
Make them happy, make them laugh,
Make them forget at least for a moment
The unpleasantness in their life.
Never let me acquire success to the point
That I discontinue calling on my Creator
In the hour of need,
Acknowledging and thanking Him
In the hour of plenty.

Chasing the Wind

When I first met Jennifer Holton as a college freshman, she seemed like an ordinary girl—with two exceptions. First, she was just exciting—such a happy person, and you could tell her happiness was real. She was high energy personified, and yet, she had an amazing calm. Just being in her presence was to feel complete and total acceptance. She had a way of allowing the spotlight to just be yours and yours alone. It was an interesting— and totally awesome—feeling. The second exception: Among her books, she always carried a Bible.

I didn't really know any religious people, but everything she said was inspiring. She gave credit for everything good in her life to God. And everything it seemed was in "good hands" because of God. She had a really clean and clear sense of direction for who she was and what she stood for. It was refreshing.

I liked her the moment I met her. She was in three of my classes. One day a class was canceled, so we decided to go to the student center to hang out until the next class. We talked about a lot of things—which was another thing I liked about her. She was easy to talk to and such a good listener. And she was excited about a lot of things: life in general, her life, and overall, I guess you could say it was sort of an "Isn't it just great to be alive!" attitude. She genuinely respected people and didn't have a bad word to say about anyone. Once I'd made a snide remark about a guy who was running for a campus student office (I thought the guy was a total jerk) and she commented, "He's just forgotten who he is, and is feeling lost and confused at the moment. Hopefully he'll talk with God and straighten himself out. The rest of us need to keep him in our prayers." One of my favorite phrases is "be proactive!" and I liked the way she'd held all of us accountable on his behalf.

Once she'd commented, "Each soul is in search of God, even if at first it doesn't seem that way." I found that interesting, too. I know I was in search of something, but I hadn't a clue what that might be. I mean, I had goals and all, but still, where was I going and why and so what? I was secretly haunted by what I saw as many people's lives (much like my own) resembling a big ant colony, whereby everyone was constantly in motion and really busy working hard. But did it make for personal happiness and joy and excitement? I wasn't so sure it did. I remember my high-school years when teachers were so dead-serious about grades as the be-all and end-all—as though the main purpose of life was to study, study, study—so you could get into college, where you stepped onto the treadmill to do it all yet again. Then after college everyone was to happily join the "rat race" where once again the cutthroat competition was on. It all looked like the ant colony way of life to me. Having met Jennifer, I now wondered, would I feel different having God in my life?

I knew I had a thirsty spirit, but I never considered that God could quench whatever it was I needed. If anything, I'd purposely kept my distance from God because I thought Christianity would be boring, and that I'd have to hang out with dull people. And I knew that I didn't want to surrender to anyone or have to live by "church rules." I mean, I'd been told that the goal of independence from parents and growing up was to "find yourself" and "own yourself"—as opposed to turning over control. And I was looking forward to getting to the point where I could "party hardy," even though my friends who did seemed rather shallow. Still, there was that nagging emptiness, a jaded feeling of "been-there, done-that" about my life—and I hadn't even turned nineteen.

As though my own identity crisis wasn't enough, Jennifer—with all her enthusiasm and joy—contradicted my image of a "Christian" and added to my turmoil. Jennifer was fun and exciting and joyous. No wallflower, she was a "step-up-to-the-plate" and get-involved sort of girl. Her brand of purpose and passion was cool, "totally cool" in fact, and I wanted to have it as my own. I wanted to see life and live life with her outlook and optimism. I wanted to look boldly into the face of the world as she did.

One day we got to talking about my feelings, and she read me a verse from Ecclesiastes: "When I surveyed all that my hands had done and what I had toiled to achieve, everything was meaningless, a vanity, a chasing after the wind; . . . Therefore I hated life . . . All of it was meaningless . . . a chasing after the wind" (2:11, 17). The message in those words was precisely what I was feeling. "The master key," she counseled, "is to synchronize your life with God's will." I knew she was right. On that day, I asked Jesus Christ to come into my heart and be the Lord of my life that I might be filled with the glory of the Holy Spirit. I can tell you firsthand that living in sync with God's will is a mighty powerful way to live.

The next year, Jennifer left to attend college in another state, one with a curriculum that was stronger in the field in which she wanted to major. We hugged, we prayed and we said our good byes. We still keep in touch by snail mail and phone calls, but I do miss her beautiful Christian presence, although I've since met and made many other great friends who love the Lord. But I'll always be thankful to this Christian sister who, in addition to helping me dispel my notion of a Christian walk as being dull, boring and constraining, helped me to stop "chasing the wind." I now know that to be a Christian is to have your life and its importance in perfect harmony with God's will. The result is clarity, the greatest surge of energy imaginable and a happiness so pure you can hardly describe it—although you really don't have to. Just as I had with Jennifer, others readily see it and feel it. Is it what you want, too? If you feel like you're ready to stop "chasing the wind," just ask God into your life. If you want to live life with the fullest sense of *everything*, if you want to live life boldly, all you have to do is allow your heart to beat in sync with God's.

Tom Reiner, 20

Doomed to Hicksville

Eight years ago, my mom married a guy named Jesse. What a disaster—especially for me!

I don't fault her, because since my real dad left when I was two, she'd been trying to support both of us alone for six years. Personally, I think she married Jesse mostly so I'd have a dad and she'd have someone to help support us. HA! What a joke that turned out to be! He couldn't—actually, it was more like wouldn't—hold a job. He couldn't get along with anybody for very long—including me. Make that, *especially* me!

Mom and Jesse had two kids together. Jesse enjoyed them, but he hated me. The older I got, the more open his hostility became. If he could make me miserable, he did. One night at dinner, I absently put my elbows beside my plate. Suddenly, he stood up, reached across the table, drew back and knocked my elbows away with such force that my plate hit the floor as I feli backward. "Pick it up!" he yelled. "That'll teach you to have some manners at my table!"

When he was drunk, it was worse. It wasn't long before I was staying away from home as much as I could. Of course, having the bad attitude I did, the friends who would accept me were the tough kids. I liked them. They had an attitude, too—a look that communicated, "Don't mess with me." We all bought our clothes at the Salvation Army—the goal being a grunge look. I dyed my hair red and cut it myself so that it stuck up in a homemade spike, my attempt at high style. I earned my own money by cleaning house for the lady next door.

My new attitude was not wasted on Jesse. As I reached official teenager status, I perfected my "I'm-bored-with-you-and-this-conversation" look. When Jesse would go off, I knew better than to be mouthy, so I'd roll my eyes and retreat to my room, leaving him to yell at my closed door.

Then everything came to a head one night when Jesse came

home drunk yet again. Mom and the kids had already gone to bed, and I was up watching TV alone. He came through the door, walked straight to the TV and changed the channel. "Could you wait just a minute?" I asked as politely as I could manage. "Then my show will be over."

"No!" he screamed back. "I won't wait just a minute, so get up off your lazy butt and fix me something to eat!"

"Fix it yourself," I shot back as I headed for my room. But I never got there. He grabbed me by the arm and hit me across the face so hard that I sailed across the room into the cupboards. From the bedroom, Mom heard the disturbance and, just as he reached me and raised his fist for another blow, she appeared in the doorway screaming at him to stop.

"I want her out of here!" he bellowed. "Tomorrow, she's gone! It's either her or me!"

Mom chose Jesse.

The next day I was put on a bus to North Carolina to live with my grandmother. Mom and I drove to the bus depot in silence, but when she put me on the bus, she hugged me. "I'm sorry, honey, I really am. It's just that he's so irrational that I can't reason with him." There were tears in her eyes as she tried to convince me. "You don't want to have to live with him—it's not good for you, either." Then it seemed to me she was trying to convince herself as she added, "And I have to think about the younger kids; they love their father, and I don't know how I'd support them without his help. You understand, don't you? I think he'll be easier for everyone else to deal with if he doesn't have you to blame his anger on." At that point I wanted to scoff out loud, but I just maintained my supremely disinterested silence. "I just know you'll be so much better off with Grandma."

"Whatever," I mumbled and rolled my eyes in boredom. My sense of pride wouldn't let me show her that my heart was breaking. Oh, I was relieved not to have to deal with Jesse, but to have my mom choose that scumbag over me—how could that be? I turned and boarded the bus and found a seat next to the window. *My life is over,* I thought. *Nobody wants me, not even my parents! If my own mother doesn't even love me, then who could? I'm a failure. A loser. Grandma has to take me in because Mom doesn't want me.*

Twenty-some hours later, I arrived in Jacksonville, North Carolina, and as we pulled into the parking lot, I saw Grandma waiting, eager to welcome me. She was tiny—maybe 100 pounds—with salt-and-pepper hair and a twinkle in her eyes. Mom looked like a younger version of Grandma, only without the twinkle. As I stepped down, Grandma rushed over to greet me. She wrapped her arms around me and hugged me with more force than I thought her frail frame could possibly manufacture. I stood stiff, feeling awkward. I hadn't seen her in five years and didn't care to be hugged. When I'd had all I could stand, coolly but gently, I kind of pushed her off. "I guess I'm a little exuberant," she responded a bit apologetically. "Oh, I'm so glad you're here, Carla! Look at how you've grown! But how are you? How was your trip? You must be exhausted! Let's get your suitcases. How is your mom? You can tell me all about it on the way home!" *A little exuberant?* I thought, as she chirped from one question to the next. *Now that's an understatement.*

In the car, I was silent. Fighting tears, I gazed out the window at the unfamiliar town that was to become home and listened to this woman with whom I was to live as she rattled on and on and on in an endless recitation of information I was too apathetic to care about. "Now you'll start school tomorrow," she informed me with far more merriment than I felt. "You're really going to like our school. He knows you're coming. He's going to have your schedule all ready for you; he said we could get your records later. And there's this lovely little girl who lives just across the street. Her name is Melissa, and she's just so thrilled you're going to be her neighbor. She's going to come over in the morning and walk to school with you and introduce you to her friends and show you where everything is. Won't that just be lovely?" She looked at me with excited anticipation.

"Yeah, lovely," I muttered, thinking, *This woman is clueless.* I wished I'd stayed on the bus and gotten off in some other city.

Sure enough, bright and early the next morning, I heard the doorbell ring. I was sitting at the kitchen table eating the eggs and biscuits Grandma had fixed me (even feeling as miserable as I was, I had to admit that they were sooooo good!), and in rushed this cutesy little feminine thing who looked like she'd just swallowed a lightbulb. "Hi! I'm Melissa!" she bubbled. She was wearing a white sweater with a red, white and blue scarf around her neck, tailored navy blue slacks, blue socks, pink and blue sparkly shoelaces and a flag beret in her hair. *I've died and gone to Hicksville,* I thought. *What has she got to be so happy about?*

As we walked to school, we must have been quite a pair. Melissa looking like she was the cover girl for Nerds-on-Parade, and me Miss Salvation Army with my spiked red hair. She chattered happily as we walked to school—evidently not noticing how different we were or that I wasn't terribly responsive to her questions. So as not to be completely rude, I smiled stiffly from time to time, but said nothing. Finally, she asked, "How old are you?"

"Fifteen."

"Oh, good! Then you're a sophomore like me!"

"No, freshman. I got held back a year because my mom and stepdad moved around so much."

"Oh, that's okay," she assured me in her ever-positive tone. "There are some really nice people in the freshman class. You'll have lots of friends. And you can always hang out with us. It doesn't matter what grade you're in here. The school is so small that everybody is friends with everybody."

Just when I was thinking things couldn't get any worse, they did! When we walked onto the campus, I didn't see anyone who was remotely dressed like me. *As usual,* I thought, *I'm a misfit.*

The other kids eyed me suspiciously as Melissa stopped and introduced me to three or four groups of people, as well as to her best friends. Everyone was dressed much like her. After we picked up my schedule from the office, Melissa showed me the layout of the school and walked me to my first period class— Algebra I. "Oh, look, you've got Mrs. Campbell. You're just going to love her. She was one of my favorite teachers last year." *Why didn't that surprise me?* "She's tough, but fair," Melissa went on brightly. "And for English you've got Mr. Evans. He doesn't smile a lot; I think he's afraid that if he does, we'll get out of control. But he's nice, too, in his own way."

Doesn't she know I don't care? I wondered. *I'm not here to learn anything or have fun; I'm only here because I have to be. Teachers are all alike. They're only here to torture us with homework and term papers and tests and constant demands that we be quiet.*

"Well, here we are!" she was still smiling. "Now, you know how to get to your other morning classes? Come sit with us at lunchtime. We'll be over by the trees in the quad."

"See ya," I mumbled as I retreated into the classroom. Kids were milling around the room, some chatting, and some obviously trying to finish their homework. When I walked in, they all stopped and stared. I walked to the back and flopped down in a desk in the corner, keeping my eyes down. In a few minutes, I saw a pair of dirty tennis shoes beside my desk. When I looked up, it was like looking in a mirror. *Yeah! Someone like me!*

Her name was Denise, and by lunchtime she and I were fast friends. She introduced me to the other kids she hung out with. As my new friends and I were crossing the quad, Melissa came running over. "Are you going to eat lunch with us? We saved you a spot. How was your morning?"

"No, I'm going to eat with Denise," I replied, without offering a smile, explanation or apology. Then I turned quickly and walked away. "That girl lives across the street from Grandma," I explained to Denise. "She kind of gets on my nerves."

"No kidding!" Denise agreed. "What a goody-two-shoes."

That afternoon I rushed away from school, trying to get home ahead of Melissa. But she saw me and raced to catch up. "Hey, how was your day? How'd you like Mrs. Campbell? And Mr. Evans? We missed you at lunch. I wanted you to get to know my friends." Evidently, she didn't notice I wasn't answering. "Maybe you can come to youth group with me at church Wednesday night. Most of my same friends from school are in it. We have a great time. Your grandma goes to the same church, but then you probably knew that already."

"Uh, yeah, maybe," I said to get her off my case. I wasn't about to go with her to any youth group. Mom used to take me to church before she and Jesse got married. I remembered some of the stories about how God created the world, about Noah and the flood, about Jonah and the whale. I used to love those stories, but obviously that God stuff was for kids. I certainly couldn't see any evidence that there was a God from my own experiences.

On Wednesday, Melissa again invited me to youth group, but I made up the excuse that I had a test the next day. It was a total lie. On Sunday, Grandma informed me that we were going to church, so I went dutifully along. I listened cynically as the minister talked about how God heals our hearts and lives. He read from Jeremiah 31:30: "For I will turn their mourning to dancing, will comfort them, and make them rejoice rather than sorrow." *Yeah, sure,* I thought to myself. Certainly, God could never heal a heart and life as broken as my own. In spite of myself, I enjoyed the music. There was actually a band with drums, and some of the people clapped in rhythm. I saw lots of smiling faces, and when Grandma introduced me to her friends, I saw their eyes do an involuntary once-over, but they tried to hide their disapproval and were polite. I was out of place, and I knew it. What a relief when, at last, it was time to get out of there!

I made excuses not to walk to school with Melissa and not to eat lunch with her, and I always tried to avoid walking home with her. But she just wouldn't take the hint! What's more, she persisted in inviting me to that youth group of hers and its string of activities. I wasn't about to go near there. No way. Church on Sunday was bad enough. After a while, I stooped to practically being rude to Melissa. Sometimes I could tell by the look on her face that I'd hurt her, but still she came back to visit and tried to walk with me to and from school every day.

One day after a couple of months, she waited for me to walk home with her. It was impossible not to like her, but I was still afraid of her "churchiness." "I've got an English test tomorrow," I told her. "On *The Red Badge of Courage*. Most boring book I've ever tried to read. I don't get it. I'll probably flunk the test."

"Oh, I read that last year," Melissa offered. "At first I didn't like it either, but then I caught on. How about if I come over tonight and help you study?"

"You'd do that?" I asked. "Why?"

"Because you're my friend, and I'd like to help you. I'll be over after dinner."

Melissa appeared right on schedule with a well-marked paperback copy of *Red Badge*. We sat down on my bed. "I'm so lost," I admitted. "I think this is the Civil War, but I can't tell where the battles are or who's winning or losing."

"You're right," Melissa began, "it is the Civil War, but that doesn't matter. What you have to understand is that the real war is not between the North and the South; the real conflict is the one in Henry's mind. Before the battle, he wonders if he will stay and fight like a man or run like a coward. He's never been there before, so Crane says he's 'an untried quantity.' When firing starts, he runs, then, when he's trying to get back to his regiment, he grabs onto another soldier seeking information and won't turn loose, so the soldier clobbers him on the head. Later, Henry's battalion thinks he sustained a 'red badge of courage' in the battle, but Henry knows the truth about himself. He's wearing a mask—looking brave on the outside but being scared to death on the inside that everyone will know he's a failure and a phony."

"Oh, I get it. He's doing a cover-up. He wants to be seen as brave, but really he's scared."

"Right on," Melissa said. And then she added, "May I say something?"

"Like you'd take no for an answer?" She laughed politely and then, choosing her words carefully, said, "Maybe you're sort of like Henry. I think maybe you're scared on the inside and afraid to let people see in."

I squirmed. "Why would you say that?"

"Because you act all tough and hard, and you don't want to be seen with me and my friends because someone might think you're like us—which isn't all that bad. We're happy, that's all. We don't have anything to prove. Of course, I'm only guessing here, but my sense is that you're not all tough- -that maybe that wall you've built around yourself is because you've been hurt and afraid you may be again."

I couldn't argue with her theory or deny that it was true. "Why did you come over here tonight to help me?" I asked. "You've been nothing but nice to me, but I've been nothing but rude and mean to you. Why don't you just give up?"

"Because I think you're worth my trouble," she said evenly. "And I don't know how many people have ever told you they love you, but God loves you, and your grandma cares a great deal about you—that's easy enough to see. And I care about you."

Without warning, tears began to pour out of my eyes. "I don't feel very lovable," I choked. "You and your friends are way too nice, and I just knew you guys wouldn't like me when you got to know me. I had to be the one to reject you—before you could reject me."

"I'm never going to reject you," she promised. "How about going to youth group with me Wednesday night?" With tears falling, I laughed. "You just don't give up, do you?"

I did go to youth group the next Wednesday night. All the kids there were very nice to me. At first all the hugging made me uncomfortable, but after a few weeks I was hugging with the best of them. It actually felt good. Melissa and the youth group were God's arms of love wrapping around me. And through their acceptance, I came to believe that God loves me, and that He will never abandon me or send me away or let me down. I now know that I am loved and cherished by the real Father—the God of the universe. When I accepted His son as my Savior, He turned my "mourning into dancing." What a powerful embrace! What unconditional love!

I remember how my mother hugged me before I climbed on the bus that day, and she said she "just knew I'd be so much better off with my grandmother." Neither she nor I ever could have realized just how true her words were. It was because of my trip to "Hicksville" that I'd come to know God and became the happy and content person I am. I have no idea what will become of my relationship with my stepfather, so for now I just leave it up to God. I have a close relationship with my mother and grandmother, and I have real friends who accept me unconditionally. All have given me the courage to give up my "red badge of courage" act. I've traded it in (that, my spiked hair and my "I'm-tough" attitude) for a life filled with lasting love and real happiness.

Carla Davis, 16

Religiously Looking

I've always been curious about how (or if) God would find His way into my life. Our family doesn't go to church, and while my parents taught me right from wrong, they never use the word God or refer to any religious rules to teach me those things. Nor have they ever said that it was important to have what my good friend Melannie calls a "personal relationship with God." I've asked my parents what religion we are, and they say we don't have one, although my mom said her family used to go to an Evangelical Lutheran church once in a while when she was growing up.

So most of what I know about religion comes from my friends, but I'd have to admit, talking with them raises more questions than answers. I have friends who are both Catholic and Protestant. One of my friends and his parents are Native American, and they go to a sweat lodge and sacred dances. Another one of my friends is Jewish, and he and his family go to temple every Saturday. Yet another one of my friends is Muslim and worships at a mosque. I even have a friend whose family is from Vietnam, and they are practicing Buddhists. Having friends who believe in different religions makes me wonder how many religions there are in the first place, and then I wonder how they are alike, and how they differ from each other. Last month, I was with two of my friends, Josh Levine and Sean Sandersohm, who got to talking about the "Golden Rule." (Sean called it a "spiritual principle." I had no idea it was a spiritual principle—I mean, I thought it was just a wise and practical "old saying.") Josh was saying that he could think of at least six religions that believed in the Golden Rule, and when Sean challenged him to name them, Josh did. I learned that the Golden Rule ("do unto others as you want them to do unto you") is shared by Buddhists, Jews, Muslims, Hindus, Christians and Confucians. Well, it was all news to me. So now that I've learned that many religions share the same ideals, I really wonder whether or not some religions are "better" or more "right" than others. And is there one that is "best"?

So I'm really curious, and I want to know more. I know that some faiths even have a different "sacred" text, or scriptures. For example, I know from talking with my friends that for Christians it's the Bible; for Jews it's the Torah; and for Muslims it's the Koran. My friend Singh, who says his faith is Hinduism, told me the sacred text for his faith is the Veda. But other than these "bits" of knowledge, I don't have a clue about what these various texts mean for followers in terms of how they should lead their lives.

I'm curious about the big deal that some make about how people of different faiths are allowed to demonstrate their spiritual beliefs. I mean, once when a classmate volunteered to lead the class in prayer before taking placement tests last year, the teacher told him he couldn't, explaining that prayer was forbidden in schools. But then I remember that after the terrorist attacks on September 11, 2001, everyone from the President of the United States to school leaders said how important it was that we all turn to prayer to find comfort and understanding. People everywhere were praying openly for the victims of the terrorists and for our nation—on radio and on television, even in the Senate. Calling on our faith was suddenly okay, and in fact, important. "God Bless America" was everywhere—on billboards and on people's lips as they sang it like a prayer across the nation. People were talking about spiritual things like the need to be kind to each other.

So, on one hand it feels good to know that I'm not alone in my search for understanding, but on the other, I'm religiously looking for a religion, because I'm certain I want God in my life.

Brad Rogers, 17
(Excerpted from A Taste-Berry Teen's Guide
to Setting & Achieving Goals)

Sweet Perfume

I so loved my grandmother, my mother's mother. I loved the way she loved me, and I deeply honored the way she lived her life. Put simply, it displayed the precious power and grace of her life as a simple and noble person. I once believed that the most grand and priceless heirloom she left was her courageous example of just how pure and simple—and unconditional—her love was. But now, I realize she left me an even greater legacy: the truth about the purpose of life.

My grandmother's love of God and the Holy Spirit poured through her. Not only did she live her life according to Christian principles, but she believed with all her heart that God was the sole reason for her life. Not only did she speak of this while she was alive, but she touched my heart with her commitment to this belief after her death through something she had written. I was looking in her Bible, which was always a very rich experience because of the way she highlighted passages and kept notes within the pages. Looking through those notes, I found one written in her beautiful handwriting, which read:

I was not born to do great works.
I was not born to belong to someone.
I was not born to be the fulfillment of someone,
    nor to fulfill someone else's life.
I wasn't even born to fulfill my own life.
I was born for God to love.
My reason for being is to be loved by God!
It is my earthly work to be filled with his Holy Spirit.
All services and duties I render in my lifetime are just my
    reasonable response to being loved by God.
I was born to praise Him.
I was born to honor Him.
I was born to be sweet perfume to God.

And so through this written legacy of love, I came to understand my purpose as well. Just as my grandmother saw her purpose was to be loved by God and to therefore love Him wholly in return, I now see that my purpose is to know God and to spend my life loving Him. My grandmother's words—and her life—echo the message Jesus gave his followers in Mark 12:30: "Love the Lord your God with all your heart and with all your soul and with all your mind and with all your strength." By loving God, my purpose and the will of God are being fulfilled. I sincerely believe, as my grandmother so eloquently stated, I was born to be sweet perfume to God.

Jennifer Leigh Youngs

"Holy Joe" and the Big Bang Theory

Do you ever feel uncomfortable when others watch your every move? I do, and that's sort of the way I felt as I walked through the halls of my high school. The students were not watching me because I wore awesome clothes or because I'd been voted Mr. Football—none of these were true. They were watching me because I had identified myself as a Christian. As one of them said, they were waiting to see if I'd "let my guard down," which was really unfair scrutiny. I mean, it wasn't as if I floated around the hallways like some guru, trying to generate an aura around myself. I didn't carry a family-size Bible under my armpit; I didn't greet everyone in the hallway with "God bless you, brother"; and I never preached a sermon in the cafeteria at lunch.

I'm being ridiculous to make my point—which is, that I didn't orchestrate my every action to make myself look holy. Not at all. I just chose not to do some of the things that others did—like cheat on tests, download term papers from the Internet, drink or do drugs. It wasn't because I was *trying* to make a statement, but because Jesus Christ had come into my life for real. His presence made a difference in my choices and activities. I realized, however, that my choice made some of my classmates see me as not exactly "fitting in"—as though my faith somehow set me apart from them. I'm sure it did, but I'm not about to be someone other than who I profess to be. Not that I wasn't liked, because I was. I had a lot of good friends. So when I got invitations to keg parties, offers of pirated term papers and things, I learned just to smile and say, "Thank you, but no thank you. I'd love to spend some time with you, but maybe when the circumstances are different." Dealing with things this way worked for me.

But I did get tired of always having to "defend" my faith. One day a couple of weeks ago in science, when we were discussing the age of the world as being billions of years old, I could feel several kids watching me as we discussed the "Big Bang Theory." Carl Bowman—someone who always gets his kicks by putting others on the spot—said, "Hey, Mr. Lehman, why don't you ask Holy Joe what he thinks of the Big Bang Theory?" Mr. Lehman looked confused. "I don't know who you're referring to, Carl." Carl laughed and repeated, "Holy Joe—that's Lance!" On the spot himself, Mr. Lehman turned to me and said, "Lance? Any thoughts on this subject?"

"Sure," I said, feeling the pressure. "The Bible speaks to how the world came into existence, and personally, I believe its teachings. As for the Big Bang Theory, well, God created the world with age, and that accounts for the discrepancy. It's obvious to me that there was a Creator. I mean, think of how intricate we are as humans, to say nothing of how all of nature works together; how we're the perfect distance from the sun, how we have oxygen to breathe, how our plants are watered with rain, how we have the seasons, how there are other galaxies—and how everything works together in perfect harmony. It could not have been by accident! There had to be a master designer—as in God."

"If there is a God, I hope He helps us out at the game Friday night," Jeff Harrelson, a friend of mine, piped in, adding, "Pray He'll take out their big running back, No. 33! That'll help!" Jeff is a pretty cool guy who played center on our football team. He's short, but stout and muscular. We tease him because he has no neck. Good-natured and fun, I like him a lot; everybody does. To this banter, Carl added, "Yeah, well, let's hope God likes our team better than theirs."

The game Friday night was the matchup of the season and the talk of the school that week. Like Jeff, I was excited about the big game. I had a big stake in it: I was the quarterback. Everyone in our town—a town that was football crazy—would turn out. We all wanted to win.

All the hype around the school's "team spirit" continued to grow throughout the week. Finally, the night of the big game arrived. Even though we were having a losing season, if we beat the Lions, we'd be a success. As quarterback, I felt the pressure. It took the whole team to win or lose a game. Nevertheless, I knew that the quarterback seemed to get more than his fair share of the blame or the applause, as the case might be. As was my habit, I silently prayed before the game. While I was praying, I heard someone say, "Oh, look! I think Mr. Holy Joe is praying." And so the remarks started up again. "Well, let's hope Lance has connections. I don't want to walk the halls next week if we lose this one!" Jason Billings said, followed by Lenny Chavez's, "Be sure and tell God we need this game."

As expected, the teams were evenly matched. On our first possession, we marched down the field to the twelve-yard line. Then I threw a pass over the middle to Ricky Hall, who was already in the end zone. It was 7–0, and we were feeling good. However, we couldn't get anything else going, and in the second quarter, the other team's big running back got loose at midfield and went all the way. Fortunately, their kicker missed the PAT (point after touchdown), so we led 7–6 at halftime. In the third quarter, we executed a plan the coach had put together in the locker room. We hit pay dirt and led 14–6, but once again the Lions came back. We just had trouble containing No. 33. This time they hit their PAT, so again we led by just one measly point as we went into the fourth quarter. We were at midfield, with a third and fifteen after a penalty. I dropped back to pass and saw the blitz coming, so I scrambled around and finally dumped the ball off to Jason. Just then, I heard a bone-crunching collision in the middle and saw a pileup involving several guys. When they started to get up and untangle themselves from each other, I saw Jeff on the bottom. He was not moving.

Immediately, I signaled for the coaches and trainers. While they were running onto the field, I turned and knelt down beside Jeff. "Jeff, can you hear me?" I asked him. Nothing. Just then, the coaches arrived, and the referees guided me away. I walked back to my team. "What do you think?" Jason asked.

"I don't know. I think he's unconscious," I said, "but it can't be good." We stood in silence and watched. Still no movement. Then a scared teammate commanded, "Lance, pray for him." To this, the other teammates standing together quickly agreed, "We have to. We have to pray for him."

"Yes," I responded, as a verse from Psalm 86:4 rang in my heart: "In the days of my troubles I will call upon thee." I removed my helmet and knelt down, the other guys following my lead. "God, we're coming to you out of our love and concern for Jeff . . ." I prayed. I don't remember the exact words I prayed after that, but when I said "Amen," I looked up and saw that the entire team had joined in by bowing their heads, some kneeling. I looked up into the bleachers and saw heads bowed as well. It was a first for the Eagles football team.

We stood in stunned silence as the ambulance came. Even though we knew help for Jeff was arriving, the presence of the ambulance was shocking. It just looked so sinister and ominous. The paramedics stabilized Jeff's neck with a white collar, carefully placed him on a stretcher and, with a piercing siren, drove off the field with our friend and teammate.

Everyone was so shaken up by the gravity of Jeff's injuries. When we went into the huddle, Jason encouraged us. "Let's do this for Jeff. He wouldn't want us to fall apart now." We hung on and won, but under the circumstances, it seemed almost unimportant.

As soon as we had dressed, we all headed to the hospital. Jeff's mom and dad were in the waiting room. We learned Jeff had sustained a subdural hematoma. If he hadn't gotten to the hospital when he did so the doctors could relieve the pressure, it could have been fatal. As a matter of fact, the doctor said it was a miracle he survived. But he was going to be okay. In a few days, he'd be out of the hospital.

As I was leaving, Jeff's father followed me out of the room.

With tears in his eyes, he thanked me for praying for his son— and for being "such a good example to everyone, especially the team." I'd like to think that it's not so much because of me but because we all had a wake-up call that day. Life is precious—and we must all think about how we live it, and what we believe about our life should we die.

As for me, I no longer pray alone before a game. In fact, now our team kneels together and prays before every game. I can sense a different attitude on our team. We're closer now, and while we love to win, we're able to put losing into perspective. The night Jeff was injured on the field, I think a lot of the guys on my team were finally able to put something else into perspective, too: the acceptance and importance of asking God to be with us in all that we do.

Lance Waldrop, 17

"*Prove* You're Not a Chicken!"

A bunch of my friends and I had just gotten out of a movie. As we were waiting for a friend's dad to pick us up, just talking about the movie and things, one of the girls lit up a joint, took a puff and then passed it on to one of her friends. The joint moved from person to person. Everyone took a puff. Then it was handed to me. I'd never smoked pot before. I was sure I didn't want to end up like Heather Comber, a girl who smoked pot and went on to do other drugs and now is in a drug rehab place. Plus, I'd also made a promise to my parents that I wouldn't do drugs.

Looking at the friend who was offering me a puff, I just froze. My parents and teachers had said, "Just say, 'No, thanks.'" That's what I always thought I'd say. But suddenly here I was with everyone acting like it was no big deal and looking at me, expecting me to take a puff. "C'mon, don't be a chicken!" one girl taunted.

"I'm not a chicken," I said, defending myself. Then my mouth got dry, and I felt like crying. "I don't want to," I blurted.

"Wimp," another accused. I stood glued to the spot for what seemed like forever. They passed the reefer around a second time. Once again, I was on the spot. Then I remembered a verse in the Bible that our youth pastor had shared with us: "God will not let you be tempted beyond what you can bear. But when you are tempted, He will also make the way of escape that you be may be able to bear it" (1 Cor. 10:13).

"No," I said simply. I backed up a couple of steps so I wasn't part of the circle. When the reefer made its way around the group for the third time, no one handed it to me, and no one said anything. It was such an enormous relief! I was proud of myself in that moment and thankful that God had made it so easy. After that experience, I knew saying no would be a natural response.

Samil Del Guercio, 14

The Darkest Corner

I suffer from depression. It's an awful thing to have because it's really tough to cope with all the ups and downs of life. I was thirteen when I first began to feel depressed, and I was diagnosed at fourteen. That's when I discovered that seventy-seven out of every thousand teens are diagnosed with it every year. Even though some people think depression is just "feeling blah" about your life, it's not. Depression isn't "just in your head"; it's an illness, as real as diabetes or cancer.

Before I knew what was wrong with me, I didn't understand the way I was feeling, and neither did my parents. Then, in eighth grade, I told one of my school counselors how my emotions were always so up and down—and that sometimes I even considered killing myself. He called my parents and told them. He also told them that I needed more help than the school counseling office could offer. My parents were shocked to learn that I could feel so depressed that I would want to end my life. That's when we found a therapist who suggested that I visit a doctor, who prescribed an antidepressant. The medicine only helped a tiny bit, and about a month later, everything still seemed so bleak that I actually tried to kill myself.

At that point, my parents placed me in the behavioral health unit of the local hospital. I spent four days there. While I was in the hospital, I went to psychotherapy sessions, and my medicine was increased several times. The goal was to help me get control of my emotions. It was a long time and a very low period for me, but it helped me get my life back in order.

It has been more than a year since I was hospitalized. I still talk regularly with a counselor and continue to take my medicine. I have also started to see a new psychologist. Although being depressed has been hard, I have learned some pretty amazing things. For one, I've learned just how much God loves me. I find a lot of comfort and strength in God's promises in 2 Corinthians

12:8–10: "My grace is sufficient for you, for my power is made perfect in weakness. Therefore I will boast all the more gladly about my weaknesses, so that the power of Christ may dwell in me; for if they have faith in me, then will I make weak things become strong unto them." Knowing God has promised to make my depression a strength in some way, and believing His grace is always "sufficient" and always there for me, has helped me through many horrible days.

Fortunately, depression is treatable. Things don't get better overnight, but you don't have to feel awful for the rest of your life. Although I'm still struggling with it, I've learned the importance of telling my parents how I'm feeling, most especially when I'm down. They're able to see that I get the treatment I need. And I've educated myself about depression so that I can do my part to ward off a "bout" when I feel one setting in.

I also surround myself with really good friends, and I've taken the time to teach them a little about depression so that when I go into a funk, rather than thinking I'm mad at them or I'm weird or "weak" on those days when everything just looks and feels hopeless to me, they can cut me a little slack while I get things under control again. Another thing that helps is finding ways to express myself and get out my emotions, such as with music, sports or art.

And so I've found ways to help myself cope with my day-to-day problems so they don't build up and turn into depression. But of all these, the most important is my faith, which remains my biggest source of comfort, support and strength. I know that I may struggle with depression for the rest of my life, but ending my life is no longer an option. Because I ask God to be with me and help me, surviving, thriving and feeling grateful for life (even on the bleakest of days) is how I live now. I have found the truth behind the words, "My grace is sufficient for you" (2 Cor. 12:9). It has made all the difference.

Emily Whitney, 16

Seventy-One

My hardest subject has always been math. I just don't have a talent for it. So for the longest time, my biggest goal in life was centered on the number seventy-one—a score I needed to pass the math portion of the TAAS (Texas Assessment of Academic Skills) exams. I'd taken this stupid—and difficult—test a number of times before and never once received a passing score! In reading and writing I always scored just above what was expected. But when it came to math, I never made above a sixty, let alone a seventy. But friends and family kept encouraging me, saying things like, "Lorenza, *this time* you'll pass." So, every time I took this darn test, I'd go in with high hopes from their encouragement. Unfortunately, their love and support didn't show up on my score!

I was really getting discouraged, plus my attitude was really bad about studying for it. Then one day, I came across 2 Timothy 2:5: "If anyone competes as an athlete, he is not crowned unless he competes according to the rules." This made me question if I had gone the distance to succeed on the test—I mean, had I really? Well, I couldn't really say that I had, so I thought I'd better make a real plan to pass the test. I developed a study schedule (a real one!), even meeting with a tutor once a week for the next two months to help me focus on studying the right things. On a regular basis, I studied. And studied same more. And I prayed, asking God to be with me on test day.

Then came test day—and I was ready. Having put every effort into preparing for the test, the evening before test day, I'd gotten a good night's rest and woke up early enough to not be in a rush. I ate a good breakfast and left the house in time to arrive early to find a seat that felt "right." (I really dislike sitting in a front row or by a door.) As the tests were being handed out, I took a deep breath and reminded myself not to panic—which was tough, because as I looked at the front of the booklet where it read

TAAS, at first I was scared to open it. But I did. *God, please let me do well on this,* I prayed. *I want this to be my last time of ever taking this test.* Then, I started in.

Time flew by, even though I was one of only six kids (out of thirty-five) who was still there when the timer reminded us that only ten minutes remained to finish up. Although I found this a little unnerving, I told myself not to be concerned and to just breathe, focus and steadily work my way through the remaining questions. Within minutes, I'd finished all except those I'd skipped—because they'd seemed like Greek to me. So I reread each one, and for those that I simply had no clue, just "bubbled" in what seemed like the most logical answer to me. Then I turned my test in—and left.

The days and weeks following the test—waiting and wondering—were nerve-wracking. Luckily, in May my English teacher gave us the results early, just so none of us would have to wait until our summer vacation to see our scores. I remember she smiled before she called me, which I thought must be a good sign. I went up to her desk, and she showed me my scores—reading, 80, which was good, then 1,520 in writing, very good, too. Then she covered the paper and said, "Congratulations! You've passed the math section, as well." My score: seventy-one! I was so proud of myself. I finally had the "crown"! Of course, my friends and family were all very proud of me, too!

I never have to worry about TAAS ever again, but passing the test holds even greater significance for me. Whenever I think of that test, I remember how I did my part for preparing to pass it and then asked God to be with me as I took it. I think that sometimes we ask God for help and support, but then ignore the guidance and help we're given. I've done this in the past, but it's not what I want to do now. So on this test, I did my part by studying and being fully prepared to do my best, and then turned the rest over to God.

I know how easy it is to say "turn over, or leave the rest to

God." While I do that sometimes, what I mostly do is talk to God, saying, "Heavenly Father, please guide me." Then I trust that He is, and know that it's then my job to attentively listen for any and all insight. I listen to my instincts, and I'm open to "hearing that small inner voice." So more and more, what I'm trying to do is, after asking God for guidance and direction, to hear it and apply it.

Having passed the TAAS, I know it works!

Lorenza A. Martinez, 17

My Boyfriend Left Me Because I Owed Him for Concert Tickets!

After my first day on campus as a high-school sophomore, I knew my year was going to be the best one yet. As I strolled from classroom to classroom with my books placed confidently at my side and my head held high, I felt that nothing could stop me. Gone were the days of freshman year and the hazing I had endured. I was now a "big kid," someone who was cool. For once in my life, I appeared to have it all together. I was a straight-A student, soccer-club captain, cross-country runner and dating my first boyfriend. Life couldn't have been better—but that left room for things to get worse.

And they did. On October 5, two months into my perfect school year, my life began to change big-time. My boyfriend suddenly broke up with me and gave no explanation. Shocked, dismayed and bewildered, I was completely clueless about how to respond. The only thing I could manage to do was cry. Over the subsequent days, I was in a mental daze, too consumed with my emotions to focus on the world around me. But my pain did not end there. The boy I thought I loved became verbally and physically abusive. During our cross-country workouts, he'd purposely trip or shove me off the course. Lunch period became his opportunity for spreading lies to defame my character.

After weeks of this ceaseless torture, I finally gathered the courage to confront him; I had taken enough of his abuse. On a Monday afternoon after practice, I demanded an explanation for his cruel actions. He responded by exploding into a fury of anger. Amid his shouts and curse words, he made it quite clear that our breakup was a result of my failure to pay for my ticket to a concert that I was unable to attend. Our five months of dating, as well as our yearlong friendship, were destroyed simply because of money. Soon after this encounter, my entire life began to unravel.

I plunged into a vicious cycle of strenuous exercise—and of basically eating as few calories as I could. If I slipped and had just an extra piece of fruit or a few pretzels, I forced myself to compensate for that mistake by doing two hundred sit-ups or running an extra half-mile. If that sounds extreme or harsh, it was. But at first I received tons of compliments from friends and family, praising me on my discipline and thin figure. However, these messages only pushed me further into my disorder. I would often rationalize with myself, *If I look this good now, imagine how much better I'll look after I lose another five pounds.*

Eventually all comments ceased, and silence was the only response to my continued weight loss. Yet in spite of this reaction, no one and nothing was going to stop me. In addition to five-mile cross-country practices and two hours of soccer three times a week, I forced myself to run an extra three to six miles a day. If I didn't work out, I couldn't focus or think until I did. Within six weeks, I began to fear food and crave exercise. It was my escape from a fate-centered world and the only thing that I felt I could still have control over. I was completely miserable, yet I couldn't stop. Instead of being in control, the behaviors were controlling me. Eventually, I hit rock bottom. Despite warnings from my doctors, therapists and parents, I continued to exercise, averaging about seven thousand crunches a day. And I also continued to lose weight.

January 11, 2002, marked my admission date to Remuda Ranch, a treatment facility for anorexia and bulimia. I weighed in at sixty-eight pounds. According to their medical team, I was lucky to be alive. My gradual journey out of mental illness had begun.

For the first month and a half, I tried so hard to be the perfect patient. I complied with their rules and always tried to wear a smile. Nevertheless, my secret plan was soon discovered. My roommates confessed to a therapist that I was continuing to exercise despite facility regulations and medical advice. Although I was able to surrender every other aspect of my disorder, I still clung firmly to this particular symptom. The endorphin high I received and the comforting feeling I felt were the only substances that elevated my spirits and kept me going throughout my stay. Soon I was placed on twenty-four-hour personal care in order to prevent me from exercising. Without this fatal coping mechanism to rely on, I gave up. I refused to eat, hardly slept and cried each day away.

Luckily, in the midst of my pain, I somehow found the Lord. I had been raised in a Christian home and had been a believer since the age of five, but I had never been forced to rely upon my faith. One evening, I made a deal with God; I promised to give recovery a try if only He would go with me every step of the way. The following morning, as I sat at the breakfast table, I decided to give this "God-thing" a try. After mumbling a quiet prayer asking for strength, I proceeded to eat my meal. For the first time, I was able to finish eating all my servings. Perplexed and somewhat confused, I began to think that maybe this time, my recovery was real. With the passing of each week, life grew easier and easier. I was finally able to break the bonds of fear and doubt that had held me captive and seek refuge in the arms of my Heavenly Father.

After my four-month stay at the Ranch, I'd gotten healthy again. And with spiritual renewal came a state of happiness and a sense of serenity and freedom. Instead of placing my trust in the hands of deceitful people, I chose to rest in the sound faith and hope in the promises of Christ.

It's now been four months since I've returned home, and things finally seem to be falling into a "normal" place. I don't diet or overexercise. My weight has been stable, and I have been able to return to competitive athletics. There are days that are still hard and sometimes almost too difficult to face. But God has not given me anything that is too hard to overcome. I find great comfort in Matthew 6:25 and 34: "Therefore I tell you, do not worry about your life, what you will eat or drink; or about your body, what you will wear. Is not life more important than food, and the soul more important than clothes? Therefore do not worry about tomorrow, for tomorrow will worry about itself." I no longer worry about what challenges each day will bring. With His strength, I have been able to stare death in the face and return to life.

This has been the most harrowing of experiences I can imagine. Because of it, I have learned a simple but profound truth: Everything in life seems so important—like who likes you and who doesn't like you. I mean, what can be more demeaning than being put down by someone you love, right? Well, the answer is that what is worse is when you think all that is happening around you is more important than your inner life, your spiritual life, your one-on-one relationship with God. More than ever, I am totally convinced that only when you have God in your life will everything else be in its proper place of importance. So now, instead of dreading the arrival of a new day, every morning I send out a prayer thanking God for the blessing that I call LIFE. With God in my life, everything is okay. Nothing is a crisis anymore, including the demands others make, and the reasons they give for loving—or not loving—me. God expects us to love and care for others, but He expects us to honor ourselves, to treat ourselves like the "temples" we are.

Jennifer Stripe, 16

"The" Dinner

I really, really wanted to attend the National Italian American Foundation conference for teens. I'd been told the competition for getting accepted was stiff, so I filled out the application carefully and made sure I mailed it in on time.

I got accepted!

One night at one of the conference dinners (which was a secular event, meaning the conference was not associated with any religious organizations), the conversation at my table turned to a discussion of religion. One teen said he didn't believe in God. Another said he had no need for God. One girl said she had no idea what she believed, and another girl said she thought of God as "anything and everything that was alive." A guy sitting next to her shared his views on the absence of moral absolutes. As I sat there listening, I thought how their views of self and life sounded so self-centered, even bleak, and knew life can feel that way when you don't believe in the truth and glory of God. But I also know it doesn't have to be this way. In John 12:46 we are promised: "I have come as a light into the world, that whoever believes in Me should not abide in darkness."

Instantly, I knew that I must share how my Christian beliefs had served my life. To my great amazement, everyone at the table listened to every word I said. One girl even got tears in her eyes. The next day, a couple of the others sought me out, wanting to know more about how they, too, could have a personal relationship with God. And so I went away from the conference feeling that I had been a ray of light to other teens—that God had worked through me to accomplish His purpose. It was one more indication to me how God uses His children to help others change their darkness into light. I feel so honored, so humbled, so loved.

Paul Cattaneo, 17

The Victorious Right Hand

Words cannot describe my fear the day I learned that my father had a malignant brain tumor. By the time the doctors had detected the tumor it was already the size of a small softball. Unfortunately, although my dad had noticed that he was having trouble with his vision, he hadn't had it checked out. So by the time the tumor was detected, something had to be done, and quickly. The surgeons said an operation was imperative—and in the same breath they told us there was an 80–85 percent chance that Dad wouldn't recognize us after the surgery. If he did pull through the surgery, he would have to learn how to walk and talk all over again. And, of course, there was always the chance that he wouldn't make it through surgery.

I couldn't imagine life without my dad.

I was thirteen at the time.

What made this news even more difficult was that my parents had gotten divorced, so my "quality time" with a dad I adored was already scarce. Now God wanted to take him away from me? I was angry at the world—and with God as well. Was this some sort of punishment?

Anxious and scared on the day of the operation, we all waited in the small waiting room. You cannot believe how slowly time passed! Personally, I just wanted to sit in the corner and pray for my dad, who was now "under the knife." Still, I knew I had to be strong for my sister and my mom, who I knew were just as scared as I was. My façade of being brave and strong didn't last long, and finally I just ran into the bathroom where I cried and cried. Hurting as much as I did, I remembered one of my favorite verses, Isaiah 41:10: "Do not be afraid, for I am with you. Do not be dismayed, for I am your God. I will strengthen you. I will help you. I will uphold you with my victorious right hand." This verse had always brought me comfort—and it especially comforted me right then.

Miraculously, my dad made it through the surgery, and he did not lose any of his memory. In fact, he pretty much went back to living a "normal" life several months after the surgery. So things seemed pretty good. Everything took on more meaning—especially being alive. But then, just one year later during his semi-annual exam, an MRI detected regrowth of the tumor.

My dad said he knew it, even without the tests.

Because my parents were divorced, my sister and I lived with my mother during the week, then went to my dad's house every other weekend. But one particular weekend, Mom told us that my dad had called and asked if they could switch weekends. He wanted us to come to his house that day, instead of waiting for the following weekend. This wasn't anything new; weekends were always being switched around.

My mom drove us over, and when my sister and I got out of the car, the first thing I noticed was that Dad's shoulder-length, sun-kissed blond hair was now short, gelled and brown. I loved it! My sister and I had always told him that we thought he should cut his hair, but we never thought he would. But within minutes, the gloomy look on the faces of everyone around— Mom, my stepmom and my dad—overcame our happy, surprised expressions. My stomach suddenly filled with knots. I knew something was seriously wrong. Then my dad told my sister and I to sit next to him. The tension in the room was so dense it was hard to breathe. Trying to hold back tears, my dad told us the tumor had come back.

The doctors gave my dad maximum amounts of radiation, and he was treated with massive doses of chemotherapy. The doctors said that if the tumor returned yet again, there was nothing they could do, and that Dad would have to accept that the tumor would eventually take his life. How do you react to the reality of something like this? I had watched him go through the radiation treatment, which sent beams of radiation through three parts of his brain, and left large bald spots on his head. But seeing him go through the chemotherapy treatment was the most difficult. He barely had enough strength to do anything. The medicine made him sick constantly, and he had no appetite. But still, he refused to give up; he wanted so desperately to live! Dad always told me that he would be there to walk me down the aisle. Dad was always one to keep his word.

Luckily, my father did not die from this second assault on his life. And there's more good news: It has now been over three years since the doctors last detected any traces of the tumor. Throughout all of the treatments, I watched him grow in his faith and his relationship with God, praising God for all that he did have and never dwelling on the negative. Watching him strengthened my own relationship with God, renewed my faith and encouraged me to honor His promise, "Do not be afraid, for I am with you." When I thought I couldn't go on, I called to mind, "Do not be dismayed, for I am your God." Questioning where I would find the strength to make it through the moments and the days, I remembered, "I will strengthen you. I will help you." When I wondered how we would ever be able to win this battle, I would focus on God's promise, "I will uphold you with my victorious right hand." I knew that if God were to take my dad away, he would go to a much happier place. Even then, we would be victorious. Every day is a blessing from God. Finally, I learned that no matter how terrible the circumstances look, God is there through it all to "strengthen," to "help" and to "uphold" us with His "victorious hand." I also know that while God did all this for me and for my family throughout my father's ordeal, he continues to do so every day and in every way in ordinary life as well. I am now in college, and as usual, life is filled with choices and decisions at every turn. Luckily, God is unfailing; He is there with me every day, everywhere. He is my rock. With God at the center of my life, I am meeting life on His terms. I am blessed. There is much I have to be thankful for.

Michelle Langowski, 19

Self-Proclaimed Princess!

I don't know about you, but I obsess constantly over my appearance. I mean, I like to look good! So I don't know what I was thinking when I signed up to head to the mountains to be a camp counselor at Indian Village for a bunch of third- and fourth-graders! Maybe it was because of the fond memories of having done the stint myself as a kid—you know, food cooked on a campfire (especially the marshmallows!) and all the sing-alongs and the games where no one gets left out. Or, maybe it was remembering how cute the boy camp counselors were—I know I was really looking forward to checking them out this time.

The idea of coming back as a counselor appealed to me—that is, right up to the first fifteen minutes of my actually being the camp counselor! Now, with all these little Indian princesses around me—ten little girls latching onto me, all needing my undivided attention and adoration—well, let's just say that this is not how a sixteen-year-old such as myself would choose to spend an entire 24/7 of a precious week of summer vacation. And how exactly was I going to have time to check out the guy counselors?

Three hours after I arrived, things hadn't improved much; I was still trying to find five minutes for myself and thinking how nice a hot shower would be. When the time for that shower actually arrived, however, I discovered ice-cold was the only temperature available—and there would be no such thing as warm water for the entire week! There were countless other small "roughing it" horrors to face, but none of the hardships could rival having to get ready in the mornings without a mirror. Unthinkable—for a self-described princess like me!

Little princesses themselves, the moment the little Indian Village campers arrived, there was immediate mayhem over where everyone would get to sleep. From pouts to shouts, cold silence to tantrums, suffice it to say that our first hour together was enough to make me wish I'd signed up to detassel corn instead of being camp counselor. One night, just after returning from taking one of the little girls on a midnight bathroom trek to the woods, I lay in my bed (which was so short that my feet hung out over the edge of the mattress) wondering what God was trying to teach me.

By the third day, I was beginning to understand what I was supposed to learn. See, the dusty mountainside is not the best atmosphere for anyone's hair and complexion. And here I was, my poor sunburned body peeling and my muscles aching from the drudgery of toil and uphill hikes. Although I knew without a doubt that I looked geeky, how I looked really wasn't even relevant. And, of course, the little girls so adored the "big teenage girl" that they didn't even see the red blotches on my face or the scarecrow hair. *Okay,* I thought, *I get it; this is all about a lesson in vanity. No problem; if bringing the focus off my outward appearance pleases God, then okay.* But God didn't allow it to be the only lesson. He wanted me to forget myself entirely, to be selfless. In James 3:13 it says, "Who is wise and understanding among you, let him show it by his good life, by deeds done in the humility that comes from wisdom."

Certainly it took humility to do the best I could in each moment and in each situation with the young girls. But the lesson was so much more. I had shifted my focus from the outside of me to the inside of me. It made all the difference. Now, by focusing on how I was doing in my job—and not just in the "looks" department—I had the privilege of becoming surrogate mother to nearly a dozen eight- and nine-year-olds. In caring for them, I had to forego any thoughts about my appearance. Between caring for chapped lips, distributing hugs and wiping away tears of homesickness, I had zero time to pay attention to how I looked. And in the end, it did not matter. Who would have guessed that it was to be the best seven days of my life to date!

Here I was, out in the wilderness at a children's camp, loving every minute of it after all. Yes, I had arrived at Indian Village with the air of a pampered princess, but I left as a princess warrior for my Lord.

Danielle Platt, 16

A Key Ring Can Tell You a Lot About Someone

When I think of God's love, the first thing I think of is the love that I see every day in our family. I have two brothers, one who is a year older than me, and a little brother who is ten months old. (He is totally cute—and my brother and I just love to play with him!) My father works with a landscaping company. My mother works as a housekeeper for about ten families. We are a very close family. My father drives my mother to each of her jobs and picks her up. He also picks us kids up from school whenever he can. I watch my parents work very hard at their jobs for the sake of their family, so I know that family is very important to them. They even send money to their parents to help them have a better life. Seeing all this, the way my parents live their lives and treat each other and us, makes me really love them—and teaches me a lot about the importance of having God be the center of your life.

I'm not the only one who recognizes that my parents are Christians. It's very clear to see that those they work for care about them and trust them implicitly. A good example can be found just by looking at my mother's key ring—which I think tells you a lot about someone. My mother's key ring holds the keys to the houses of the people she works for—which are some of the most beautiful homes you can imagine. People trust her with the care of their homes and all the possessions inside. When homeowners are away, they give my mom the security code and allow her to come into their homes to look after their very pampered pets. (I know for a fact that in some instances, they don't even give their relatives a key!) She is so appreciated that her employers sometimes even give her nice gifts. And one of the people she works for is a writer who has acknowledged my mother in her books.

Seeing the way that my parents live their faith has given me a great appreciation for both them and what they believe. I can tell that it is valuable and real. And while my parents tell me about God's love, the love that they live each day has taught me the very most about God's love. It is my parents' example of Christianity that makes me want to serve the Lord by living the same way. As it says in Joshua 24:15, "As for me and my house, we shall serve the Lord." When I read it, I believe it's really true, because with parents who live God's love the way mine do, I can't see how it could be any other way.

Noeli Rios, 12

Snow Cave

Snowmobile trips to the mountains of Wyoming are a regular event for my family. We love it because to experience the beauty of nature while flying over the glistening snow and through the towering trees is both peaceful and exhilarating.

On one beautiful winter morning, our trip began with the usual routine: Get up extra early (which no one complained about) and stop for breakfast at Kate's Beanery—always a treat—then a stop for gas and to buy some last-minute items (which on this trip included a compass and a whistle). The only thing that made this trip different from the others was that my uncle (who had the most knowledge and experience of the mountains) wasn't able to join us.

A lunch of cold sandwiches and cookies had brought us to about halfway in our loop of the mountain. Our choice resting spot was an old, abandoned, single-room shack that had lost its door and windows. Our first snowmobile trip without my uncle had gone well, and we were feeling pretty proud of ourselves! We then packed up the food and headed back out to the trail to finish the day's ride.

As if to make up for the morning's perfection, misfortune struck soon after our break: My mom's snowmobile broke down. It took over an hour before we could get it started again. During this time, the brilliance of the morning sun turned into ominous clouds that gave our surroundings a whole new look. About the same time we were getting back on the trail, the snow began to fall and our environment changed yet again—this time to white-out conditions.

It wasn't long before we were unable to identify anything that even remotely resembled the path we had been on. Our compass did little more than tell us we were traveling in a straight path; it did not reveal that the path we were traveling was, in fact, a big circle. When my dad dropped off a four-foot cliff, we knew it was not smart to blindly drive around an area that had 100- and 200-foot drops, so we decided we'd better get back to the cabin where we had eaten lunch only a few hours earlier.

Our effort to make it over "the pass," the largest hill on the mountain, didn't happen. Soon we were forced to face the fact that we would be spending the night on the highest point of the Snowy Range Mountains. Gathering a few supplies from our snowmobiles, we began our search for a rock that would offer protection from the blowing wind and snow. Exploring the surrounding area—knowing we needed to get settled in before the sun went down and made seeing even more difficult—we settled for a fair-sized rock and began digging in.

The digging itself was not bad, since working our muscles warmed us up. But not long after we started digging, we hit ground, so then our plan for a snow cave turned into hopes for more or less any kind of shelter. We still had one bag of cookies, but that was all we had. So it was cookies or nothing for dinner— although the stress of our situation pretty much did away with our appetites. Then we all crawled into our snow "shelf."

Without room for all four of us to lie on our backs, my dad volunteered to take the even more uncomfortable position on his side. Conversation faded in and out as we tried to pass the time and keep our minds off the cold. My mom's classes in outdoor survival had been extremely helpful in helping prepare the snow cave. Now they were again useful in keeping us from a state of shock or hypothermia. In an attempt to maintain coherency, she had us take turns counting. It wouldn't usually be a struggle to say the right number every third or fourth time, but now it was unbelievably difficult. We just couldn't remember whose turn it was or what number we were on. Although we didn't know it at the time, this was pretty much what the next fourteen hours would be like.

There wasn't enough room to lie completely stretched out, so around two hours after we had entered the snow cave we all began to suffer from leg cramps. This unbearable pain forced everyone to get out of the shelter and into the blizzard. Each time we slid back into our cave, a little more snow was pushed to the bottom. This made it smaller and exposed more of our bodies to the severe cold. At around 10:00 P.M., the agonizing wait for daylight and the hopes of a rescue team became almost too much to handle. Sensing our anxiety, my mom said, "Let's all pray together." Everyone instantly agreed with her—even though we each had been praying on our own. Together we asked God to keep each person in our family safe.

I cannot describe the feeling that overflowed my soul as we prayed together. Each of my family members also felt a similar kind of serenity. In that moment, Philippians 4:6-7 became an experience instead of just a verse. "Do not be anxious about anything, but in everything, by prayer and petition, with thanksgiving, present your requests to God. And the peace of God, which transcends all understanding, will guard your hearts and your minds in Christ Jesus." As we prayed, I was filled with the peace of God even though it was freezing and our circumstances were dire. Yet, I had faith that since we asked God to watch over us—and are told that when two or more are gathered in His name He hears—God was there with us, looking after us. Each of us that night talked about our faith and took comfort that we each "knew" God; each of us had our own personal relationship with God. Such faith—and prayer—continued to provide us with the reassurance of God being with us in that little snow cave and watching over us. Each of us "knew" it was so.

Morning came. We had made it through the night without freezing to death! We started our day by giving thanks, and then, with every ounce of energy we could gather, got to our snow-mobiles now totally buried in snow. Since my uncle had planned to meet us the next morning to ride with us, we knew he would eventually arrive at our truck and realize that we had not made it off the mountain. With this in mind, our wait was filled with silence as we tried to listen for the sounds of some sort of help coming.

Eventually, my uncle and help did arrive. My uncle, along with a few of his friends, helped get us off the mountain and into the camper of some other riders. Lying beneath blankets and drinking hot chocolate, we retold our story and waited for the mountain patrol to come and check our condition. After the mountain patrolman's inspection, he shook his head and said, "I'm amazed that you spent a night on that mountain—and survived!" He looked from one of us to the next. "It's been totally closed off now because the weather condition is so serious. Yes, this weather will make a believer out of many!"

Yes, it was amazing, but to us, we knew in our hearts that we would make it. To this day, we continue to believe that our family was under God's protection while in the snow cave. We really got the opportunity to live that "peace that transcends understanding" (Phil. 4:7). I know without a doubt that if God can bring peace to us in a snow cave in the middle of the blizzard, He will be there to comfort and protect each of His children wherever they go. Christians call upon God in good times and frightening times, and thank God daily for the blessings He bestows.

As I remember back, I think about the patrolman's comment, ". . . will make a believer out of many." I think there's a lot of truth to that. Even those who say they do not believe, when confronted with a serious crisis, may very well call upon God. So for anyone who questions if there is a God or if there is life after death, I'm betting a crisis experience converts a good many people!

Mandy Pohja, 17

Together—For Always

To say that my father and I didn't have the typical father/ daughter relationship was an understatement! At times, I felt it was because I was a girl. I mean, my dad spent a lot of time with my brother, doing "guy things"—like going to action movies and being computer geeks together. This was good news and bad news. The good news was that I spent time with my mother, and we had a totally awesome relationship. We also had a lot in common—like our love for horses. Yet, I wanted to spend more time with my father; I yearned for his acceptance more than he knew.

Up until sixth grade, life seemed okay for me. Then suddenly, everything—especially school—seemed suffocating. To me, it seemed everyone was negative, and I didn't exactly feel like the most popular kid around. I begged my parents to let me go to a different school. My mother agreed to look into it and made calls requesting information from various schools in our area. This was how I came across a school by the name of Santa Fe Christian. Reading over the brochure, deep in my heart I felt certain that this was the right school for me. Looking over the brochure, I could just tell that the smiles on the kids' faces were genuine. And the idea of having God at the center of my life seemed like the way it ought to be, so this school especially sparked my interest.

"I want to go to this school, Dad," I announced one evening after dinner.

"You don't want to go there; they'll force religion on you," he retorted. So sensing his objections—and being so young at the time—the subject of moving schools dropped. But I always kept Santa Fe Christian in my mind. Besides, as my dad had said, "Maybe you can go *later*." I held onto the hope of that "later."

Later arrived one day. As eighth grade rolled around, I brought up the discussion of changing schools again. Once again my father voiced his doubts, but this time I was more assertive and told him I was positive this *was* the school for me. Seeing how adamant I was, my father relented. To this day, it is a decision he doesn't regret. My attending school at Santa Fe Christian has been such a great experience for me. I have literally become one of the genuine smiles I'd seen in the brochure. I've gone from a rowdy tomboy who cussed like a sailor to a confidant and respectful young woman. And God is the center of my life.

But other miracles are at work as well. Because I am filled with the grace of His Spirit, my father can see the outpouring of God's amazing love at work. Never was this more evident than one evening when my dad and I were talking. He told me he was proud of me and that he could see the many ways God had changed my life—and that it was a beautiful thing. Although my father has yet to say it, my faith is "speaking" to him. For this I feel so thankful, so grateful. And so I've come to honor a favorite Scripture, Psalm 40:1–3: "I waited patiently for the Lord; he turned to me and heard my cry. He set my feet on a rock and gave me a firm place to stand. He put a new song in my mouth."

I want to believe that one day my dad will know God as I do. I believe in eternal life, and I want to believe that when our earthly lives are over, my *entire* family will be together with God. Even so, I know that if my dad accepts God as his personal Savior into his life, it is his to do. But I never understate that living my life with the love and joy that I have because I am a Christian can be a turning point for my dad (or others).

Martha Haake, 17

Good Luck with the Tough Guys!

There I was, 36,000 feet in the air, on my way to a country others had described as filled with lush, green forests—and many, many poisonous snakes! I'd been told, "What a lucky guy to have such an awesome opportunity to see a 'new and different' culture—one where your presence is 'really, really needed.'" Embarking on the "experience of a lifetime"—and not quite a freshman in high school—I was feeling a little unsure of myself at the moment and not really "lucky." Why had I said yes to this journey?

It all happened one day while I was in church, listening to our youth pastor announce that the church would be "accepting applications" for a mission trip to Costa Rica. I remember thinking, *Hmmm. Interesting.* But I completely forgot about it until a couple of weeks later when one of my friends asked me if I had already submitted my application. When I told him I'd forgotten about it, he produced an "extra" one. Without giving it too much thought, I filled it out later that day and handed it in.

Now here I was, literally in the air as well as completely "up in the air" about what I'd have to say that was valuable or would make a difference to those I'd never met, and no doubt would never, ever see again.

Little did I know that my travels to Costa Rica would prove valuable and make a difference—most especially in my own life. My mission was to assist with the running of a three-day camp for 130 kids, ages twelve to nineteen. Our goal was to witness and share God's word. I was assigned to run the ropes course and to help the camp kids feel successful and make it through without getting hurt. Looking around, sizing up the kids and their abilities, I spotted six older, rough-looking kids. Like a badge of honor, written all over their faces they wore "I'm big and tough and don't mess with me" expressions. Momentarily worried, I remember thinking, *Okay, God, I'm going to focus on the little guys and leave the big guys to you! I'll pray for them, but the rest is all yours: Good luck!*

Every evening we held a special session, all of us praying that one by one, each boy would learn about God and desire a personal relationship with Him. I'd always believed in the power of prayer, just as it says in James 5:16, "Pray for one another, so that you may be healed. The effective prayer of a righteous man can accomplish much." It was particularly wonderful to watch as life by life, each one would make a decision to walk with God. I remember one of those altar calls very clearly. I was praying that God would speak to the hearts of the six tough guys. Just then, I looked up, and three of them stood up—they were making the decision to accept Christ into their lives. It was the most amazing miracle. It was awesome to see God at work.

Throughout the week, 102 out of 130 boys made decisions for God in some way. Imagine that! God's mercy and grace had been shown to 102 lives! But that's when I realized God had done more than work miracles in their lives—He had worked through mine as well. Seeing others grasp the grace of God was awesome, but realizing that through sincere prayer I can be part of such a miraculous grace was humbling. Imagine—through prayer we can bring others to God. How truly, truly awesome. And so my faith was strengthened.

On the flight home, I reflected how God had used my life to witness to others and to help them come closer to God. In exchange, He filled my heart with gratitude and a sense of purpose that can only be gained when we are living His plan, living our lives for Him. I just think God is so great, and it is my choice to always give Him glory.

Greg Wright, 16

When You Can't Answer "Why?"

Have you ever wondered why God allows suffering? I sure have, most especially when tragedy and suffering struck my family. First, my youngest sister, Christina, was diagnosed with Type 1 diabetes when she was only six years old. I can remember how shocked my whole family was and how devastating it was to face the reality that this little girl would have to live the rest of her life with such a complex disease. I remember thinking, *Why does such an innocent little child have to come down with a disease that will change her life forever?* I could accept that trials and tribulation are a part of life, but I was still upset that my sweet little sister would have to grow up with something like diabetes.

Fortunately, my sister's condition could be managed. But it meant she would now have to check her blood sugar and prick her finger about four times a day, and have two shots of insulin before breakfast and dinner! Even so, Christina was remarkably brave and mature, and displayed an incredible attitude about it all. Every day she made the best of it. And through her amazing attitude and outlook on life, she influenced everyone around her. Certainly, the way she dealt with her illness changed how I looked at things. Proverbs 3:5 took on greater meaning for me: "Trust in the Lord with all your heart, and lean not on your own understanding." Seeing how Christina was able to cope and really touch others, I came to the conclusion there were some things I just would never be able to understand. I decided to trust that God would never give us more than we could handle. Little did I know that this trust in God would soon be put to the test yet again.

If you had told me at the time that in just two years both my sisters and I would be left to live the rest of our lives without our mother, I never would have believed it. No one ever wants to think that God's plan for His "children" would allow something that terrible. But less than six months ago, my mom died at the young age of forty-three from melanoma. Diagnosed with the cancer only a few weeks after New Year's Day, immediately she began treatment. However, the chemo didn't work, and things grew steadily worse. She died that April.

The following months were a total blur. I was so filled with grief that life became an exercise of putting one foot in front of the other in order to get through each day. I still can't believe my mom is gone, and that I must face my life without her. I miss her more than anything. She was my everything—and the most amazing woman. As an example, my dad worked in Los Angeles during the week, so my mom was the primary constant parent, taking my sisters and I to three different schools, cooking, cleaning, volunteering, running a photo business and taking care of my little sister's special needs with diabetes. I know there had to be a lot of stress involved, but she always managed to give so much to everyone around her and to fill our lives with positive thinking, encouragement and joy. I will never forget her explaining her illness to me and saying, "You must never blame God for this."

While I didn't blame God, I certainly wondered, *What does God have in store for this family? Why is He allowing all this pain?* I mean, you can only imagine how our hearts were feeling the morning my father and I had to walk into my little sister's room and explain to her, "Mommy has gone to heaven." It is in such times that trusting God and having faith is all you can do because sometimes "real life" doesn't have a "neat" answer. So I remind myself that God will never give us more than we can handle, and while I may not always understand "how" or "why," I can always ask Him for strength to cope with all I'm going through. But this, too, is a part of the "answer." I've discovered we can survive tragedy, and that tough and harrowing times can make you lean on God even more. Certainly, you can't lean solely on your understanding! I've learned how important it is not to overlook the blessings I have in life, blessings that include the love of family and friends, my faith, a home and my health, to name just a few. Throughout it all, I readily turn to God knowing I can trust in Him "with all my heart"—and He will help me through my pain and heartache. Sometimes this is understanding enough.

Jenny King, 17

How Would You Feel if Your Father Didn't Want You?

I was born at twenty-six weeks—which means I was fourteen weeks premature. I only weighed a pound and a half, and I was just ten inches long. I had to spend my first three months in the hospital. At three days old, I had open-heart surgery to close a bad heart valve. I was connected to all kinds of machines to help me breathe and monitor all my vital signs. I still have the marks on my hands and feet. I was famous; they put my picture in the paper.

After three months, I went home with my mom. She said all the nurses cried the day I left. My father came to see me at my grandparents' house. I've been told he was too immature to want a family, and he took off, never to be seen again. So I never got to know him. When I started school and saw that most of the other children had fathers who spent time playing with them, helping them with their homework and taking them places, I started to wonder why my dad didn't want anything to do with me. I was very hurt, confused and angry. To this day I still feel really unwanted and unloved by my dad. There has never been communication of any kind between us, and our relationship is still nonexistent.

At first, I was naïve enough to ask God to bring my father back into my life—even though my father obviously didn't want any part of it. But my dad never came back. Once I realized my dad was never going to be a part of my life, it made me angry and hurt all over again. So I decided God wouldn't be part of my life either. I shut Him out and stopped asking Him to be with me in my daily life.

I haven't "walked with God" since I was thirteen years old. Now, as a seventeen-year-old high-school senior, I might question my decision sometimes—but I haven't yet returned to Him. If I'm being completely honest, I have to say that I don't feel like

I'm ready to turn to God for help with anything, at least not yet. However, most of my friends believe in God, and whenever I'm in the middle of heartache or crisis, they often suggest that I pray and ask God for His forgiveness and for the strength to make it through the day. A few times, I actually tried praying again, but I know I'm still relying on myself. I also know this is because I have a lot of anger over my father. I've never gotten past the emptiness, and I still do battle with my feelings of being abandoned and hurt. I am overcoming it—I mean, I've learned how to live without having a father—sometimes I don't even think about it for weeks. But a strange thing can happen when someone so important in your life deserts you, the way my father deserted me: You start to wonder what's wrong with you. You ask yourself, *What makes me so unlovable?* After thinking this way awhile, you can even stop loving yourself. I know this is what I've done.

The fact that I don't love myself is actually the biggest reason I think I should try reaching out to God: I mean, I do know God loves me. And I do know He has not abandoned me. I know it is ironic that because my earthly father rejected me, I reject my Heavenly Father. I guess I'd have to say that on one level, I believe the very incident that caused me to stop believing in God has created exactly what may bring me back to Him. Sometimes when I am most hurting, I recall Deuteronomy 31:6: "God goes with you; He will never leave you nor forsake you." So I guess it's fair to say that one day I do hope to be back with God—to really accept and commit to Him, to walk with Him and to really be able to believe that He walks with me. I believe this because deep within me is a feeling that cannot be explained except to know that it is Him—just waiting for me to once again ask Him to come into my life and to allow myself to be loved only in the fullness that God can do.

Justina Jasper, 17

I'm Listening

Dear God,

I'm writing because I need your help.
It's been a long time since we've communicated.
I meant to keep in touch,
but I've been busy keeping up the payments
on my house, the cable, electricity and such.
Guess I'm one reason why your world's a mess.
I didn't help you much to make it better,
so I'm ashamed to ask you to even
read this letter.

But . . .
I have teenage great-grandkids,
who I love as you well know.
I want them to have all the joy
and good as they live and grow.
I wonder what their world will be
if most of us have been like me.
As with your servant Paul,
my prayer for them would be
that their "love may abound more and more
in knowledge and depth of insight,
so that (they) may be able to discern what is best
and may be pure and blameless until the day of Christ,
filled with the fruit of righteousness . . ."
(Phil. 1:9–11).

And although my promises
are long past due,
please God, for them
help me to help you.
My love for them assures
this time, I'm listening . . .
I'll do whatever you ask of me
Please guard them, and
guide them.
Give them the desire to
live a life that pleases you.

Elmer Adrian, 94
father, grandfather and great-grandfather

Epilogue

Dear Readers,

If we've succeeded in what we set out to do with this book, we've answered some questions for you, but also raised some. Of course, it really isn't possible to cover every detail from A to Z in one book. It is our prayer and hope that you will want to learn even more about God's Word and what it can mean in your life. You may want to check out some of the books we've mentioned in the Suggested Readings and Resources. And as we've suggested in various places throughout the book, we hope you will talk with a youth counselor, your minister and, of course, your parents about the things that are on your heart and mind. As always, we encourage you to surround yourself with other teens whose faith is at the center, the core, of their lives. All these things can help and support you in your Christian Walk.

It's important that you know that each of us authors has traveled a road similar to the one you're on now. Life has had its ups and downs for us. Sometimes we've made the right choices; sometimes we've made the wrong ones. Nevertheless, God has been faithful. We've grown stronger and wiser with each passing day, and so will you. You are embarking on a wonderful adventure—the rest of your life. The world can be a frightening place, but it is also a place of wonder. Step out into it boldly, knowing that God is on your side!

In closing, we want you to know that you are dear to our hearts. We work with teens worldwide and know of the struggles you face as you look to find your place in the world— and the challenges you face as you strive to live "close to the bone"—to face daily life with heart as you do. As always, we'd like to know how you found this book helpful and the ways it

made a difference in your life—or in the lives of friends or family
members to whom you gave it. You can write us at:

Teen Team
3060 Racetrack View Drive
Del Mar, CA 92014

Or visit our Web site at *www.tasteberriesforteens.com*

Godspeed, dear friends,
Bettie, Jennifer and Debbie

Abbreviations for Books of the Bible

The following abbreviations for books of the Bible are used throughout the text. (Other references to books of the Bible are spelled out.)

Old Testament		New Testament	
1 Chronicles	1 Chron.	1 Corinthians	1 Cor.
2 Chronicles	2 Chron.	2 Corinthians	2 Cor.
Deuteronomy	Deut.	Ephesians	Eph.
Ecclesiastes	Eccles.	Galatians	Gal.
Exodus	Exod.	Hebrews	Heb.
Genesis	Gen.	Matthew	Matt.
Isaiah	Isa.	Philippians	Phil.
Jeremiah	Jer.	Romans	Rom.
Joshua	Josh.	1 Timothy	1 Tim.
Leviticus	Lev.	2 Timothy	2 Tim.
Numbers	Num.	1 Thessalonians	1 Thess.
Proverbs	Prov.	2 Thessalonians	2 Thess.
Psalms	Ps.		
1 Samuel	1 Sam.		
2 Samuel	2 Sam.		

Appendix:
Simple Prayers
for Christian Living

The Lord's Prayer

Our Father who art in heaven,
Hallowed be thy name;
Thy kingdom come.
Thy will be done on Earth
as it is in heaven.
Give us this day our daily bread.
And forgive us our debts,
As we forgive our debtors.
And lead us not into temptation,
But deliver us from evil:
For thine is the kingdom,
and the power, and the glory, forever. Amen.

The Serenity Prayer

God grant me the serenity
to accept the things I cannot change,
courage to change the things I can
and the wisdom to know the difference.

A Prayer for Salvation

Dear Father, I realize that I am a sinner
And that I cannot change anything I have done.
But You can give me a new life, Lord,
if I give my old one to You.
Forgive me for my sins and accept me into Your holy family.
I know that You sent Your only son, Jesus,
into the world to die for my sins. I believe that he is
the way, the truth and the life,
and I accept him now as my personal Savior.
Thank You, Lord, for hearing my prayer
and for giving me eternal life.

A Prayer of Thanksgiving

Heavenly Father, I offer You praise and thanks
for who You are and for all that You have done.
You have created this wondrous universe
and all things are under Your control.
You made me, Father, just the way You wanted me,
and You put in me your Holy Spirit
so that I could be more like You.
Your blessings are too numerous to count.
You have always been there with what I need
just when I need it.
I know I can bring any problem, no matter how small, to You
and You will help me work it out according to Your will.
I promise to love and serve You all of my life
because You want what is best for me.
May I always seek You first, above all else.

A Prayer for Healing

Dear God, today I am in need of Your healing touch.
You know just what ails me, even before I speak it.
You understand all that I am feeling because
You have suffered all things in the form of Jesus Christ.
Take my pain, Lord, and use it to show me Your truth.
If it is Your will, heal me and remove my pain.
If You have some purpose for this affliction,
Show me what it is, Lord.
"I can do all things through Him who gives me strength."
If You wish to make me stronger through this pain, Lord,
then so be it.
Give me the courage to withstand it
and the grace to be an example to others.
Forgive me if I sin in my pain and selfishness.
Show me that all things are working for good through You.

A Prayer for Courage

Father, today I need Your strength
to help me get through the challenges I am facing.
I know that You have not given me a spirit of fear,
but of courage and a sound mind.
Yet, I am frightened when I think of what I must do.
Strengthen me, Lord, and help me to shed my fear.
You are the God who delivered Daniel from the lion's den,
And I know You can deliver me if You choose to.
Father, show me how to stand tall
and to be bold in the midst of this situation.

Help me to do whatever I must to bring glory
and honor to Your name.
If you choose not to deliver me, then stand beside me
and help me to get through this.
Thank you, God, for being my help and my strength.

A Prayer for Peace

God, as I look around me I see people absorbed in conflicts.
The world is in turmoil because too many people
do not know You.
Open their eyes, Lord, and show them that You have the answer.
Send your Holy Spirit to convict and change hearts.
Only then will people understand what is truly important.
Father, help me to do my part in sharing Your truth
with others who do not know You.
Give me courage and wisdom
to know how to set a godly example for others around me to see.
As we all long for peace in the world, Father,
so we also long for peace in our hearts.
Touch the hearts of those who are suffering and oppressed,
Especially help those who are too weak to help themselves.
And, Father, give us the grace to forgive the oppressors.
You sent Your Son into the world to be the Prince of Peace.
May the world know that peace.

A Prayer for Grace

Dear God, You know what I am facing today.
I cannot face it on my own. Give me Your grace
and send Your peace to comfort me in my confusion.
You have said that Your grace is sufficient
and that Your strength is made perfect in our weakness.
Father, I feel so weak today.
You know exactly what I need even before I ask.
My prayer is that You will give me a calm spirit
and a clear mind so that I can see which way to go.
Be my rock, Lord, and let me hold onto You.
Your Word is a lamp for my feet and a light to my path.
Guide me in Your truth.

A Prayer for Wisdom

Lord, I am struggling today with a decision I must make.
There are so many ways I could go.
Is there a best way, Lord? If so, will You show me?
You have said that You will make our paths straight
if we commit all our ways to You.
I am laying this decision at Your feet, Father.
Open my eyes to Your truth. Send Your Holy Spirit to guide me.
Help me to accept the decision I make
and to do everything in my strength to make it right.
If You close a door, I know You will open a window.
Your ways are higher than my ways.
Give me Your peace and clear vision to see the road ahead.
Thank You for being my strength.

A Prayer for the Needs of Others

Dear Father, someone I love is in need of Your touch today.
Please bring Your grace to my friends.
Help them to wait before You and to seek Your strength
instead of trying to do it by themselves.
You can provide for their needs because You are God.
If it is Your will, You can heal or You can change circumstances.
Show them that you are in control and give them Your peace.
Help them to have the courage to know what they can change
and the serenity to know what they can't.
Give them a deeper knowledge of who You are through this struggle.
Strengthen their trust and help them to glorify You in all their trials.

Suggested Readings and Resources

Aranza, Jacob and Josh McDowell. *Making a Love That Lasts: How to Find Love Without Settling for Sex.* Ann Arbor, Mich.: Servant Publications, 1996.

Arterburn, Stephen and Fred Stoeker. *Every Young Man's Battle: Strategies for Victory in the Real World of Sexual Temptation.* New York: Waterbrook Press, 2002.

Beers, V. Gilbert and Ronald A. Beers (eds.). *Touchpoints for Students.* Wheaton, Ill.: Tyndale House Publishers, Inc., 1996, 1999.

The Bible Promise Book. Urichsville, Ohio. Barbour and Company, Inc., 1990.

Cloud, Dr. Henry, and Dr. John Townsend. *Boundaries in Dating: Making Dating Work.* Grand Rapids, Mich.: Zondervan, 2000.

Dobson, James. *Life on the Edge: A Young Adult's Guide to a Meaningful Future.* Dallas: Word Publishing, 2000.

Doud, Guy. *Stuff You Gotta Know: Straight Talk on Real Life Issues.* St. Louis: Concordia Publishing House, 1993.

Dunn, Sean. *I Want the Cross: Living a Radical Faith.* Grand Rapids, Mich.: Fleming H. Revell Co., 2001.

Fuller, Cheri and Ron Luce. *When Teens Pray.* Sisters, Ore.: Multnomah, 2002.

Graham, Franklin. *Living Beyond the Limits: A Life in Sync with God.* Nashville, Tenn.: Thomas Nelson Publishers, 1998.

———. *Rebel with a Cause.* Nashville, Tenn.: Thomas Nelson Publishers, 1995.

Grieger, Mike. *Personal Prayers for Teens: Brief Meditations and Prayers Dealing with Experiences Common to Teenagers.* Nashville, Tenn.: Dimensions for Living, 2001.

Haas, David. *Prayers Before an Awesome God: The Psalms for Teenagers.* Winona, Minn.: St. Mary's Press, 1998.

Hanegraaff, Hank. *The Prayer of Jesus.* Nashville, Tenn.: W Publishing Group, 2001.

"How to Know You're in Love." Two-part tape series by Dawson McAllister. Available from Focus on the Family.

347

Hunt, Angela Elwell. *Keeping Your Life Together When Your Parents Pull Apart: A Teen's Guide to Surviving Divorce.* iUniverse, 2000.

Johnson, Kevin Walter. *Get God: Make Friends with the King of the Universe.* Minneapolis: Bethany House, 2000.

————. *Does Anybody Know What Planet My Parents Are From?* Minneapolis: Bethany House, 1996.

————. *Can I Be a Christian Without Being Weird?* Minneapolis: Bethany House, 1992.

Lucado, Max. *He Chose You* (adapted from *He Chose the Nails*). Nashville, Tenn.: Thomas Nelson Publishers, 2002.

Luce, Ron. *Extreme Promise Book.* Nashville, Tenn.: J. Countryman Press, 2000.

————. *The Mark of a World Changer.* Nashville, Tenn.: Thomas Nelson Publishers, 1996.

McDowell, Josh and Bill Jones. *The Teenage Q & A Book.* Dallas: Word Publishing, 1990.

McDowell, Josh and Bob Hostetler. *13 Things You Gotta Know to Make It as a Christian.* Nashville, Tenn.: W Publishing Group, 1992.

Myers, Bill. *Just Believe It: Faith in the Real Stuff.* Eugene, Ore.: Harvest House, 2001.

No Apologies: The Truth About Life, Love & Sex. Colorado Springs, Colo.: Focus on the Family Pubs., 1999.

Peterson, Lorraine. *How to Get a Life . . . No Strings Attached: The Power of Grace in a Teen's Life.* Minneapolis: Bethany House, 1997.

Raunikar, Don. *Choose God's Best: Wisdom for Lifelong Romance.* Sisters, Oreg.: Multnomah Pubs., 1998.

Shellenberger, Susie. *Help! My Friend's in Trouble! Supporting Your Friends Who Struggle with . . . Family Problems, Sexual Crises, Food Addictions, Self-Esteem, Depression, Grief and Loss.* Ann Arbor, Mich.: Servant Publications, 2000.

Speck, Greg. *Sex: It's Worth Waiting For.* Chicago: Moody Press, 1989.

Stroebel, Lee. *Case for Faith—Student Edition.* Grand Rapids, Mich.: Zondervan, 2002.

Thurman, Debbie. *From Depression to Wholeness: The Anatomy of Healing.* Monroe, Va.: Cedar House Publishers, 1998.

————. *Hold My Heart: A Teen's Journal for Healing and Personal Growth (For Girls)*. Monroe, Va.: Cedar House Publishers, 2002.

————. *Sheer Faith: A Teen's Journey to Godly Growth (For Boys)*. Monroe, Va.: Cedar House Publishers, 2003.

Trujillo, Michelle. *Teens Talkin' Faith*. Deerfield Beach, Fla.: Health Communications, Inc., 2002.

Waggoner, Brittany. *Prayers for When You're Mad, Sad, or Just Totally Confused*. Ann Arbor, Mich.: Vine Books, 2002.

Wallace, RaNelle. *The Burning Within*. Grand Rapids, Mich.: Phoenix Society, 1994.

Wilkinson, Bruce. *Secrets of the Vine for Teens*. Sisters, Ore.: Multnomah, 2003.

Youngs, Bettie B. *Safeguarding Your Teenager from the Dragons of Life: A Guide to the Adolescent Years*. Deerfield Beach, Fla.: Health Communications, Inc., 1998.

————. *Taste-Berry Tales: Stories to Lift the Spirit, Fill the Heart and Feed the Soul*. Deerfield Beach, Fla.: Health Communications, Inc., 1999.

————. *A String of Pearls: Inspirational Stories Celebrating the Resiliency of the Human Spirit*. Holbrook, Mass.: Adams Media, 2000.

————. *Gifts of the Heart: Stories That Celebrate Life's Defining Moments*. Deerfield Beach, Fla.: Health Communications, Inc., 1999.

————. *Values from the Heartland*. Deerfield Beach, Fla.: Health Communications, Inc., 1998.

————. *Helping Your Child Succeed in School*. Marietta, Ga.: Active Parenting, 1998.

Youngs, Bettie B. and Jennifer Leigh Youngs. *365 Days of Taste-Berry Inspiration for Teens*. Deerfield Beach, Fla.: Health Communications, Inc., 2003.

————. *A Taste-Berry Teen's Guide to Managing the Stress and Pressures of Life*. Deerfield Beach, Fla.: Health Communications, Inc., 2001.

————. *A Taste-Berry Teen's Guide to Setting & Achieving Goals*. Deerfield Beach, Fla.: Health Communications, Inc., 2002.

————. *A Teen's Guide to Living Drug-Free*. Deerfield Beach, Fla.: Health Communications, Inc., 2003.

————. *More Taste Berries for Teens: A Second Collection of Short Stories and Encouragement on Life, Love, Friendship and Tough Issues*. Deerfield Beach, Fla.: Health Communications, Inc., 2000.

———. *Taste Berries for Teens: Inspirational Short Stories and Encouragement on Life, Love, Friendship and Tough Issues.* Deerfield Beach, Fla.: Health Communications, Inc., 1999.

———. *Taste Berries for Teens #3: Inspirational Stories on Life, Love, Friends and the Face in the Mirror.* Deerfield Beach, Fla.: Health Communications, Inc., 2002.

———. *Taste Berries for Teens Journal: My Thoughts on Life, Love and Making a Difference.* Deerfield Beach, Fla.: Health Communications, Inc., 2000.

Youngs, Bettie B., Jennifer Leigh Youngs and Debbie Thurman. *12 Months of Faith: A Devotional Journal for Teens.* Deerfield Beach, Fla.: Health Communications, Inc., 2003.

Youngs, Jennifer Leigh. *Feeling Great, Looking Hot & Loving Yourself: Health, Fitness and Beauty for Teens.* Deerfield Beach, Fla.: Health Communications, Inc., 2000.

Support Resources

Focus Adolescent Services
An information and referral service for families of troubled teens, *not* a hotline.
877-FOCUS-AS (877-362-8727)
www.focusas.com

AIDS Hotline for Teens
800-234-8336

Alcohol and Drug Abuse

National Council on Alcoholism and Drug Dependence
Hope Line
twenty-four hours: 800-622-2255

Al-Anon and Alateen Family Headquarters
800-356-9996

National Association for Children of Alcoholics
301-468-0985

Teen Challenge International USA Headquarters
3728 W. Chestnut Expressway
Springfield, MO 65802
417-862-6969
www.teenchallengeusa.com

Child Abuse, Rape, Sexual Abuse

Childhelp USA
twenty-four hours: 800-4-A-CHILD

Rape Crisis Center
800-352-7273

Faithful and True Ministries
6542 Regency Lane
Eden Prairie, MN 55344
www.faithfulandtrueministries.com

Eating Disorders

American Anorexia and Bulimia Association
165 W. 46th Street, Suite 1108
New York, NY 10036
212-501-8351

National Eating Disorders Association
603 Stewart St., Suite 803
Seattle, WA 98101
206-382-3587
www.NationalEatingDisorders.org

Mental Health Issues

National Alliance for the Mentally Ill
Colonial Place Three
2107 Wilson Blvd.
Arlington, VA 2201
800-950-NAMI (6264)
www.nami.org
(Check your phone book for local chapters.)

Christian Mental Health Services, Inc.
2180 Pleasant Hill Road, A5-225
Duluth, GA 30096
770-300-9903
www.christianmh.org

Ministries, Family Counseling

Focus on the Family
Colorado Springs, CO 80995
719-531-3400
www.family.org
Maintains a national referral network for counselors.

American Association of Christian Counselors
1639 Rustic Village Road
Forest, VA 24551
(434) 525-9470
www.aacc.net
Maintains a national referral network for counselors.

Pornography, Sexual Addictions

National Center for On-Line Internet Pornography
Usage and Addictions
eBehavior, LLC
P.O. Box 72
Bradford, PA 16701
877-CYBER-DR (292-3737)
www.netaddition.com

PureIntimacy.org
Developed by Focus on the Family

Porn-Free Ministries
www.porn-free.org

Turning Point
A Ministry of Teen Challenge
See contact information above.

Pregnancy Counseling

Birthright International
777 Coxwell Ave.
Toronto, Ontario M4C 3C6
Canada

Birthright USA
P.O. Box 98363
Atlanta, GA 30359
800-550-4900
Information about abstinence, safe sex, infant care and adoption
services.

Runaway, Homeless Teens

National Runaway Hotline (twenty-four hours)
800-621-4000

Suicide

Suicide hotline: 800-SUICIDE

Permissions *(continued from page vi)*

Testimony of Gianna Jensen from a hearing on H. R. 4292, the "Born-Alive Infants Protection Act of 2000." House Judiciary Subcommittee on the Constitution, July 20, 2000. From the *Congressional Record*.

Statistics on New Age spirituality from *www.religioustolerance.org*.

Testimony of Rick, Tim, Curt and Carolyn Goad used by permission of Goad Ministries International, 8825 Boggy Creek Road, Orlando, FL 32824.

Taleen Kullukian's recollections of the Armenian Mission Trip of 2000 used with her permission.

"The ABCs of Spiritual Growth" reprinted from the New Life Ministries Web site. Rights reserved by New Life Ministries (*www.newlife.com*). Used by permission.

Statistics on general religious beliefs of the U.S. population from Barna Research Group Ltd. Web site (*www.barna.org*). Used by permission. All rights reserved.

List of nine fundamental beliefs of the Christian faith was prepared by the editors of *Christianity Today* magazine. Used by permission, *Christianity Today*, Feb. 8, 1993.

Religiously Looking. Reprinted with permission by publisher Health Communications, Inc., Deerfield Beach, Florida, adapted from *A Taste-Berry Teen's Guide to Setting & Achieving Goals* by Bettie B. Youngs, Ph.D., Ed.D. and Jennifer Leigh Youngs. ©2002 Bettie B. Youngs, Ph.D., Ed.D. and Jennifer Leigh Youngs.

I'm Listening. Reprinted with permission by publisher Health Communications, Inc., Deerfield Beach, Florida, adapted from *Taste Berries for Teens: Inspirational Short Stories and Encouragement on Life, Love, Friendship and Tough Issues* by Bettie B. Youngs, Ph.D., Ed.D. and Jennifer Leigh Youngs. ©1999 Bettie B. Youngs, Ph.D., Ed.D. and Jennifer Leigh Youngs.

About the Authors

Bettie B. Youngs, Ph.D., Ed.D., is a Pulitzer Prize–nominated author of thirty books translated into thirty-one languages. She is a former Teacher-of-the-Year, university professor and executive director of Instruction and Professional Development, Inc. A long-acknowledged expert on family and teen issues, Dr. Youngs has frequently appeared on *The Good Morning Show, NBC Nightly News,* CNN and *Oprah. USA Today,* the *Washington Post, Redbook, U.S. News & World Report, Working Woman, Family Circle, Parents Magazine, Woman's Day* and the National Association for Secondary School Principals (NASSP) have all recognized her work. Her acclaimed books include: *Taste Berries for Teens: Inspirational Short Stories and Encouragement on Life, Love, Friendship and Tough Issues; Safeguarding Your Teenager from the Dragons of Life; A Teen's Guide to Living Drug-Free;* the Pulitzer Prize–nominated *Gifts of the Heart: Stories That Celebrate Life's Defining Moments* and the award-winning *Values from the Heartland.* Dr. Youngs is the author of a number of videocassette programs and is the coauthor of the nationally acclaimed *Parents on Board,* a video-based training program to help schools and parents work together to increase student achievement.

Jennifer Leigh Youngs is a speaker and workshop presenter for teens and parents nationwide. She is the author of *Feeling Great, Looking Hot & Loving Yourself: Health, Fitness and Beauty for Teens* and coauthor of *Taste Berries for Teens: Inspirational Short Stories and Encouragement on Life, Love, Friendship and Tough Issues; Taste Berries for Teens Journal; More Taste Berries for Teens; A Taste-Berry Teen's Guide to Managing the Stress and Pressures of Life* and *Taste Berries for Teens #3*. Jennifer is a former Miss Teen California finalist and Rotary International Goodwill Ambassador and Exchange Scholar. She serves on a number of advisory boards for teens and is a Youth Coordinator for Airline Ambassadors, an international organization affiliated with the United Nations that involves youth in programs to build cross-cultural friendships and delivers humanitarian aid to those in need worldwide.

Debbie Thurman—author, journalist and speaker—has been actively involved in many facets of Christian ministry for more than twenty years. She now runs her own ministry, Sheer Faith, in Central Virginia where she leads a weekly support group and works with local and state officials and churches to improve mental health care and family support. She and husband Russ Thurman have been married for twenty-one years and have two teenage daughters. Debbie is a former Marine Corps public affairs officer, and is the author of *From Depression to Wholeness: The Anatomy of Healing, Journaling From Depression to Wholeness: A 12-Week Program for Healing, Hold My Heart: A Teen's Journal for Healing and Personal Growth* and *Sheer Faith: A Teen's Journey to Godly Growth*. In addition to her writing and speaking, Debbie mentors teens and families in crisis and works in Christian mental health advocacy.

To contact Bettie and Jennifer Youngs, write to:

Youngs, Youngs & Associates
3060 Racetrack View Drive
Del Mar, CA 92014

Web site: *www.tasteberriesforteens.com*

To contact Debbie Thurman, visit her Web site:

www.debbiethurman.com

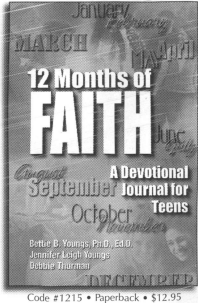

More From
Bettie and Jennifer Leigh Youngs

Have you ever had a day when you felt overwhelmed, down-and-out or simply "at wit's end"? On the days when stress sets in, pressures mount and anxiety lingers this book is yours.

With contributions
from teens for teens
Bettie B. Youngs,
Ph.D., Ed.D.
Jennifer Leigh Youngs
Authors of the national bestseller
Taste Berries™ for Teens

Code #9322 • Paperback • $12.95

Want to be more in charge of your life? This book will help you set and achieve goals to shape the direction of your life.

Bettie B. Youngs, Ph.D., Ed.D.
Jennifer Leigh Youngs
Authors of the bestselling
Taste Berries™ for Teens series and
Feeling Great, Looking Hot & Loving Yourself!

Code #0405 • Paperback • $12.95

For more great books by Bettie and Jennifer Youngs
Go to hcibooks.com